INTERPRETING
DEUTERONOMY

INTERPRETING DEUTERONOMY

Issues and Approaches

Edited by David G. Firth
and Philip S. Johnston

APOLLOS (an imprint of Inter-Varsity Press)
Norton Street, Nottingham NG7 3HR, England
Website: www.ivpbooks.com
Email: ivp@ivpbooks.com

First published 2012

British Library Cataloguing in Publication Data
A catalogue record for this book is available from the British Library.

UK ISBN: 978-1-84474-597-5
Set in Monotype Garamond 11/13pt
Typeset in Great Britain by CRB Associates, Potterhanworth, Lincolnshire

CONTENTS

CONTRIBUTORS

Paul A. Barker lectures in Old Testament at Seminari Theoloji, Malaysia and is Adjunct Professor of Old Testament at Myanmar Evangelical Graduate School of Theology. He is a Visiting Lecturer also at Zarephath Bible Institute, Rawalpindi, Pakistan. He is author of *The Triumph of Grace in Deuteronomy* (Paternoster).

Jenny Corcoran is a PhD student at St John's College, Nottingham, and Associate Priest at St Barnabas, Lenton Abbey, Nottingham.

David Firth is Old Testament Tutor and Director of Research, St John's College, Nottingham. He is author of *1 and 2 Samuel* (Apollos).

Greg Goswell is Lecturer in Old Testament, Presbyterian Theological College, Melbourne.

Christian Hofreiter is curate and chaplain to postgraduates at St Aldates, Oxford and associate chaplain at the Oxford Pastorate. His doctoral research at Oxford University focuses on the Christian reception of *ḥērem* texts and is funded by the Arts & Humanities Research Council (http://www.ahrc.ac.uk).

Philip S. Johnston is Senior Tutor, Hughes Hall, Cambridge. He is author of *Shades of Sheol* (Apollos).

James Robson is Tutor in Old Testament and Hebrew, Wycliffe Hall, Oxford. He is author of *Word and Spirit in Ezekiel* (T&T Clark).

Csilla Saysell was Temporary Old Testament Tutor at St John's College, Nottingham and has now been appointed as Old Testament Lecturer at Carey Baptist College, Auckland, New Zealand. She completed her PhD under Walter Moberly at Durham in 2009. Her dissertation is to be published as *'According to the Law': Reading Ezra 9 – 10 as Christian Scripture*, JTISup (Eisenbrauns, 2012).

Heath A. Thomas is Assistant Professor of Old Testament and Hebrew and Director of PhD Studies at Southeastern Baptist Theological Seminary. He is author of *Poetry and Theology in Lamentations: The Aesthetics of an Open Text* (Sheffield Phoenix, 2012) and a forthcoming commentary on Habakkuk (Eerdmans).

Peter T. Vogt is Professor of Old Testament, Bethel Seminary. He is author of *Deuteronomic Theology and the Significance of Torah* (Eisenbrauns) as well as a number of other books and articles on Old Testament issues.

John H. Walton is Professor of Old Testament, Wheaton College. He is author of (among others) *Ancient Near Eastern Thought and the Old Testament* (Apollos).

ABBREVIATIONS

AB	Anchor Bible
ABD	*Anchor Bible Dictionary*, ed. D. N. Freedman, 6 vols. (New York: Doubleday, 1992)
ANE	Ancient Near East(ern)
AOTC	Apollos Old Testament Commentary
BA	*Biblical Archaeologist*
BBR	*Bulletin for Biblical Research*
BETL	Bibliotheca ephemeridum theologicarum lovaniensium
BHQ	*Biblia Hebraica Quinta: Deuteronomy*, ed. C. McCarthy (Stuttgart: Deutsche Bibelgesellschaft, 2007)
BHS	*Biblia Hebraica Stuttgartensia*, ed. K. Elliger and W. Rudolph (Stuttgart: Deutsche Bibelstiftung, 1983)
Bib	*Biblica*
BIS	Biblical Interpretation Series
BJS	Brown Judaic Studies
BZAW	Beihefte zur Zeitschrift für die alttestamentliche Wissenschaft
CBQ	*Catholic Biblical Quarterly*
ConBOT	Coniectanea biblica: Old Testament Series
COS	*The Context of Scripture*, ed. W. W. Hallo, 3 vols. (Leiden: E. J. Brill, 2003)
CTH	Catalogue des Textes Hittites

DJD	Discoveries in the Judaean Desert
DL	Deuteronomic Laws
EN	Ezra–Nehemiah
ESV	English Standard Version
ET	English translation
FAT	Forschungen zum Alten Testament
FRLANT	Forschungen zur Religion und Literatur des Alten und Neuen Testaments
HTR	*Harvard Theological Review*
HUCA	*Hebrew Union College Annual*
ICC	International Critical Commentary
Int	*Interpretation*
IOS	*Israel Oriental Studies*
JBL	*Journal of Biblical Literature*
JETS	*Journal of the Evangelical Theological Society*
JGRChJ	*Journal of Greco-Roman Christianity and Judaism*
JHS	*Journal of Hebrew Scriptures*
JPS	Jewish Publication Society
JPSV	Jewish Publication Society Version
JSOT	*Journal for the Study of the Old Testament*
JSOTSup	Journal for the Study of the Old Testament, Supplement Series
JTISup	Journal of Theological Interpretation, Supplement Series
LHB/OTS	Library of the Hebrew Bible/Old Testament Studies
LNTS	Library of New Testament Studies
LXX	Septuagint
MT	Masoretic Text
NAC	New American Commentary
NASB	New American Standard Bible
NCB	New Century Bible
NCBC	New Century Bible Commentary
NEB	New English Bible
NETS	*New English Translation of the Septuagint*
NIBC	New International Biblical Commentary
NIBCOT	New International Biblical Commentary on the Old Testament
NICOT	New International Commentary on the Old Testament
NIDOTTE	*New International Dictionary of Old Testament Theology and Exegesis,* ed. W. A. VanGemeren, 5 vols. (Carlisle: Paternoster; Grand Rapids: Zondervan, 1996)
NIV	New International Version
NJB	New Jerusalem Bible

NJPS	New Jewish Publication Society Tanakh
NRSV	New Revised Standard Version
NSBT	New Studies in Biblical Theology
OBO	Orbis Biblicus et Orientalis
ÖBS	Österreichische Biblische Studien
OBT	Overtures to Biblical Theology
OTC	Old Testament Commentary
OTG	Old Testament Guides
OTL	Old Testament Library
OTS	Old Testament Studies
OtSt	Oudtestamentische Studiën
PBM	Paternoster Biblical Monographs
RB	*Revue biblique*
RBL	*Review of Biblical Literature*
ResQ	*Restoration Quarterly*
RTR	*Reformed Theological Review*
SBLAB	Society of Biblical Literature Academia Biblica
SBLDS	Society of Biblical Literature Dissertation Series
SBLMS	Society of Biblical Literature Manuscript Series
SBT	Studies in Biblical Theology
SBTS	Sources for Biblical and Theological Study
SHBT	Smyth and Helwys Bible Commentary
SJT	*Scottish Journal of Theology*
SOTBT	Studies in Old Testament Biblical Theology
TOTC	Tyndale Old Testament Commentary
TThZ	*Trierer Theologische Zeitschrift*
TynB	*Tyndale Bulletin*
VTE	Vassal Treaty of Esarhaddon
VT	*Vetus Testamentum*
WBC	Word Biblical Commentary
WTJ	*Westminster Theological Journal*
WUNT	Wissenschaftliche Untersuchungen zum Neuen Testament
ZA	*Zeitschrift für Assyriologie*
ZABR	*Zeitschrift für altorientalische und biblische Rechtsgeschichte*
ZAW	*Zeitschrift für die alttestamentliche Wissenschaft*

INTRODUCTION

David G. Firth and Philip S. Johnston

The book of Deuteronomy has been immensely influential. It is among the most frequently cited books of the Old Testament in the New, and among the most frequently occurring manuscripts at Qumran. To note one example, in Matthew's Gospel it is the book of Deuteronomy which Jesus twice cites in rejecting temptation. Its influence is also widely seen within the Old Testament itself. Perhaps the best evidence for this is that it has spawned two scholarly adjectives – 'Deuteronomic' to describe elements of its own content, and 'Deuteronomistic' to describe those texts which show its influence. Of course, determining exactly what constitutes a 'Deuteronomistic' text is difficult; but even if the boundaries of its influence cannot be marked absolutely, there is little doubt about its wide influence. A text which has been so formative for the people of God down through the centuries is thus worthy of further reflection, and this collection of papers aims to contribute to that ongoing process.

As with so many other books of the Old Testament, study of Deuteronomy is in the midst of great change. A generation ago the dominant questions revolved around interpreting it within the framework of the Documentary Hypothesis, for which of course Deuteronomy was 'D'. But even that one siglum indicated something important: where the first four books of the Pentateuch were divided among three interwoven sources (JEP), Deuteronomy stood largely alone. However, while for many scholars the Documentary Hypothesis has continued to provide a framework for interpreting Deuteronomy, it no longer commands the status of an 'assured result'. Instead, other approaches have been developed, engendering their own debates. This means that questions of date and origin, theological themes and continued significance are now discussed from a variety of angles. Indeed, one of the healthier aspects of this methodological diversification has been a greater awareness of the book's theological themes and significance. It would be premature to say that we have a settled new paradigm for its interpretation, as origins and purpose continue to be debated, but clearly the emerging approaches are more open to consider its message and communication strategies. Yet throughout recent as well as older study, it is affirmed that Deuteronomy represents a distinctive theological voice within the Pentateuch.

As the study of Deuteronomy changes, so too must books about Deuteronomy. While many excellent resources are currently available, they tend to fall into two categories. Many are introductions aimed at beginning students, offering an overview of scholarship on Deuteronomy. Others contain highly learned articles, often focusing on the minutiae which contribute to the goals of scholarship. But there is less literature which bridges the gap between the two, building on introductory work and helping readers to take the next steps in the study of Deuteronomy. Like its companion volumes on Psalms and Isaiah,[1] this book aims to meet that need, assuming some foundational knowledge and guiding readers through current issues and approaches.

The chapters within this book fall into three groups. The first pair (James Robson, Paul Barker) present overviews of current scholarly approaches to Deuteronomy and arguments for how we approach the book, thus creating a context for the discussions which follow. The second set (John Walton, Peter Vogt, Philip Johnston, David Firth, Heath Thomas) examine particular themes within Deuteronomy, including both specific issues and more general matters relevant to the whole book. A third group (Csilla Saysell, Greg Goswell, Jenny Corcoran, Christian Hofreiter) then consider different aspects of the reception of Deuteronomy. Because reception is such a developing but diverse area of study, we feel it important to offer a range of perspectives here, looking at how the book has been and is read as well as potential areas of continuing significance. A range of different approaches to Deuteronomy is thus modelled.

As with the volumes on Psalms and Isaiah, this book was produced by a collaborative effort. Draft chapters were written by selected members and guests

---

1. Philip S. Johnston and David G. Firth (eds.), *Interpreting the Psalms: Issues and Approaches* (Leicester: Apollos, 2005); David G. Firth and H. G. M. Williamson (eds.), *Interpreting Isaiah: Issues and Approaches* (Nottingham: Apollos, 2009).

of the Tyndale Fellowship Old Testament Study Group, circulated electronically, and then discussed at the annual conference in July 2011 (in Cambridge, UK). So although all the contributors are responsible for their own chapters, each of us has benefited from the input of the other contributors and the significant body of scholars who attended the conference. The editors have not sought to impose a standard interpretative approach on the contributors and considerable diversity remains, reflecting the Tyndale Fellowship itself. Further diversity is evident among the contributors – some are established scholars whose writing is well known, while others are still establishing themselves as scholars. It is precisely because there is so much in the interpretation of Deuteronomy that requires continued discussion that we believe such diversity is essential, though of course all the contributors are committed to the authority of Scripture and therefore to faith-based scholarship.

Finally, we would like to thank all contributors for their happy acceptance of suggested changes, some substantial, in order to keep to strict word limits and to fulfil the book's aims. Bringing this book to completion has not always been easy, but it has been immensely facilitated by the collegial spirit of those involved.

PART I

APPROACHING DEUTERONOMY

1. THE LITERARY COMPOSITION OF DEUTERONOMY

James Robson

Introduction

Over the last two hundred years, Deuteronomy has played a pivotal role in critical scholarship. In 1805, de Wette precipitated a paradigm shift in Deuteronomy studies, not so much by arguing that the kernel of Deuteronomy (Deut. 12 – 26) was the book of the law linked with Josiah's reforms,[1] but by proposing that it was written just before its discovery, and separately from Genesis–Numbers. Scholarship in general developed from this base, and the work of two later scholars in particular illustrates Deuteronomy's significance. In the 1870s Julius Wellhausen's Documentary Hypothesis regarded Deuteronomy (D) and Josiah's reforms (622 BC) as an anchor point by which other parts of the Pentateuch and historical writings are to be dated and evaluated.[2] Then in 1943 Martin Noth linked Deuteronomy with what followed rather than

---

1. Jerome (AD 342–420) had already suggested that the book of the law found in Josiah's reign was Deuteronomy.
2. Julius Wellhausen, *Prolegomena to the History of Ancient Israel: With a Reprint of the Article 'Israel' from the Encyclopaedia Britannica* (Gloucester: Peter Smith, 1983; German original, 1878).

what preceded.[3] Together, its law code and narrative prologue introduced and shaped the portrayal of theology and history in the books of Joshua to 2 Kings. The resultant 'Deuteronomistic History' served the purpose of explaining why the exile happened.

The work of these two scholars has spawned innumerable articles and books, their theories variously deemed sophisticated or implausible. Rather than summarize them, this chapter will examine seven main areas, outlining key pieces of evidence and the main arguments that are advanced in reaching conclusions on the composition of Deuteronomy.[4] I will start within the book of Deuteronomy itself, then move to the rest of the Bible and on to extrabiblical evidence, making brief evaluative points *en route*, before finally giving my view.

It should be noted at the outset that there is a spectrum of positions held, from essentially Mosaic authorship to non-Mosaic authorship or origin, which, on some readings, subverts the agenda found in earlier parts of the Pentateuch. I have avoided using loaded terms to describe the two ends, because such an approach runs the risk of short-circuiting the careful sifting of evidence.

Nuanced analysis is necessary. First, Mosaic *authorship* is not the same as Mosaic *origin*. Authorship is a claim about the *book* of Deuteronomy. Within this can be discerned a strong and a weak version. The strong version would claim that Moses wrote the book, *in toto*. The weaker version would claim that essentially Moses wrote Deuteronomy, but post-Mosaica may be present. To talk about Mosaic origin is to make a claim about Moses as the *source* of the book of Deuteronomy. Although the 'weaker' version of Mosaic authorship can tend towards Mosaic origin, the difference is one of perspective and attitude. With the former, post-Mosaica are something to be explained away, while with the latter, they are something to be embraced, and the book is to be understood and read from the editor's perspective.

Second, the questions of dating and of relationship to Moses are logically separable. The date of Deuteronomy may be earlier than Josiah's reform, yet the material may neither be authored by nor originate with Moses. Similarly, the final date of the book of Deuteronomy may be during or soon after the exile, but the material may have significant links with Moses.

---

3. Martin Noth, *The Deuteronomistic History*, trans. D. Orton, JSOTSup 15 (Sheffield: JSOT Press, 1981; 2nd ed. German original, 1957).

4. For a concise summary of most scholars' understanding of the composition of Deuteronomy, see Richard D. Nelson, *Deuteronomy*, OTL (Louisville: Westminster John Knox, 2002), pp. 4–9; or Alexander Rofé, *Deuteronomy: Issues and Interpretation*, OTS (Edinburgh: T&T Clark, 2002), pp. 1–9.

Third, the weight placed upon the different types of evidence adduced varies significantly. For some, it is the explicit testimony of Deuteronomy, or of other parts of the Old and New Testaments, which gives the definitive perspective. For others, it is the testimony that lies beneath the surface of the text. With these in mind, we now turn to the first area.

The explicit testimony of Deuteronomy[5]

The source

Almost all of Deuteronomy is said to consist of the words of Moses, as he addresses Israel in the plains of Moab before he dies and they cross the Jordan. After the prologue in 1:1–5, Moses' first speech runs from 1:6 – 4:40. His next speech begins in 5:1 and continues until the end of chapter 26. Chapter 27:1–10 breaks the flow, as others speak alongside him (elders, v. 1; levitical priests, v. 9). Moses speaks again on his own from 27:12, continuing until the end of chapter 28. Moses' final speech starts in 29:2 and continues until the end of chapter 30. In chapter 31, Moses' words are embedded within a narratival context. Deuteronomy 32:1–43 gives Moses' song, and is followed by his brief exhortation to take all his words seriously (32:46–47). Chapter 33 consists of the blessings of Moses, his final words recorded in the book, and chapter 34 narrates his death.

The prima-facie testimony of the book of Deuteronomy, then, is that Moses is the *source* of much of it as its speaker. Although the hearer is encountering Yhwh's words, they are mediated through Moses, as mandated in 5:22–33. Strikingly, the first time that Yhwh's voice is heard unmediated by Moses' direct speech is in chapter 31. It is only heard directly in five places, in thirteen verses.[6] Almost everywhere else we encounter the voice of Moses.

The time and place

The overt testimony is also clear about the *time* of speaking: the prologue introduces Moses' first speech as happening on 'the first day of the eleventh month', 'in the fortieth year' (Deut. 1:3).[7] Although Josephus regards Moses' death as

---

5. For much fuller presentations, see Jean-Pierre Sonnet, *The Book within the Book: Writing in Deuteronomy*, BIS 14 (Leiden: Brill, 1997); Daniel I. Block, 'Recovering the Voice of Moses: The Genesis of Deuteronomy', *JETS* 44 (2001), pp. 385–408.

6. Deut. 31:14b, 16b–21, 23b; 32:49–52; 34:4b.

7. Unless otherwise identified, Scripture quotations in this chapter are the author's own translation.

having taken place on the first day of the twelfth month,[8] Deuteronomy seems to present the first day of the eleventh month not only as the date of Moses speaking, but also as the day of Moses' death (see 32:48, 'on that very day'; cf. 27:9, 11).[9] The 'fortieth year' indicates the end of the wilderness period and imminent entry into the Promised Land, from which Moses is barred (3:25–26). So at the outset, Moses' impending death dominates the book.[10]

Deuteronomy is also clear about the *place* of speaking. Although there is some debate as to whether the list of places in 1:1b should be taken with verse 1a to give the locations of Moses' speaking *en route*, or with verse 2 simply to give place names on the journey, 1:5 states explicitly that Moses is speaking in the plains of Moab, east of the Jordan.

Different voices, different stages

However, it is both possible and desirable to go further, for two reasons. First, while Moses is the dominant voice heard in the book, he is not presented as the narrator. Instead, the book depicts Moses in the third person, 'He . . . ', or 'Moses . . . ', rather than 'I'. As Block helpfully identifies, the voice of the narrator is heard in three contexts: where Moses is spoken of in the third person, in 'historical notes' or parenthetical comments (2:10–12, 20–23; 3:9, 11, 13b–14; 10:6–9), and finally, 'indirectly in the material he chooses to include in or exclude from the book, as well as in his arrangement of the materials'.[11] Theoretically it is possible that Moses uses the persona of narrator to introduce his speaking. However, this is implausible given the post-conquest perspective of some narratorial comments (e.g. 2:12) and the third-person account of Moses' death.[12]

---

8. Josephus, *Antiquities* 4.8.

9. Jan van Goudoever, 'The Liturgical Significance of the Date in Dt 1, 3', in Norbert Lohfink (ed.), *Das Deuteronomium: Entstehung, Gestalt und Botschaft*, BETL 68 (Leuven: Leuven University Press, 1985), p. 145.

10. See especially Dennis T. Olson, *Deuteronomy and the Death of Moses: A Theological Reading*, OBT (Minneapolis: Fortress, 1994), though surprisingly Olson does not comment on this link at the start.

11. Block, 'Recovering the Voice of Moses', p. 392.

12. In addition, some scholars regard the reference in 1:1 to *bĕ'ēber hayyardēn* (NRSV: 'beyond the Jordan') as conclusive evidence that the narrator is not Moses, for he is writing from inside the land. Although the phrase is often used as a term designating a place as seen from the writer's perspective, it sometimes designates a specific geographical region (e.g. Deut. 3:8). The phrase should not be marshalled as conclusive evidence for establishing the location of the narrator.

That Moses is not the narrator is a point of the greatest importance. The narrator takes the hearers of the book back to the plains of Moab and invites the hearers to adopt that perspective, but the narrator is not writing *for* Israel in the plains of Moab.

Second, there are different stages in its formation that the book of Deuteronomy *itself* identifies, both within Moses' words and in the narrator's recounting. The initial stage is the writing down of the Decalogue, the 'ten words', by Yhwh at Horeb (4:13; 5:22; 9:10). Intermediate stages are apparent from references to both an oral and a written Torah.[13] A significant milestone is Moses *writing* 'the words of this law' and 'this song' (31:9, 22, 24). To this the narrator has appended chapters 33 – 34.

Evaluation

This testimony is a crucial piece of evidence for those holding to Mosaic authorship or origin in the strong sense. How should it be evaluated?

Few critical scholars feel constrained by the claims to Mosaic involvement that the book itself gives. Some regard Deuteronomy as an 'impious fraud', essentially a work that is designed to deceive its hearers, inculcating a new agenda while 'troping' an assumed existing agenda as 'deviant'.[14] Others view the attribution of Deuteronomy to Moses as a serious attempt to respect Mosaic tradition and to articulate for a new situation what the author(s) believe Moses would say.[15] Still others find themselves somewhere in between these two views.

Lying behind such views is the recognition that prima-facie claims to authorship within a book need to be interpreted historically like all other data. This is very different from what Marshall terms the 'so-called "dogmatic" approach', where 'one simply records what the biblical writers themselves say about matters

---

See further B. Gemser, 'Be'ēber hajjardēn: In Jordan's Borderland', *VT* 2 (1952), pp. 349–355.

13. Block, 'Recovering the Voice of Moses', pp. 394–402.

14. E.g. Bernard M. Levinson, *Deuteronomy and the Hermeneutics of Legal Innovation* (Oxford: Oxford University Press, 1998), p. 150.

15. See especially S. R. Driver, *A Critical and Exegetical Commentary on Deuteronomy*, ICC (Edinburgh: T&T Clark, 1895), pp. lvi–lix. Care is needed in understanding scholarly language. For example, Kenton M. Sparks distinguishes between the notion of a 'pious ruse' and 'a mendacious attempt to mislead', *Ancient Texts for the Study of the Hebrew Bible: A Guide to the Background Literature* (Peabody: Hendrickson, 2005), p. 250. Others might think it impossible to make such a distinction.

of authorship and the like and for the rest ignores historical investigation'.[16] Marshall insists on the desirability and necessity of historical investigation of such statements, and comments, 'Scholars who affirm that Moses wrote Deuteronomy but then separate off the last chapter because it inconveniently records the author's death are also practising a kind of literary criticism. In short, one cannot avoid historical and literary study.'[17]

Those who question the Mosaic authorship or origin of Deuteronomy on historical and literary grounds are not necessarily being sceptical about its explicit statements. They may be attributing them to literary convention, extending the reasoning concerning Moses' death to other parts of Deuteronomy. On the other hand, Mosaic authorship or origin should not be lightly dismissed, given the book's prima-facie claims and its excoriation of false witness.

Further, it is a mistake to focus on Moses' words and the book's forward-looking perspective, while being defensive about post-Mosaica and later shaping, since the book itself demands to be read from a different perspective. As with the Gospel writers presenting Jesus' words, so the narrator who *presents* Moses' words should be a critical factor in determining our reading perspective. Deuteronomy demands to be read both against the rhetorical time frame *in* the book and against the rhetorical time frame *of* the book. Readers need to adopt the perspective of the addressees of *both* Moses *and* the narrator.

Implicit evidence from Deuteronomy

Distinctive style
The main implicit ground for regarding Deuteronomy as a unity is its style. Driver summarizes:

> The literary style of Dt. is very marked and individual. In vocabulary, indeed, it presents comparatively few exceptional words . . . but particular words, and phrases, consisting sometimes of entire clauses, recur with extraordinary frequency, giving a distinctive colouring to every part of the work.[18]

He lists no fewer than seventy words or phrases as characteristically Deuteronomic. This is not to claim that they never occur elsewhere in the Pentateuch,

---

16. I. Howard Marshall, *Biblical Inspiration* (London: Hodder & Stoughton, 1982), p. 83.

17. Ibid., p. 84.

18. Driver, *Deuteronomy*, p. lxxvii.

though in some cases that is true (e.g. the verbal roots *lmd* ['learn', 'teach'], *ndḥ* ['stray', 'lead astray'], *kʿs* ['vex']), but rather that they are typical of Deuteronomy and not of other books. For example, the phrase 'which Yhwh ... is giving you' occurs thirty-seven times in the Old Testament, all in Deuteronomy except for one in Exodus 20:12. In many cases these are not incidental items of vocabulary or phrasing, but are indicative of a distinctive theological outlook. Examples include 'love' ('*hb*), both Yhwh's love of his people and vice versa; 'choose' (*bḥr*), of Yhwh's choice, particularly of Israel and of the place for Yhwh's name; and 'other gods'. To this observation about distinct literary style could be added the 'pedagogy of saturation'[19] that characterizes Deuteronomy's parenesis: repetition and exhortation mark even the laws themselves.

Nonetheless, alongside the distinctive style that points to a substantial unity, there is also evidence pointing to a complex process of composition.

Temporal perspective

First, some texts seem to envisage a significant time gap between the narrated events and the author. In 34:10, the narrator declares, 'Never since has there arisen a prophet in Israel like Moses.' This is hardly the perspective of one writing within a few years of Moses. Similarly, there is the language of 'to this day' or 'as this day'.[20] Sometimes these phrases are on Moses' lips and the time frame reads naturally as before entry into the land (e.g. 2:30; 26:16; 27:9). But sometimes the perspective is that of the narrator, indicating some distance between Moses' day and his own (e.g. 2:22; 34:6). At other points, the perspective could equally be Moses' addressees and the narrator's addressees (4:20; 10:15).

Intriguingly, in three places the two time horizons seem to blur. In two of these, the phrase 'as this day' looks to the future, in a father's instructions to his son (6:24) and in the nations' witnessing of Israel's exile (29:28). At one level, these are simply comments anticipated by Moses. But at another, the horizons merge, as though the *future* for Moses is the *present* for the narrator. Perhaps these words are a narrative intrusion, such that the 'then' of Moses is the 'now' of the narrator?[21] The clearest evidence for this occurs in 4:38. Here, the possession of the land is a present reality, yet the land was *not*

---

19. Walter Brueggemann, *Theology of the Old Testament: Testimony, Dispute, Advocacy* (Minneapolis: Fortress, 1997), p. 722.

20. 'to this day': Deut. 2:22; 3:14; 10:8; 11:4; 29:4; 34:6; 'as this day': Deut. 2:30; 4:20, 38; 6:24; 8:18; 10:15; 29:27.

21. Cf. Moshe Weinfeld, *Deuteronomy 1 – 11*, AB 5 (New York: Doubleday, 1991), p. 172.

possessed by Moses but *is* possessed by the author's contemporaries.[22] Von Rad puts it bluntly: 'in v. 38, the preacher has forgotten the fiction of Moses' speech before the conquest'.[23] But rather than the preacher forgetting, this could be seen as a narratorial aside, where the narrator breaks out of retelling the relationship between Moses and his hearers, and addresses *his own* hearers. At the very moment of affirming distance between *that* day and *his* day, the narrator blurs the distinction, affirming the relevance of Moses' words for his own hearers (cf. the subsequent 'know this day'). The two 'todays' merge together with powerful rhetoric.

Rhetorical perspective

Second, there is a shift in rhetorical perspective from a *warning* of Israel's declension and exile, 'if', to a *certainty*, 'when'.

In three places fairly early in Deuteronomy, Moses warns the Israelites of the danger, once they have eaten and are full, 'lest' (*pen*) they forget Yhwh and turn to other gods (6:11–12; 8:10–14; 11:15–16). Yet later, in 31:20, Moses is convinced not merely of this danger, but of the certainty of apostasy after they have eaten their fill (same terms). The 'if' has become a 'when'.

This move is replicated in the curse section in chapter 28. The chapter as a whole has two main sections. One outlines the blessings of the covenant appropriated through obedience (vv. 1–14), whereas the other (vv. 15–68) emphasizes the curses resulting from disobedience. Both blessings (vv. 1, 2) and curses (v. 15) are introduced by 'If ... obey the voice of Yhwh'. The latter part of the chapter – the curses – may be subdivided into verses 15–44, 45–57, 58–68. Each of these sections begins with language of keeping (*šmr*, vv. 15, 45, 58) Yhwh's words. Verse 45 begins a new section, partly because of the repetition of *šmr*, and partly because there is a repetition of 'obey the voice of Yhwh' (cf. vv. 1–2, 15). However, the 'if' at the start of previous sections becomes a factual 'these *will* happen ... *because* ... '.[24] This certain fate is reinforced by verse 47: 'Precisely because you did not serve ... '. It is now a 'foregone conclusion'.[25] This is not a matter of the plausibility or otherwise of predictive prophecy: sieges were commonplace in the ancient world, so these curses could

---

22. Unless what is meant is the land *east* of the Jordan, but that hardly equates to possession of the whole land.

23. Gerhard von Rad, *Deuteronomy*, trans. Dorothea Barton, OTL (London: SCM, 1966), p. 51.

24. Olson, *Deuteronomy*, p. 122.

25. Nelson, *Deuteronomy*, p. 332.

simply be stereotypical language, rather than based on experience of the final siege of Jerusalem. The temporal gap is inferred from the rhetorical shift, not from the details of the siege.

A third place where this rhetorical shift may be seen is in the notion of 'acting corruptly' (*šḥt*). In 4:16, Moses warns the Israelites to be careful not to 'act corruptly' by making idols. In 4:25, it seems as though the 'if' has become a 'when'. It is true that NRSV, NIV and ESV assume there is an unmarked, implicit conditional here and introduce 'if' before 'act corruptly'. However, the syntax seems more naturally to envisage a sequence outlining an expected future where 'when you beget sons' (presumably a certainty) continues seamlessly to 'act corruptly'. The assumption is that corrupt action will be as much part of the future as having children and growing old in the land. Thus NJB and NASB continue with 'when'. This view is reinforced by Moses' statement in 31:29 that echoes the language found in 4:25.[26]

One synchronic explanation for these shifts in rhetorical perspective is of a crescendo within a developing argument. A difficulty with this is that the shifts occur throughout the book. A different synchronic explanation distinguishes between the *form* (unconditional statements) and the *force* (warning).[27] This is more plausible in chapter 28 than in chapter 31. A diachronic explanation regards these shifts as deriving from different historical situations. This again raises the question of whether ascribing to Moses all such words from different rhetorical situations (akin to *vaticinium ex eventu*) was conventional practice, or something profoundly deceptive.

Literary structuring

A third indication of a more complex process of composition comes from evidence of literary structuring and growth. We shall look at three places.[28]

First, there is the location of chapter 27. This chapter raises many other questions for the interpreter, including when and where to erect the steles (vv. 2–4) and what to write on which stones (vv. 3–8). So Nelson is typical of many

---

26. Other examples include 30:1 (curses as well as blessings) and Yhwh's declaration in 31:16–22.

27. In speech-act theory this is the difference between locutionary and illocutionary acts. Cf. Karl Möller, 'Words of (In-)evitable Certitude? Reflections on the Interpretation of Prophetic Oracles of Judgment', in Craig G. Bartholomew, Colin Greene and Karl Möller (eds.), *After Pentecost: Language and Biblical Interpretation*, Scripture and Hermeneutics Series 2 (Carlisle: Paternoster, 2001), pp. 352–386.

28. Other evidence includes the superscriptions of different sections (esp. 4:44, 45).

scholars when he speaks of its 'disjointed' nature.[29] But there is also evidence which points to its location as purposely redactional. Chapter 28 seems a more natural conclusion to chapters 12 – 26.[30] This is apparent from 28:1, where the opening 'and it will be if . . . ' follows naturally from the command to obedience in 26:16–19, but is abrupt after chapter 27; from the blessings and curses in chapter 28 that follow on well from 26:19, but hardly seem necessary after the curses of chapter 27; and from the language of Israel being 'high above the nations' in 28:1 that echoes 26:19. Further, chapter 27 seems loosely connected to chapters 26 and 28. There is the sudden appearance (and subsequent disappearance) of the narrator's voice in 27:1; the locational shift (prospectively) to Mounts Ebal and Gerizim, near Shechem; and the unmarked transition from the Mount Ebal curses back to Moab.[31] Finally, chapter 27 expands on 11:26–30, where the blessing and curse pronounced in Moab is repeated in the ceremony of blessing and curse in the land itself. All these factors suggest that the position of chapter 27 is best explained in terms of intentional literary structuring.

Second, there is the relationship between chapters 4 and 29 – 30.[32] Most significant is the shared temporal perspective. Both sections have a distant horizon, beyond disaster to possible restoration (4:25–31; 29:23 – 30:10). They also have many common motifs and phrases: 'bowing down' and 'serving' gods 'allotted' to the nations (4:19; 29:26); heaven and earth as witnesses against Israel (4:26; 30:19); 'standing' 'before Yhwh (y)our God' (4:10; 29:15); gods or objects of 'wood and stone' (4:28; 29:17); an international perspective (4:6, 32–33; 29:24); Israel responding to Yhwh after destruction 'with all your heart and all your soul' (4:29; 30:2, 6, 10); 'all these things' coming upon Israel and precipitating a 'return' to Yhwh (4:30; 30:1–2); the phrase 'you shall/should take to heart' (4:39; 30:1); knowledge of Yhwh as God as the purpose of Israel's experiences (4:35, 39; 29:6). Some of these motifs and phrases occur elsewhere in Deuteronomy; others are only found in chapter 4 and chapters 29 – 30. These instances could be explained by rhetorical flourish. For many, though, literary shaping is more plausible.[33]

---

29. Nelson, *Deuteronomy*, p. 316.

30. See Block, 'Recovering the Voice of Moses', p. 391 n. 35; Nelson, *Deuteronomy*, p. 315; J. G. McConville, *Deuteronomy*, AOTC (Leicester: Apollos; Downers Grove: InterVarsity Press, 2002), p. 387.

31. Note the first-person speech of Moses in Deut. 28:1 and the resumption of 'today' in 28:13–15 (cf. 26:16–18). For these, see McConville, *Deuteronomy*, p. 401.

32. Several comments here come from the work of a former student, Chris Thomson.

33. See e.g. Jon D. Levenson, 'Who Inserted the Book of the Torah', *HTR* 68 (1975), pp. 203–233.

Third, there is the structuring of chapter 31. Tigay comments, 'More than any other chapter in Deuteronomy, it is characterized by doublets, inconsistencies, interruptions, and variations in vocabulary and concepts that scholars take as evidence of different literary sources.'[34] One example for Tigay is that verses 16–22 interrupt the sequence of Yhwh's planned commissioning of Joshua (vv. 14–15) and the event itself (v. 23). This interruption would explain the unmarked shift in subject from Moses in verse 22 to Yhwh in verse 23 (so most English versions; the Hebrew does not have 'Yhwh', just 'and he commanded'). Yet, as Tigay goes on to note, the structure of the chapter is anything but haphazard. There is, on the one hand, a neat alternating of long and short speeches, and, on the other, a palistrophic structure based around verses 16–22, with different speakers and addressees in view. The effect is to make close connections between Moses' song and the rest of Moses' words; both will serve as instruction and as witnesses against Israel for future generations. The commissioning of Joshua in the middle of this shows Yhwh as 'the driving force in the history of God's people'.[35] It also introduces a delicate dialectic: the optimism fuelled by Yhwh's presence with his chosen leader is tempered by anticipated failure. Failure is not the last word, though. Yhwh's enduring word in song and law not only acts as a witness against Israel, but also tells the story of restoration on the other side of that failure.

Other evidence of different hands at work

The discerning of different sources within a text is controversial. Evidence adduced usually includes language, theme, syntax, structure, discontinuity of thought and similarity to other works.[36] The predisposition of the interpreter makes a significant difference to the approach adopted and the level of confidence expressed. In so far as the distinctive style noted above can be used as an argument for the unity of Deuteronomy, departures from that style may well point to the presence of different hands.

The most egregious examples are Moses' Song (32:1–43) and Blessing (33:2–29). Naturally the different, poetic genre may account for some of the differences, including the large number of unique words. Also for Moses' Song,

---

34. Jeffrey H. Tigay, *Deuteronomy*, JPS Torah Commentary (New York: Jewish Publication Society, 1996), p. 502.

35. Norbert Lohfink, *Theology of the Pentateuch: Themes of the Priestly Narrative and Deuteronomy*, trans. Linda M. Maloney (Minneapolis: Fortress, 1994), p. 247.

36. For most of these, see Richard E. Friedman, 'Torah (Pentateuch)', *ABD* 6:616.

at least, there are many connections with the literary context. The basic narrative of Yhwh's past faithfulness, Israel's current failure and Yhwh's restoration of them means that the song functions largely as a 'summary of the Torah'.[37] Further, many of its words are also found in chapter 31 (e.g. Yhwh 'hiding' his 'face' (31:17–18; 32:20); 'eating, being full, and growing fat' (31:20; 32:15);[38] 'foreign' (*nēkār*; 31:16; 32:12; the only two instances in Deuteronomy). Both of these links point to the careful integration of the song into the present context. But there are also distinctive features. In particular, the retelling of salvation history is very different, as McConville outlines:

> There is no express reference to Israel's deliverance from Egypt, or to Yahweh's bringing them to the promised land. The twin covenants of Horeb and Moab are passed over, as are the comprehensive temporal panorama (patriarchs to return from exile), the journey through time and place, the vision of a nation governed by Yahweh's law as mediated by a diffused administration, and the people most truly itself when worshipping Yahweh at his chosen place.[39]

For some scholars, Deuteronomy 32 is from a different theological tradition.[40] For McConville, it is preferable to say that 'Deuteronomic themes have been deliberately eschatologized'.[41]

Other examples where many scholars have greater confidence that material comes from another hand are those in which several strands of evidence converge. In that vein, Friedman says that 'Dt. 4:25–31; 8:19–20; 28:36–37, 63–68; 29:21–27; 30:1–10, 14–20 . . . show signs of having been composed after the destruction and exile of Judah' because of the 'combination' of the factors noted above and because of a 'thematic commonality' in that 'all refer to apostasy, destruction, exile, and dispersion'.[42]

Other evidence includes the striking change in Moses' address from 'you' singular to 'you' plural (the so-called *Numeruswechsel*); apparent changes in the

---

37. Nathan MacDonald, *Deuteronomy and the Meaning of 'Monotheism'*, FAT 2/1 (Tübingen: Mohr Siebeck, 2003), p. 145. Cf. Olson, *Deuteronomy*, p. 129.

38. Following the Samaritan Pentateuch. See *BHQ: Deuteronomy*, p. 144*; Nelson, *Deuteronomy*, p. 367 n. i.

39. McConville, *Deuteronomy*, p. 461.

40. A. D. H. Mayes, *Deuteronomy*, NCBC (London: Marshall, Morgan & Scott, 1979), p. 380; Tigay, *Deuteronomy*, p. 510.

41. McConville, *Deuteronomy*, p. 461.

42. Friedman, *ABD* 6:616.

referent of a word (e.g. 'covenant' in ch. 4;[43] 'Torah' as sometimes oral, sometimes written; and 'fathers' as sometimes the exodus generation and sometimes the patriarchs).[44]

Evaluation

Two points need to be held together. First, there is the striking unity that is present in the text. It makes sense to speak of a 'Deuteronomic' style. It is no surprise that many scholars regard all, or almost all, of Deuteronomy 5 – 26 as from the same hand. On the other hand, there are signs of a depth perspective within the book as a whole. This accords with the conclusion above that the book demands that we listen both as Moses' hearers *and* as the narrator's hearers.

The testimony of tradition

There are two interlocking issues as we turn to explicit testimony outside Deuteronomy. First, there is testimony that might give further indications on the existence and availability of the book. Second, there is testimony that might illuminate the relation of Moses to it.

The phrase which designates Deuteronomy in the book itself is 'the book of the law' (28:61; 29:20; 30:10; 31:26). This occurs elsewhere (sometimes as 'the book of the law of Moses/God') in the Old Testament: repeatedly in Joshua (1:8; 8:31, 34; 23:6; 24:26); once more prior to Josiah (2 Kgs 14:6); in Josiah's reform (2 Kgs 22:8, 11); and in post-exilic works (2 Chr. 17:9; 34:14–15; and five times in Neh. 8:1 – 9:3).

The references in the book of Joshua are part of the depiction of Joshua as the ideal leader (perhaps kingly; cf. Deut. 17:18–20), a depiction that Nelson in particular associates with Josiah.[45] The referent of the phrase is arguably not

---

43. Nelson, *Deuteronomy*, p. 62.

44. Thomas Römer, 'Deuteronomy in Search of Origins', in Gary N. Knoppers and J. Gordon McConville (eds.), *Reconsidering Israel and Judah: Recent Studies on the Deuteronomistic History*, Sources for Biblical and Theological Study 8 (Winona Lake: Eisenbrauns, 2000), pp. 112–138.

45. See especially Richard D. Nelson, 'Josiah in the Book of Joshua', *JBL* 100 (1981), pp. 531–540. It could, though, be 'the standard for all leaders'. See J. Gordon McConville and Stephen Williams, *Joshua*, Two Horizons Old Testament Commentary (Grand Rapids: Eerdmans, 2010), p. 14.

what was later called the Pentateuch, but some version of Deuteronomy.[46] The reference in 2 Kings 14, quoting the law of individual responsibility from Deuteronomy 24:16, could either indicate the existence of a version of Deuteronomy during the reign of Amaziah, or be a post-Josianic description of where that law is now to be found.[47] The reference in 2 Chronicles 17:9 could, on its own, indicate the existence of Deuteronomy during Jehoshaphat's reign. However, 'though by the Chronicler's own day such a designation would probably refer to the Pentateuch, one cannot insist on that significance for the time of Jehoshaphat'.[48] In similar vein, the referent of the phrase in Nehemiah *may* be Deuteronomy, or some version of the Pentateuch, but it is not possible to be certain.[49]

The explicit testimony of the Old Testament, then, is of the existence of some version of Deuteronomy within the lifetime of Moses' successor. Further, Moses is closely linked with this book. This is evident from the title, 'the book of the law of Moses' (Josh. 8:31; 23:6) and from the fact that the book contains what Moses is said to have commanded (e.g. Josh. 1:7; 8:31).

In other places, while a book itself is not mentioned, laws attributed to Moses form the basis for action. In some places, the language is closely connected to that in Deuteronomy. Three examples illustrate this. First, David charged Solomon with keeping the law of Moses (1 Kgs 2:3). Second, Jehu 'was not careful to follow the law of the LORD the God of Israel with all his heart' (2 Kgs 10:31). He neglected to turn from the self-devised religion of Jeroboam, consisting of the wrong people offering sacrifices to wrong deities in the wrong place at the wrong time (1 Kgs 12:25–33). Third, Hezekiah's reform (2 Kgs 18:4–6) resembles that prescribed in Deuteronomy 12:1–7 in 'breaking standing stones' and in dealing with Asheroth. There is a further link in the crushing (*ktt*) of Nehushtan, since this verb is used in 9:21 of Moses' action with the golden calf, but not in the Exodus account.

The explicit testimony, then, is of the early and ongoing availability and Mosaic origin of the commands found in Deuteronomy. This Old Testament testimony is matched by that of the New. Moses is said to have given the

46. McConville and Williams, *Joshua*, p. 14.

47. Mordechai Cogan and Hayim Tadmor, *II Kings*, AB 11 (New York: Doubleday, 1988), p. 155.

48. Raymond B. Dillard, *2 Chronicles*, WBC 15 (Waco: Word, 1987), p. 134.

49. For a succinct statement of the options, see Michael W. Duggan, *The Covenant Renewal in Ezra–Nehemiah (Neh. 7:72b – 10:40): An Exegetical, Literary, and Theological Study*, SBLDS 164 (Atlanta: Society of Biblical Literature, 2001), p. 20.

command about divorce (Matt. 19:7–8; cf. Deut. 24:1–4) and to have spoken about God's provoking to jealousy (Rom. 10:19; cf. Deut. 32:21). Further, Jesus says that Moses *wrote* about him (John 5:46), which may, as Carson observes, be a reference to Deuteronomy 18:15,[50] and the Sadducees speak of Moses' writing the law about levirate marriage (Luke 20:28; cf. Deut. 25:5–10). The later Babylonian Talmud also speaks of Moses writing his book (*Baba Bathra* 14b).

The significance given to this testimony relates very closely to the significance given to the testimony of the book of Deuteronomy itself. For some scholars it is irrefutable proof of Mosaic origin and authorship. For others, it is relativized by other data. As with Deuteronomy's explicit testimony, interpreting these statements historically is essential.

Deuteronomy's relationship to the rest of the Pentateuch

Continuity
First, at the most basic level, Deuteronomy recapitulates and continues the story begun in Genesis 1. The analogy of Yhwh 'hovering' like an eagle matches the wind of God 'hovering' over the water (*rḥp*; Gen. 1:2; Deut. 32:11);[51] the 'formlessness' of creation matches the 'formlessness' of the wilderness (*tōhû*; Gen. 1:1; Deut. 32:10); so at the end of Deuteronomy God's act of redemption is associated with his act of creation.[52]

Deuteronomy describes the land in creation terms, as 'good' (Deut. 1:25–35; cf. Gen. 1), with Edenic abundance. There are many parallels between Adam in Eden and Israel in the land. Dumbrell notes:

> Like Adam (Gn. 2:8), Israel was formed outside of the land. Placed in the land by God, she was given a code which was to regulate life there. In the land she was promised particular access to the divine presence, but the threat existed that if the regulations were not kept, she would be expelled from the land.[53]

---

50. D. A. Carson, *The Gospel According to John* (Leicester: Inter-Varsity Press, 1991), p. 266.

51. These are the only two occurrences of the piel of *rḥp* in the Old Testament.

52. Deuteronomy's connection of redemption with creation is also apparent in its grounding of the sabbath command in deliverance from Egypt, mirroring Exodus's grounding of it in creation.

53. William J. Dumbrell, *The Faith of Israel: Its Expression in the Books of the Old Testament*, 1st ed. (Leicester: Apollos, 1988), p. 56.

Further, Israel as the son of God inheriting the land (14:1; 32:5–6; cf. 8:5) matches Adam as son of God receiving the gift of Eden.[54] The sanctuary nature of the garden where Yhwh walks about is matched by the sanctuary nature of the camp where Yhwh walks about (hitpael of *hlk*; Gen. 3:8; Deut. 23:14), and ultimately by the sanctuary nature of the land where Yhwh will make his name dwell (Deut. 12) and where he will be near his people (4:7). The choice of life or death, prosperity (lit. 'good', *ṭôb*) or destruction (lit. 'evil', *rā'*) confronting the people on the edge of the Promised Land is precisely the same choice that confronted Adam and Eve in the garden (Deut. 30:15; Gen. 2:17). Finally, 'the verbs "multiply" and "bless" [in Deut. 1:10–11] recall the creation account (Gn. 1:28); God's initial words of blessing are enacted in Israel, who is the carrier of YHWH's will for all creation'.[55]

Second, Deuteronomy is part of a wider story driven by the promises made to Abraham (1:8; 30:20; 34:4). This is no surprise, given that Genesis presents Abraham as the one through whom Yhwh's purposes for creation will be fulfilled. Hence the apparently conditional nature of the blessings in Deuteronomy must be interpreted within the wider context of the covenant made with Abraham. Also, the boundaries of the land in Deuteronomy 1:7 match those envisaged in Genesis 15:8–10.

Third, Moses, the dominant figure since the start of Exodus, dies as Deuteronomy ends. There is a sense of closure, notwithstanding the fact that the land itself remains to be possessed.

Finally, although God's people at the end of Deuteronomy are no nearer to the land geographically than at the start, they are nearer narratively. The death of Moses, anticipated from Numbers 20, climaxes the book, and a successor is nominated and commissioned.

Discontinuity

Language and style

Alongside this evident continuity, though, there are some striking discontinuities. As noted above, Deuteronomy is distinctive within the Pentateuch in both turn of phrase and vocabulary. This is not to say that such phrasing and vocabulary are necessarily unique to Deuteronomy; indeed, a number of

---

54. The notion of Adam as God's son, articulated in Luke 3:38, is clear from the language of 'image' and 'likeness' used both of Adam's son Seth (Gen. 5:3) and of God's creating Adam (Gen. 5:1).

55. Walter Brueggemann, *Deuteronomy*, Abingdon OTC (Nashville: Abingdon, 2001), p. 27.

scholars have seen Deuteronomic material in Genesis–Numbers.[56] It is rather to point out that there *is* something distinct. The death of Moses' mouthpiece Aaron (Num. 20:28) cannot account for the different style in Deuteronomy because of the significant stylistic differences between Numbers 21 – 36 and Deuteronomy.

Laws

Deuteronomy is also distinctive in regard to its laws.[57] Although it often covers the same ground as the several codes elsewhere,[58] many of the laws have a distinctive slant. To illustrate, I shall focus on four passages where Deuteronomy differs from Exodus.[59]

Perhaps most famously, the Decalogue in Deuteronomy (5:6–21) differs from that in Exodus (Exod. 20:2–17). The main contrast concerns the sabbath (Exod. 20:8–11; Deut. 5:12–15). In Deuteronomy, the injunction is to 'observe' (*šmr*) rather than 'remember' (*zkr*) the sabbath, possibly because it self-consciously appeals to an already established command (cf. v. 12b) and because it uses 'remember' of historical events.[60] In Deuteronomy 5:14, there is an additional motivational clause founded in the ethical concern that slaves also rest. Most strikingly, the observance of the sabbath is rooted in redemption, not creation as in Exodus. Other significant differences in the Decalogue are the connecting

---

56. See e.g. Joseph Blenkinsopp, *The Pentateuch: An Introduction to the First Five Books of the Bible* (London: SCM, 1992), pp. 186–194.

57. See Kenton L. Sparks, *God's Word in Human Words: An Evangelical Appropriation of Critical Biblical Scholarship* (Grand Rapids: Baker Academic, 2008), p. 91.

58. The Book of the Covenant (BC; Exod. 21 – 23); the Priestly Code (P; including Lev. 1 – 16); the Holiness Code (H; Lev. 17 – 26). Some laws occur in several codes; the wording and order in Deuteronomy is closer to BC than to P/H.

59. The relationship between Deuteronomy and P/H is harder to assess, because of the ways the laws are framed. For some scholars, P/H is later because it assumes what is commanded in Deuteronomy, and Deuteronomy makes no reference to laws it would be expected to mention; older traditions may be found in P/H, but Deuteronomy is prior. For others, it is possible to demonstrate Deuteronomy's indebtedness to P/H, but not vice versa. For the former, see G. I. Davies, 'Introduction to the Pentateuch', in John Barton and John Muddiman (eds.), *The Oxford Bible Commentary* (Oxford: Oxford University Press, 2001), pp. 12–38; for the latter, see e.g. Jacob Milgrom, *Leviticus 1 – 16: A New Translation with Introduction and Commentary*, AB 3 (New York: Doubleday, 1991), pp. 8–10.

60. Nelson, *Deuteronomy*, p. 82.

waw ('and') in Deuteronomy 5:18–21, which unifies the second group of five, and the change in order and in verbs in the final commandment (Exod. 20:17; Deut. 5:21). In Exodus, the command is not to 'covet' (*ḥmd*) your neighbour's 'house' and not to 'covet' (*ḥmd*) his 'wife . . . '; in Deuteronomy, it is not to 'covet' (*ḥmd*) your neighbour's 'wife' then not to 'long for' (*'wh*) his 'house . . . '.

A second place is the Passover celebration. In Exodus the animal for that first Passover is to be a lamb or kid (*śeh*); it is to be eaten 'roasted over the fire' and not 'raw' or 'boiled in water' (*bšl*) and is to be eaten in their homes. This is to be celebrated as a 'perpetual ordinance' for 'your generations' (Exod. 12:3–9, 21–24). In Deuteronomy the animal is to be taken from 'flock' (*ṣō'n*) or 'herd' (*bāqār*); they are to 'cook' (*bšl*; 'boil'?) it and 'eat it', not in their own towns but in the place Yhwh will choose as a dwelling for his name. The next day they may return to their tents (16:1–7).[61]

A third place where there are significant differences is in laws concerning the release of slaves (Deut. 15:12–18; Exod. 21:2–11; cf. Lev. 25:39–46, though it uses different vocabulary, particularly the fifty-year Jubilee). The laws in Deuteronomy and Exodus have points of similarity:[62] release is in the seventh year; the law has to do with 'Hebrew' people; those released will be 'free'; there is the option for the slave to make service permanent; 'love' for the master is involved in that decision; permanence (*'ōlām*) is sealed by 'ear-piercing' 'in the door' with an 'awl'. But there are also significant differences: the initiating agent is the poor person (Deut. 15:12: 'sells himself', or perhaps, 'is sold') or the master (Exod. 21:2: 'buys'); the person sold is designated *'āḥ*, 'brother'/'kinsman' (Deut. 15:12) or 'slave' (Exod. 21:2). In Deuteronomy alone women are included equally (as *'āḥ*), there is generous giving on release, and motivation is rooted in the experience of Yhwh's blessing and Israel's slavery. Finally, in Exodus alone the decision of the slave to remain is also shaped by the desire to stay with his wife and his children born while a slave.

A fourth area of difference concerns the place of sacrifice, mentioned at the start of both sets of legislation. For Levinson, for instance, the authors of Deuteronomy reapply the language of Exodus to give authority to their own agenda, though the latter actually contradicts the original law. The Deuteronomists are fostering two main reforms: from sacrifice at any place to sacrifice at one place, and from limiting animal slaughter to the cult to allowing it in a non-cultic context. Deuteronomy modifies the Exodus law by:

---

61. Cf. 2 Chr. 35:13.

62. The majority of similarities and all the differences are noted in McConville, *Deuteronomy*, pp. 261–264.

1. prohibition: 'in every place' (Exod. 20:24) becomes 'not . . . in every place' (Deut. 12:13);
2. requirement: sacrifice must be 'in the place which Yhwh will choose' (12:14);
3. permission: 'you may slaughter . . . in every one of your settlements' (12:15).[63]

In other words, this new law 'conforms both in substance and in formulation to the older legal norm' as found in Exodus 20, but it is in fact a 'rhetorical straw man erected by the authors of Deuteronomy' that 'camouflages the real point of the exercise: functionally to abrogate that law with its affirmation of multiple altar sites as legitimate for sacrifice'.[64]

Theology/concepts

Many scholars also highlight distinctive Deuteronomic theology and concepts. I will give one example in more detail, then mention a few others.

The notion of Yhwh's presence is articulated differently: Deuteronomy speaks of Yhwh as dwelling in heaven (Deut. 26:15), while in Exodus Yhwh's dwelling is the sanctuary (e.g. Exod. 25:8). Similarly, in Deuteronomy Yhwh is present *by his word* and the Israelites have not *seen* Yhwh. Thus, when Deuteronomy emphasizes sight in 4:34–36, what is seen is Yhwh's actions or his great fire. Where the focus is on experiencing Yhwh, it is hearing his voice *from heaven* (4:36a) or, strikingly, seeing a voice (4:12).[65] For some scholars, this is evidence of a sharp disjunction between the secular Deuteronomic conception and the sacral priestly one. Yhwh is present on earth in Deuteronomy by means of his 'name' or 'word',[66] in contrast to God's immanence ('real presence') in the tabernacle in Exodus and Leviticus.

Other Deuteronomic distinctives include *desacralization*,[67] since Deuteronomy shows little concern for sin, guilt and how offerings and sacrifices are to be made, unlike Leviticus–Numbers; *holiness*, 'inherent' in Israel's 'biological nature'

---

63. Levinson, *Deuteronomy*, pp. 28–36.

64. Ibid., p. 31.

65. Compare also Deut. 5:24 and Exod. 33:20.

66. The seminal essay is Gerhard von Rad, 'Deuteronomy's "Name" Theology and the Priestly Document's "Kabod" Theology', in *Studies in Deuteronomy*, SBT 9 (London: SCM, 1953), pp. 37–44. See also Moshe Weinfeld, *Deuteronomy and the Deuteronomic School* (Oxford: Clarendon Press, 1972); Weinfeld, *Deuteronomy 1 – 11*.

67. So, especially, Weinfeld.

in D, but presented as an 'ideal' or task for Israel in H, J and E;[68] *priesthood* as the domain of all the tribe of Levi in Deuteronomy, but reserved for the Aaronites in Leviticus–Numbers; *governance*, since Deuteronomy has a law on kingship and a developed conception of distributed constitutional powers, unlike the other law codes; *women and sex*, since Deuteronomy is interested in ownership and protecting a man's property rights, while Leviticus is concerned for classification and the preservation of boundaries.[69]

Recounting of history

A fourth distinctive between Deuteronomy and the rest of the Pentateuch concerns the recounting of history, with varying degrees of discontinuity.[70] Deuteronomic mention of what is not noted elsewhere (e.g. 1:6–8) is hardly significant. Elsewhere there are differences that are striking but ultimately reconcilable through harmonization and the discerning of a distinctive rhetorical purpose. For instance, in the appointing of judges (1:9–18) and spies (1:22), Moses identifies the significant role played by the people, a characteristic theme in the democratizing Deuteronomy. Other passages, though, make it harder for many scholars to envisage the same author. A case in point is the number of visits that the Israelites made to Kadesh-barnea and the length of time they spent there.[71] Deuteronomy 2:14 seems to indicate that they left Kadesh thirty-eight years before entering the land, during which they wandered around Edom (2:1). Numbers 14:25 gives instructions for the Israelites to leave Kadesh-barnea, dovetailing with the Deuteronomy account. However, whether they actually did or not, the Israelites are back at Kadesh in Numbers 20:1, at the end of the wilderness wandering.[72]

Evaluation

Among many readers, there is an understandable concern for harmonization and reconciliation. Some differences *may* be more apparent than real. Concerning differences in law codes, it has been suggested that Exodus's altar law

---

68. Jacob Milgrom, 'Holy, Holiness, OT', in Katharine D. Sakenfeld (ed.), *The New Interpreter's Dictionary of the Bible*, 5 vols. (Nashville: Abingdon, 2006–9), vol. 2, p. 853.

69. Deborah L. Ellens, *Women in the Sex Texts of Leviticus and Deuteronomy: A Comparative Conceptual Analysis*, LHB/OTS 458 (London: T&T Clark, 2007).

70. See Driver, *Deuteronomy*, pp. xxxv–xxxvii.

71. See ibid., pp. xxxvi, 32–33; Tigay, *Deuteronomy*, p. 426.

72. Note that this is the time of Miriam's death. That Kadesh is an alternative name for Kadesh-barnea is clear from Deut. 1:19, 46.

could be read as distributive, envisaging not multiple simultaneous sites but multiple sequential ones. This is improbable, though, given the existence of multiple simultaneous sites subsequently and Deuteronomy's picking up of Exodus's language and changing it. An alternative is that Deuteronomy allows certain sacrifices to take place at other sites, but restricts some sacrifices to a single site, the place Yhwh will choose.[73] With regard to purportedly different theologies of Yhwh's presence, reticence about seeing God should not be taken to assume that Yhwh is not present. At the end of Moses' first speech (4:36c), 'his words you heard from the midst of the fire' removes the sharp distinction between 'hearing Yhwh' from 'heaven' and 'seeing fire' on 'earth'.[74] Further, Yhwh brings them out 'with his own presence' (4:37; cf. Exod. 33:14; Isa. 63:9). 'Invisibility does not mean absence.'[75] It is possible to scrutinize every difference and attempt to harmonize. However, reconciliation and harmonization are not my focus, though I am not trying to suggest ultimate contradiction. What I am trying to do is outline differences discerned and to explore explanations for these differences. On any reading, Deuteronomy *is* different in significant ways.

Every scholarly explanation is articulated in terms of change of the rhetorical situation that gave rise to the laws, but the precise change differs. Some account for the differences by saying the laws in Exodus 20 – Numbers 10 were given for life in the desert rather than life in the land. This explanation is inadequate because many laws in Exodus are explicitly about life in the land (e.g. Exod. 22:5–6). Another explanation is that the laws in Deuteronomy are reflective of the forty-year gap, where Israel's faithlessness has come to the fore and in other ways they have changed. Those doubting Mosaic origin or authorship find this explanation of the change of situation less plausible than one that posits different authorship and a more significant change of social situation.[76] Driver's preface to his commentary captures the response of many scholars: Deuteronomy would be 'intelligible . . . as a work of the Mosaic age . . . if it stood perfectly alone'. However, this opinion is no longer 'intelligible' when looking at the book (especially chs. 12 – 26) 'in the light shed upon it by other parts of the Old

---

73. See Jeffrey J. Niehaus, 'The Central Sanctuary: Where and When?', *TynB* 43 (1992), pp. 3–30.

74. Cf. Nathan MacDonald, 'The Literary Criticism and Rhetorical Logic of Deuteronomy i–iv', *VT* 56 (2006), p. 215.

75. McConville, *Deuteronomy*, p. 106. Cf. Ian Wilson, *Out of the Midst of the Fire: Divine Presence in Deuteronomy*, SBLDS 151 (Atlanta: Scholars Press, 1995), pp. 45–53.

76. Indeed, most contemporary scholarship denies to Moses *both* Deuteronomy *and* the other law codes.

Testament'; in short, 'a study of it in that light reveals too many features which are inconsistent with such a supposition'.[77]

What is at stake in favouring one of these explanations over another is not one set of presuppositions against another, at least not directly. Rather, what is in view is the relative significance granted to different types of evidence.

Deuteronomy and Josiah's reforms

A further aspect thought by many scholars to 'anchor the origins of Deuteronomy in the first three-quarters of the seventh century'[78] is the relationship between it and the reforms of King Josiah (2 Kgs 22 – 23; 2 Chr. 34 – 35). The putative relation between Deuteronomy and Josiah's reforms is complex and controversial, but essentially the debate can be reduced to four questions. First, was Deuteronomy the book found in the temple? Second, did it provide the impetus for Josiah's reforms? Third, was it written for Josiah's reforms? Finally, what precisely was the extent of the book in the first three questions?[79] The following discussion will answer the questions *en route* rather than take them directly, since many of the issues are interlocking.

The account in Kings intends to connect Josiah's reforms with Deuteronomy.

1. Deuteronomy insists that worship must occur at the place where Yhwh will choose to put his name (chs. 12 – 16); similar language elsewhere refers to Jerusalem (2 Sam. 7; 1 Kgs 8:29; 2 Kgs 21:4; 23:27).
2. The reforms that Josiah undertook mirror those demanded in Deuteronomy: the purging of idolatrous practices;[80] the celebration of the Passover in one place (Deut. 16:6; in contrast to the family home in Exod. 12; 2 Kgs 23:21–23).[81]

---

77. Driver, *Deuteronomy*, p. xii.
78. Nelson, *Deuteronomy*, p. 6.
79. That the account is utopian and has no basis in fact is wholly implausible. There are no obvious reasons for the reforms documented to be so different from those of other righteous Davidic kings unless the discovery is rooted in an historical event. See Rofé, *Deuteronomy*, p. 4.
80. Note particularly the prohibitions against male temple prostitutes (*qādēš*; Deut. 23:18).
81. Note also the identical language: 'make [*ʿśh*] a Passover [*psḥ*] to Yhwh [*lyhwh*] your God [*ʾlhyk(m)*]' (Deut. 16:1; 2 Kgs 23:21). Elsewhere (Exod. 12:48; Num. 9:10, 14), 'your God' is missing.

3. Deuteronomy is a strongly covenantal work; Josiah makes a covenant (2 Kgs 23:2, 21).

4. Deuteronomy 28 gives curses for disobedience; 2 Kings 22:13, 19 speaks of Israel as an object of 'wrath' and a 'curse'.

5. Josiah was unique in turning to Yhwh with all his 'heart', 'soul' and 'might' (2 Kgs 23:25); the only other conjunction of these three words is in Deuteronomy 6:5.

6. The book found is described as the 'book of the law' (2 Kgs 22:11), which is the self-designation of Deuteronomy (Deut. 28:61; 29:20; 30:10; 31:26).[82]

7. Deuteronomy insists on consulting prophets, rather than mediums or spiritists (Deut. 18:9–22); Josiah consulted a prophetess, Huldah (2 Kgs 22:14) and removed mediums (2 Kgs 23:24), 'establishing' the 'book of the law' in the process.

8. Deuteronomy defined the rule of the king, insisting that he should read it (Deut. 17:14–20); Josiah took the law seriously, hearing it (2 Kgs 22:11) and reading it (2 Kgs 23:2–3).

9. The focus on all of Israel involved in the covenant in Moab (Deut. 29) is matched by the emphasis on all Israel making the covenant in Josiah's day (2 Kgs 23:2–3, 21).

Cumulatively, the writer of 2 Kings intends to connect Josiah's reforms with the book of Deuteronomy.[83]

The close connections between the Kings account of Josiah's reforms and Deuteronomy have led many scholars, beginning with de Wette, to regard Deuteronomy as *written for* the reforms. Reference to the 'place' that 'Yhwh will choose' to put his 'name' is then seen as an unsubtle reference to Jerusalem, given verisimilitude by the reticence actually to *name* the place in Deuteronomy. The account in Chronicles is regarded as derivative of Kings, and of less historical value.

However, the connection between Deuteronomy and both Jerusalem and Josiah's reforms is not as straightforward as this view might suggest, for several

---

82. Although the term 'book of the covenant' is used in Exod. 24:7 of the covenant code, in 2 Kgs 23:1 it must indicate a different book, presumably Deuteronomy, since there is no Passover celebration in the covenant code.

83. See further Ernest W. Nicholson, *Deuteronomy and Tradition: Literary and Historical Problems in the Book of Deuteronomy* (Philadelphia: Fortress, 1967), p. 3; Weinfeld, *Deuteronomy 1 – 11*, pp. 81–82.

reasons. First, chapter 12 does not sanction one *permanent* centre (Jerusalem?) but simply one centre, which could conceivably change. This fits with evidence elsewhere that Yhwh made his name dwell first at Shiloh.[84] Deuteronomy itself mandates altar-building and sacrifices on Mount Ebal (27:1–8) and implies the existence, indeed sanctioning, of other altars (16:21; 33:19). So it hardly makes sense to see it as *written* to limit worship to Jerusalem. One response to this is to suggest that the 'core' of Deuteronomy (*Ur-Deuteronomium*) found in the temple was more limited in scope. In an already full day, it was read at least twice (2 Kgs 22:8, 11; 23:1).[85] Driver identified *Ur-Deuteronomium* as chapters 5 – 26 and 28, on the basis of their strong stylistic unity;[86] others limit it to chapters 12 – 26, though recent scholarship discerns many layers in these chapters.[87] We noted above that chapter 27 breaks the flow in some ways. However, excluding this chapter from *Ur-Deuteronomium* raises a significant problem: how and why would northern emphases (Mounts Ebal and Gerizim in chs. 11 and 27) be incorporated into Deuteronomy long after the northern kingdom had been annexed?[88]

Second, the account of Josiah's actions does not relate straightforwardly to Deuteronomy. One of the key terms in 2 Kings 23:4–20, 'high places' (*bāmôt*), does not occur in Deuteronomy; there is no mention of the book of the law in these verses; and some of the reforms cannot be derived from Deuteronomy alone (e.g. the desecrations in vv. 6b, 14).[89] Further, some scholars draw distinctions between the account of the reforms themselves (2 Kgs 23:4–20) and the surrounding account, patterned after covenant renewal (2 Kgs 22:3 – 23:3, 21–23).[90] Perhaps, then, Deuteronomy influences not so much the reforms

---

84. Jer. 7:12; cf. Josh. 18:1; 19:51; 22:12; 1 Sam. 1 – 3. There may have been other locations, possibly on rotation, such as Bethel (cf. Judg. 20:18), Shechem (Deut. 27 implicitly; Josh. 8:30–35; 24) and Gilgal.

85. Weinfeld, *Deuteronomy 1 – 11*, p. 84.

86. Driver, *Deuteronomy*, p. lxv.

87. See the brief summary in Carsten Vang, 'The So-Called "Ur-Deuteronomium" – Some Reflections on Its Content, Size and Age', *Hiphil* 6 (2009), pp. 3–5, available at www.see-j.net/index.php/hiphil.

88. Cf. Gordon J. Wenham, 'The Date of Deuteronomy: Linch-Pin of Old Testament Criticism: Part Two', *Themelios* 11/1 (1985), p. 16.

89. For this and others, see Nelson, *Deuteronomy*, pp. 6–7.

90. For a succinct summary, see Gwilym H. Jones, *1 and 2 Kings: Based on the Revised Standard Version*, 2 vols., NCB (London: Marshall, Morgan & Scott, 1984), pp. 607–609, 615–617.

themselves of 23:4–20, but more the depiction of events in this latter account. It is true that some features, such as the permitting of non-sacrificial slaughter (Deut. 12:13–25), the provision for converting tithes to money (14:22–27) and the passover provision (16:1–8) fit with a programme of centralizing worship to one place.[91] However, for Josiah, even in the 'covenant' account, the problem is not lack of centralized worship, but of idolatry, abandoning Yhwh and serving other gods (2 Kgs 22:17).

Third, the depiction of kingship in Deuteronomy is not something that would be written to strengthen Josiah. It is true that Josiah embodies the piety that the king of 17:14–20 is expected to display. However, in Deuteronomy as a whole, the role of the king is ignored. Yhwh, not the king, is land-giver, war-fighter and law-maker. Yhwh's son is Israel, not the king (1:31; 14:1; contrast Ps. 2:7). Justice and righteousness are the people's responsibility rather than the king's. It would be foolhardy to downgrade even a young king.

Fourth, the account of Josiah's reforms in Kings stands in some chronological tension with that of 2 Chronicles. It may well be that the book of the law was not quite as central to the reforms as first appears. Both the order of events and the regnal year ascribed to them differ in the two accounts.[92]

	2 Chronicles			**2 Kings**		
	Order	Year	Ref.	Order	Year	Ref.
Seeking God	1	8th	34:2	–	–	–
Purging pagan cults	2	12th–18th	34:2–14	4	18th	23:4–20, 24
Temple repairs	3	18th	34:8–28	1	18th	22:2–7
Law book discovery	4	18th	34:15	2	18th	22:8
Covenant renewal	5	18th	34:29–33	3	18th	23:3
Passover	6	18th	35:1–19	5	18th	23:21–23
Death	7		35:20–27	6		23:29–30

Both accounts are stylized, reflecting the concerns of their respective authors. Chronicles stresses retribution, especially with Josiah's death, and the celebration of the Passover. Kings stresses the role played by the book of the law.

---

91. Evidence that there were not many centres includes the language of 'choosing' (see Nelson, *Deuteronomy*, p. 148); the place may be far away (12:21); the tiers of the judicial system and the place for hard cases (16:18 – 17:13; cf. 1:9–18).

92. Other main differences are the amount of space devoted to the celebration of the Passover and the reasons for Josiah's death.

There is much to be said for seeing Chronicles as connecting more closely with the events themselves, not least because its chronology fits well with the Assyrian decline and the death of Ashurbanipal in 627 BC. This does not mean that political expediency alone was the reason for the reforms, for the deities purged were mostly not Assyrian (though there were horses dedicated to the sun god; 2 Kgs 23:11). In any case, it was not Assyrian custom to impose deities, despite the imposition of temple tax and religious tribute.[93] The critical point is that Chronicles indicates that the purge of pagan cults started *before* the discovery of the law book. In Kings, the fact that Josiah was already repairing the temple when the law book was found may point to reforming activity prior to the book's discovery, but it is somewhat different from the full-scale reforms which Chronicles seems to indicate.

Fifth, a century earlier Hezekiah undertook reforms (2 Kgs 18:4–6) which also seem to echo Deuteronomy 12:1–7. Although these reforms are not explicitly said to be in accord with the book of the law, one cannot conclude simply on this basis that no written book existed then. After all, Hezekiah 'kept the commandments that Yhwh commanded Moses' (2 Kgs 18:6). The glowing commendation of Hezekiah (v. 5) suggests a pre-Josianic version of Kings climaxing with Hezekiah.[94] The juxtaposition of this commendation with mention of Hezekiah's obedience shows this pre-Josianic version is aware of Mosaic commands on the purity of worship.

In summary, the book of Kings makes a strong connection between Josiah's reforms and (some version of) Deuteronomy, but Deuteronomy was not *written* for Josiah's reforms, which had already started. Notwithstanding issues surrounding the time taken to read it, it is likely that at least Deuteronomy 5 – 28 was found and that it provided some further impetus for the reforms.

Deuteronomy and other Old Testament material

Deuteronomy is often regarded as the centre of the Old Testament and of Old Testament theology because Deuteronomic thought-forms and phrasing are to be found across a substantial cross-section of the Old Testament. In this section we will look at four such connections.

---

93. See Mordechai Cogan, 'Judah Under Assyrian Hegemony: A Reexamination of Imperialism and Religion', *JBL* 112/3 (1993), pp. 403–414. Cf. 2 Kgs 17:27–28.

94. Baruch Halpern and David S. Vanderhooft, 'The Editions of Kings in the 7th – 6th Centuries BCE', *HUCA* 62 (1991), p. 207.

Deuteronomistic History (DtH)

Ever since the work of Martin Noth, the dominant scholarly paradigm has treated Deuteronomy–Kings as a unity of some kind. Most scholars have moved from Noth's single exilic author to either two redactions, at the time of Josiah and then in exile (the 'Cross school'), or three redactions, all in exile (the 'Göttingen school'). Others have returned to essentially one exilic work with later additions, while others still have been sceptical about the notion of a Deuteronomistic History at all.[95] For the vast majority of scholars, the writers were working with an already existing *Ur-Deuteronomium*.

Some data indicates a connection between Deuteronomy and these books (and a distinction between these and the rest of the Pentateuch), in addition to the obvious point that there is a narrative flow and continuous storyline.[96] First, there is the distinctive thematic link of idolatry, evidenced, for example, in the phrase 'other gods' (*'ĕlōhîm 'ăḥērîm*). Second, the threat of being cast out of the land frames the account (e.g. 4:26–31; 28:63, 68; 29:28; 2 Kgs 25:11, 21). Third, Moses' speech in Deuteronomy provides a pattern for the speeches at pivotal moments within DtH (Josh. 23; 1 Sam. 12; 1 Kgs 8). Fourth, Deuteronomy establishes the importance of prophets (18:9–22) who are major characters in the subsequent books, with history happening according to the word of Yhwh. Fifth, there are significant connections between Deuteronomy and the individual books. Deuteronomy and Joshua are connected by events (e.g. the ceremony anticipated in Deut. 27 is carried out in Josh. 8), motifs, speeches and language.[97] Deuteronomy and Judges are related by the problems of doing what is evil in Yhwh's sight, a certain ambivalence about kingship,[98] and by the depiction of inveterate faithlessness, judgment in anger, appeal to Yhwh and 'grace' the other side of judgment. Deuteronomy and Samuel are connected by concerns for kingship and by the implicit portrayal of Samuel as a prophet like Moses.[99]

---

95. For a summary, see Thomas C. Römer, *The So-Called Deuteronomistic History: A Sociological, Historical and Literary Introduction* (London: T&T Clark, 2006), pp. 13–44.

96. See ibid., pp. 40–41, for the first three.

97. See especially Gordon J. Wenham, 'The Deuteronomic Theology of the Book of Joshua', *JBL* 90 (1971), pp. 140–148.

98. In Judges the regret over the lack of a king in chs. 17 – 21 is matched by Gideon's refusal to be king and the negative portrayal of the first king, the 'bramble' Abimelech, in ch. 9.

99. As the first major prophetic figure after Deuteronomy, Samuel appears to be the fulfilment of Deut. 18:15–19. Like Moses, he is Yhwh's servant (1 Sam. 3:9), who intercedes for the people (1 Sam. 7:5–6; 12:19, 23), none of whose 'words' 'fell' (1 Sam. 3:19; cf. Josh. 21:45; Deut. 12:10).

Deuteronomy and Kings are connected by the intimate link between doing evil in Yhwh's sight, idolatry and judgment climaxing in exile. There are further verbal echoes between Deuteronomy and these books.[100] Cumulatively, then, the notion of one work from Deuteronomy to Kings makes sense of the data.

On the other hand, there is also a distinctiveness of Deuteronomy from DtH that makes a straightforward unity of authorship implausible. Two examples demonstrate this. First, Deuteronomy envisages a speedy destruction and expulsion from the land if there is idolatry (4:26; 7:4; 11:17; 28:20; cf. 7:10). This is different from the portrayal found in the rest of DtH.[101] Second, some of the language and terminology differs between Deuteronomy and DtH: 'high places' (*bāmôt*) are tolerated (e.g. used by Samuel) until 1 Kings 3:2 and then roundly condemned, but the term never occurs in Deuteronomy; language of 'plundering' (*šsh*; Judg. 2:14, 16) and being 'sold into the hand of' (*mkr běyad*; Judg. 2:14; 3:8; 4:2, 9) is missing from Deuteronomy; talk of a 'whole heart' (*lēbāb šālēm*; 1 Kgs 8:61; 11:4; 15:3, 14; 2 Kgs 20:3) is not found in Deuteronomy;[102] language used to describe the exile in Deuteronomy ('bring', *bw'*; 'lead', *nhg*; 'scatter', *pwṣ*; 'banish', *ndḥ*) is different from the more specific language of captivity (*glh*) found in Kings (and several prophets).[103]

This evidence suggests both that there has been a conscious production of a work which we could term DtH, linked to but distinct from Deuteronomy. The Deuteronomic distinctives also suggest that *Ur-Deuteronomium* is not exilic: in particular, sections often thought exilic because exile is envisioned may not in fact be so, since the speed with which exile occurs in Deuteronomy differs from that of the historical accounts.

Jeremiah

There are many connections between Jeremiah and Deuteronomy, both linguistically and conceptually. For Driver, 'Jeremiah exhibits marks of it on nearly every page.'[104] The covenantal pattern is found in both: stubbornness and rebellion (Jer. 5:23; Deut. 21:18, 20; 29:18), not fearing Yhwh, turning to 'other gods', so that curses come, the rain does not fall (Jer. 3:3; Deut. 11:14, 17) and

---

100. Deut. 31; 34 and Josh. 1; Deut. 13 and Judg. 20; Deut. 17 and 1 Sam. 8; Deut. 12 and 2 Sam. 7; Deut. 28 and 1 Kgs 8; 2 Kgs 23 – 25.

101. Cf. Vang, 'So-called "Ur-Deuteronomium"', pp. 13–15.

102. For other phrases found in Kings, but not in Deuteronomy, see Driver, *Deuteronomy*, p. xcii.

103. For the last point, see Vang, 'So-called "Ur-Deuteronomium"', pp. 12–13.

104. Driver, *Deuteronomy*, p. xlvii. For a list, see p. xciii.

the people are scattered (Jer. 9:15; 20:21; 13:24; 18:17; Deut. 4:27; 28:64; 30:3), but this is not the last word if there is repentance.

Assessing the significance of these similarities for the formation of Deuteronomy is not straightforward, for at least two reasons. First, the book of Jeremiah itself experienced a complex process of formation: it is made up of heterogeneous material; it lacks a straightforward structure; and it is significantly shorter and has a different order in the Septuagint. Second, there is a complex web of putative relationships between Deuteronomy, the Deuteronomistic History, the reforms of Josiah and the book of Jeremiah.

For our purposes, there are two main ways in which the book of Jeremiah impacts upon the formation of Deuteronomy. First, the substantial overlap in vocabulary and thought-forms needs explanation. Many scholars regard the similarities as indicative of a similar time of composition. The reply has sometimes come that religious language tends to be conservative in style. While this is true in general, its relevance is doubtful. If Deuteronomy were much earlier, a work of such significance would surely have influenced literature in the intervening period, especially since DtH acknowledges the ongoing existence of the book of the law. The question then is raised about the intervening period. We will look below at the connections between Deuteronomy and Hosea.

Second, given that Jeremiah seems so indebted to (some version of) Deuteronomy, there is the question of Jeremiah's lack of appeal to Deuteronomy for corroboration of his message of judgment: does it indicate that the parts of the book that speak of exile as an unavoidable reality post-date Jeremiah's prophesying?[105] This is an important observation, but it is dangerous to argue from silence. Jeremiah, for example, makes no reference to Jerusalem as the place Yhwh has chosen to place his name,[106] but few scholars would insist that such references in Deuteronomy were later. Further, it may be the case, as noted above, that the illocutionary force of Deuteronomy's declaration of exile is more to warn than to predict.

Hosea

The connections between Deuteronomy and Hosea are great at every level, from traditions through to words and phrases. Wolff summarizes many of them concisely:

---

105. For this latter conclusion, see Sparks, *God's Word*, pp. 90–91.
106. Beyond the oblique reference, when speaking of Shiloh as the place where Yhwh first chose to place his name, in the prose sermon in 7:12.

we find reminiscences of the exodus from Egypt, of divine guidance through the wilderness, and of the entry into the arable land, combined with the themes of Israel's satiation, presumption, and forgetting of Yahweh. In addition, there is the struggle against Israel's political alliances; the manner in which *tôrâ* (Torah) is spoken of; Yahweh as Israel's 'teacher'; Yahweh's 'love'; 'redemption'; the genuine prophet who is 'with God'; 'brotherhood'; the *maṣṣēbôt* [standing stones] of the Canaanites; 'grain, new wine, and olive oil'.[107]

To these could be added a covenantal theology, reservations about kingship, Yhwh's gift of the land, enthusiasm for prophets and returning to Egypt.[108]

Accounting for the obvious affinities between Hosea and Deuteronomy is not straightforward. Wolff represents scholars who see Hosea and his contemporaries as 'forerunners'[109] of the Deuteronomic movement. On this reading, Deuteronomy looks to implement the prophetic vision of Hosea. On the other hand, Andersen and Freedman assert that 'Hosea's discourses are threaded with Deuteronomic ideas in a way that shows they were already authoritative in Israel'.[110] Their observation in itself does not *prove* the contemporary existence of *Ur-Deuteronomium*. It could be that there were authoritative traditions to which Hosea could appeal, which later became codified in Deuteronomy. Also 'there seems to be no instance of a prophetic indictment based explicitly on a law'.[111] But it is a mistake to read too much into the fact that Hosea does not appeal directly to the authority of *tôrâ*. Prophets did not characteristically appeal to *tôrâ*: one reason may be that *tôrâ*, while a divine verdict and part of a judicial system (cf. 17:11), is still far removed from 'statute law' in the Western legal tradition; another may be the limited availability of texts.[112]

107. Hans W. Wolff, *A Commentary on the Book of the Prophet Hosea*, trans. Gary Stansell, Hermeneia (Philadelphia: Fortress, 1974), p. xxxi.

108. For the first three of these, see J. Gordon McConville, *Exploring the Old Testament: Volume 4 – Prophets* (London: SPCK, 2002), p. 136. See further Nicholson, *Deuteronomy and Tradition*, pp. 56–82; Weinfeld, *Deuteronomy 1 – 11*, pp. 44–50.

109. Wolff, *Hosea*, p. xxxi.

110. Francis I. Andersen and David Noel Freedman, *Hosea: A New Translation with Introduction and Commentary*, AB 24 (Garden City: Doubleday, 1980), p. 75.

111. Joseph Blenkinsopp, 'Prophecy and the Prophetic Books', in A. D. H. Mayes (ed.), *Text in Context: Essays by Members of the Society for Old Testament Study* (Oxford: Oxford University Press, 2000), pp. 338–339.

112. See Thomas Renz, 'Torah in the Minor Prophets', in J. Gordon McConville and Karl Möller (eds.), *Reading the Law: Studies in Honour of Gordon J. Wenham*, LHB/OTS 461 (New York: T&T Clark, 2007), pp. 77–78.

It should also be noted that some distinctive vocabulary suggests a more complex relationship than straightforward indebtedness. For example, Hosea lacks some characteristically Deuteronomic verbs ('command', *ṣwh*; 'bless', *brk*; 'choose', *bḥr*; 'perish', *'bd*; 'curse', *'rr*) and nouns ('commandment', *miṣwâ*; 'statute', *ḥōq*, *ḥuqqâ*; 'inheritance', *naḥălâ*; 'servant', *'ebed*; 'sojourner', *gēr*; 'abomination', *tô'ēbâ*; 'blessing'/'cursing', *bĕrākâ*/*qĕlālâ*). Hosea in turn has some words that are absent from Deuteronomy. Verbs include 'be guilty' (*'šm*), 'offer incense' (*qṭr*), 'reject' (*m's*), 'rebel' (*pš'*); nouns include 'fornication' (*zĕnûnîm*), 'idols' (*'ăṣabbîm*).[113] Sometimes, significantly, different words have the same referents (e.g. 'idol'; 'rebel'). Further, the dominant motif for the relationship between Yhwh and Israel is different. In Deuteronomy, Israel is Yhwh's son, while in Hosea, Israel is Yhwh's errant wife (except in Hos. 11:1); in Deuteronomy, the command for Israel to love Yhwh is foundational, while in Hosea it is absent.[114]

When put alongside Deuteronomy's interest in places Mounts Ebal and Gerizim, the similarities demonstrate a connection between Deuteronomy and the northern kingdom. At the same time, it is implausible that Deuteronomy arose *directly* from northern prophetic circles such as that of Hosea.[115] Apart from the distinctive vocabulary, prophets themselves do not have as high a position in Deuteronomy as might be expected on such a reading.[116] The similarities between the language of Deuteronomy and Hosea also have implications for our discussion of Jeremiah's relationship to Deuteronomy. While undoubtedly connections between Jeremiah and Deuteronomy are strong and suggestive of a similar time of writing/updating, the significant affinities between Deuteronomy and Hosea make certainty ill-advised.

Wisdom

The close links between Deuteronomy and wisdom are apparent from a number of features. I will give three instances here.[117] First, there are many verbal and conceptual similarities between Deuteronomy and Proverbs, in particular.

---

113. Also the specific geographical terms 'Assyria', 'Samaria'.

114. Cf. William L. Moran, 'The Ancient Near Eastern Background of the Love of God in Deuteronomy', *CBQ* 25 (1963), pp. 77–78.

115. As proposed by Nicholson, *Deuteronomy and Tradition*, pp. 58–82.

116. See Ronald E. Clements, *Deuteronomy*, OTG (Sheffield: JSOT Press, 1989), p. 78.

117. For a thorough articulation of these links, see Weinfeld, *Deuteronomic School*, pp. 244–281, and more briefly Weinfeld, *Deuteronomy 1 – 11*, pp. 62–65.

There is similar language: 'fearing Yhwh', 'fear' leading to 'life', two destinies, 'abomination of Yhwh';[118] the call to 'listen' and 'obey'; and the emphasis on instructing the next generation. Second, some phrasing in Deuteronomy is more closely connected to wisdom phrasing than occurs in other parts of the Pentateuch. For example, the qualities predicated of judges in Deuteronomy 1:13, 15 are more obviously oriented towards wisdom than the corresponding terms in Exodus 18:21. Third, Deuteronomy 4:6 correlates obedience and wisdom, identifying obedient Israel as 'a wise and understanding people'.

For Weinfeld, such connections fit with his thesis that scribes and wise men involved in governmental administration were instrumental in Deuteronomy's composition.[119] However, the lack of mention of such officials in the book, the doubtful connection between wisdom and such administration, and the striking points of difference between Deuteronomy and wisdom (e.g. on the prominence of covenant) make such a proposal problematic.

Evaluation

The above links, by no means exhaustive, demonstrate Deuteronomy's centrality within the literature and theology of the Old Testament. For Wright and Block, the extensive similarities between Deuteronomy and such a wide variety of Old Testament material are best explained by Deuteronomy influencing the other books.[120] Another explanation is to see those who produced the book of Deuteronomy as profoundly influenced by almost every strata of the literature of the Old Testament.[121] Who the writers were, though, is by no means straightforward.

We have already noted and queried the proposal that sees the origins of Deuteronomy in northern prophetic circles. The connection with Josiah's reforms might suggest origins among scribes associated with the royal court, but the downplaying of the role of the king, democratization and the absence of any such officials in the book militate against this. A third proposal, derived from the catechetical style and the links to the northern kingdom, is that the origins of the book lie with northern Levites who fled south after

---

118. Eight times in Deuteronomy, eleven times in Proverbs, and nowhere else in the Old Testament.

119. Weinfeld, *Deuteronomic School*.

120. Christopher J. H. Wright, *Deuteronomy*, NIBC (Peabody: Hendrickson, 1996), p. 7; Block, 'Recovering the Voice of Moses', pp. 388–389.

121. This is true, even if subsequent Deuteronomic influence on these works is also acknowledged.

722 BC.[122] However, it is not easy to conceive of the process by which such theology was accepted within a country strongly influenced by Zion and David traditions; further, although provision is made for such impoverished Levites (Deut. 18:6–8; cf. 12:12, 18, 19; 14:27, 29), they remain firmly within the underclass along with orphans and widows, and the abolition of local sanctuaries ensures they remain there. To propose 'Deuteronomists' as the origin, while in one sense necessary given the problems with other proposals, also has its own problems since such a group is otherwise unknown.

Deuteronomy and the Ancient Near East

Social situation envisaged

Two aspects of Deuteronomy's connections with the Ancient Near East merit examination. One concerns the belief that the social situation envisaged in Deuteronomy, particularly its law code, will reveal clues as to the social situation contemporary with its writing. In other words, the world *in* the text reveals the world *of* the text. However, what seems self-evident to some is disputed by others. Three examples will illustrate this.

First, Rofé thinks that the judicial structures envisaged (16:16–18; 17:8–13) reflect a time after Sennacherib's invasion when the long-prevailing role of elders diminished.[123] On the other hand, the elders are prominent in a number of other ways, especially in chapters 21 – 25.

Second, Na'aman believes Sennacherib's invasion lies behind some of the Deuteronomic terms and the laws which deal with them. He traces the origin and rise of two distinct landless and property-less groups, the 'sojourner/resident alien' (*gēr*) and the Levite, to the displacement and migration of refugees in the wake of this invasion.[124] Knauf, however, thinks that the problem was not permanent, especially given the prosperity of Manasseh's reign.[125]

Third, Clements thinks that 'the overwhelming point of view which is assumed, argued for, and striven for, in Deuteronomy is that of a progressive,

---

122. So Gerhard von Rad, *Studies in Deuteronomy* (Chicago: H. Regnery Co., 1953); idem, *Deuteronomy*.

123. Rofé, *Deuteronomy*, p. 5.

124. Nadav Na'aman, 'Sojourners and Levites in the Kingdom of Judah in the Seventh Century BCE', *ZABR* 14 (2008), pp. 237–279.

125. Ernst Axel Knauf, 'Observations on Judah's Social and Economic History and the Dating of the Laws in Deuteronomy', *JHS* 9, Article 18 (2009), p. 1.

organized and prosperous nation-state'.[126] Urbanization and the reality of commerce lie behind much of the legislation, as, for example, in the use of money (14:24–27) and in laws about wealth and poverty.[127] On the other hand, Vang insists that the society envisaged is 'a predominantly agricultural society consisting of herds and peasants'; further, there is no evidence of disputes between merchants and officials that would be expected in a society posited by Clements,[128] and there is no mention of a capital, or hint of a temple. The 'money' that is mentioned is silver, and coinage is not in view.

One problem here is potential circularity. A plausible setting may be posited, but care needs to be taken lest this postulated setting then becomes in itself grounds for drawing other conclusions, not least the exclusion of data that does not fit. At the same time, looking for a 'fit' and for the kind of society envisaged is desirable, and not every setting is equally likely. In the case of Deuteronomy, it is certainly a settled society.

Treaty links

Connections between Deuteronomy and ANE treaty texts have been discussed extensively since the 1950s, both Hittite treaties from the second millennium and Assyrian treaties of the seventh century.[129] For ease of presentation I shall examine first the former, then the latter, before making some concluding observations.

Hittite treaties

In 1954 Mendenhall published two important studies in which he compared Hittite treaties with different accounts of Yhwh's covenant with Israel.[130] These treaties, dating from the fourteenth to the twelfth centuries, were between a suzerain, or major power, and a vassal, or minor one. They had a characteristic form, which Mendenhall outlined with the following six elements:[131]

---

126. Clements, *Deuteronomy*, p. 87.

127. Ibid., pp. 86–91.

128. Vang, 'So-called "Ur-Deuteronomium"', p. 10.

129. All millennium and century dates in this section are BC/BCE.

130. George E. Mendenhall, 'Ancient Oriental and Biblical Law', *BA* 17/2 (1954), pp. 26–44; George E. Mendenhall, 'Covenant Forms in Israelite Tradition', *BA* 17/3 (1954), pp. 49–76. These were reprinted as *Law and Covenant in Israel and the Ancient Near East* (Pittsburgh: Biblical Colloquium, 1955).

131. Mendenhall, 'Covenant Forms', quotations variously from pp. 58–60.

1. Preamble, identifying the covenant's author.
2. Historical prologue, in which the history of the previous relationship between suzerain and vassal is documented, including instances of the suzerain's benevolence; thus 'the vassal is exchanging future obedience to specific commands for past benefits which he received without any real right'.
3. Stipulations, which 'detail the obligations imposed upon and accepted by the vassal'.
4. 'Provision for deposit in the temple and periodic public reading.'
5. 'The list of gods as witnesses', including deified natural elements.
6. Curses and blessings, with the curses enacted by the gods, even if, presumably, the suzerain actually enforced the sanctions.

Building on this, Kline argued that Deuteronomy as a whole was modelled on this form, rather than on first-millennium Assyrian treaties dating from the ninth to the seventh centuries.[132] This had two important corollaries for Kline. First, Deuteronomy is to be regarded as a unity. Second, because its structure mirrors the second-millennium Hittite treaties, Deuteronomy should be dated to the second millennium.

The parallels are outlined below:

Hittite Treaty	Deuteronomy
1. Preamble	1:1–5
2. Historical prologue	1:6 – 4:49
3. Stipulations	5 – 26 (general, 5 – 11; detailed, 12 – 26)
4. Deposit and reading	31:9, 24 – 26 (deposit); 31:9–13 (reading)
5. Witnesses	30:19; 31:26; 32:1
6. Blessings and curses	27 – 28

Although there are some variations between the ordering in the characteristic Hittite treaty form and Deuteronomy, according to Kitchen these can be explained. First, Deuteronomy has blessings before curses, while every Hittite treaty has curses first. This is explicable because Deuteronomy is analogous not just to ANE treaty documents, but also to ANE law codes, where the order found in Deuteronomy is characteristic.[133] Second, blessings and curses precede

---

132. Meredith G. Kline, *Treaty of the Great King: The Covenant Structure of Deuteronomy* (Grand Rapids: Eerdmans, 1963).

133. K. A. Kitchen, 'The Fall and Rise of Covenant, Law and Treaty', *TynB* 40/1 (1989), pp. 124–128.

both deposit/reading and witnesses in Deuteronomy, unlike in most Hittite treaties. However, there is some variation in the placement of witnesses and blessings and curses in Hittite treaties, such as in the treaty between Tudkhalia IV and Ulmi-Tesup.[134] Third, the fourth element above (deposit/reading) is 'very rarely found' in Hittite treaties,[135] so some scholars have expanded the third element to comprise two sets of stipulations, general and detailed. However,

> it should be no surprise if some variations do occur. (1) We have here a covenant, not a treaty, so differences may be expected. (2) A new category ('covenant') a confluence of two other related ones (law, treaty) may follow its own path in how elements from both may be combined. (3) Exodus–Leviticus, Deuteronomy and Joshua 24 are *not* themselves formal treaty (or even covenant) documents, like the cuneiform records. They are the retrospective *narrative reports* of the covenant and renewals actually being enacted.[136]

Assyrian treaties

This picture needs to be set alongside the Vassal Treaty of Esarhaddon (VTE), first published in 1958.[137] Esarhaddon was the king of Assyria, the major super-power in the first part of the seventh century BC. He became king after the violent death of Sennacherib in 682 BC, and died in 669 BC. The VTE, dating from this time, was concerned to ensure that his son Ashurbanipal would succeed him. Given that neither Esarhaddon nor Ashurbanipal was an eldest son, Esarhaddon presumably tried to avoid opposition by insisting on a pledge of loyalty.[138]

It was not long before scholars noted similarities between VTE and Deuter-onomy, and began to argue for parts of Deuteronomy's indebtedness to VTE,[139]

---

134. K. A. Kitchen, *On the Reliability of the Old Testament* (Grand Rapids: Eerdmans, 2003), p. 288.

135. Dennis J. McCarthy, *Old Testament Covenant: A Survey of Current Opinions*, Growing Points in Theology (Oxford: Basil Blackwell, 1972), pp. 26–28.

136. Kitchen, 'Fall and Rise', pp. 129–130; *Reliability*, pp. 288–289.

137. D. J. Wiseman, 'The Vassal-Treaties of Esarhaddon', *Iraq* 20/1 (1958), pp. 1–99.

138. See Markus Zehnder, 'Building on Stone? Deuteronomy and Esarhaddon's Loyalty Oaths (Part 1): Some Preliminary Observations', *BBR* 19/3 (2009), p. 359.

139. See especially Moran, 'Ancient Near Eastern Background'; Rintje Frankena, 'The Vassal Treaties of Esarhaddon and the Dating of Deuteronomy', *OtSt* 14 (1965), pp. 122–154; Moshe Weinfeld, 'Traces of Assyrian Treaty Formulae in Deuteronomy', *Bib* 46 (1965), pp. 417–427.

in particular chapters 6, 13 and 28. Zehnder has recently analysed the data on all three chapters, and Berman on chapter 13.[140] Space only allows a brief discussion of chapter 13 as illustrative of the arguments adduced. In summary, they argue that both VTE and *Ur-Deuteronomium* have many similarities in common both with loyalty oaths and Hittite vassal treaties from the fourteenth to thirteenth centuries, and with Aramaic treaties of the ninth to eighth centuries; further, there are significant dissimilarities between VTE and Deuteronomy, such that any assertion of the supposed *Ur-Deuteronomium*'s dependence on VTE is unwarranted.

Deuteronomy 13 has a number of verbal connections with VTE §10, lines 108–122. Both give warnings of death for those who advocate breaking faith. Common language includes 'not to conceal', 'not to listen', 'not to consent' and 'to kill'. Some groups of people occur in order (e.g. brother, son, daughter). Further, there are some phrases in common, e.g. 'speaking of rebellion' (Deut. 13:6; *dibber-sārâ*; cf. VTE §57, line 502, *da-bab sur-ra-a-te*).[141] However, as Berman has pointed out, the parallels are significantly closer to a second-millennium Hittite treaty, CTH 133, 'the treaty between Aruwanda I of Hatti [fifteenth century] and the Men of Ismerika'.[142] Many features that are not found in the Neo-Assyrian treaties are to be found in both Deuteronomy 13 and CTH 133. Five examples Berman gives are:

1. 'reference to the beneficence of the sovereign king as the basis for the vassal's loyalty';
2. 'the concern for due process when a loyal vassal is suspected of seditious acts';
3. 'laws of the rebellious city';
4. 'the specific concern for the vassal's loyalty when confronted with seditious family members';
5. the 'script' of the agitator to disloyalty, which is in both cases 'let us . . .'[143]

---

140. Zehnder, 'Building on Stone? (1)'; Markus Zehnder, 'Building on Stone? Deuteronomy and Esarhaddon's Loyalty Oaths (Part 2): Some Additional Observations', *BBR* 19/4 (2009), pp. 511–535; Joshua A. Berman, 'CTH 133 and the Hittite Provenance of Deuteronomy 13', *JBL* 130/1 (2011), pp. 25–44.

141. Zehnder, 'Building on Stone? (1)', pp. 348–351.

142. Berman, 'Hittite Provenance', p. 28.

143. Ibid., p. 41.

Admittedly there is no parallel in CTH 133 to the danger of divination leading the people astray, as in Deuteronomy 13:2 and VTE §10, and conversely there is an attractive contact between Neo-Assyria and the reforms of Josiah. However, neither point demands that Deuteronomy 13 is better seen as influenced by VTE. There are parallels of vassals employing divination in other contexts, so the lack of a specific parallel here should not be seen as conclusive.[144] Yhwh's conduct is closer to a more 'amicable' Hittite suzerain than to a Neo-Assyrian 'despot'.[145]

Evaluation

Any evaluation of connections between ANE texts and Deuteronomy needs to account for their extent, their type (verbal, conceptual, structural), the plausibility of indebtedness and the variety of possible explanations. One text could be borrowing from the other, both could have a common source, or similarities could arise from common conceptual landscape. The plausibility of indebtedness is an intriguing one. It raises questions about how long a given treaty form would be available, how much a form would change over time to match historical circumstances, and how and why those drawing on such a form would do so.

Two points need to be made. First, Deuteronomy is closer in form and nature to second-millennium Hittite treaties. The combination of elements and ordering found in Deuteronomy is unparalleled in extant first-millennium Aramaic or Assyrian treaties.[146] With one possible 'rudimentary' exception, the Assyrian treaties lack a historical prologue.[147] They also lack 'gratitude for previous benefits conferred, the blessing, and the provision for deposit and public reading'.[148] In addition, they lack expression of the sovereign's love for the vassal. The similarities that are observable between Deuteronomy and Assyrian treaties do not demand a later date for Deuteronomy, partly because the parallels are often closer to second-millennium treaties anyway, and partly because there are good alternative explanations for the aspects of Deuteronomy which are closer to first-millennium treaties.

Second, while Deuteronomy contains many echoes of ancient treaties, it is not in its present form a treaty document. As Mayes points out, the final three

---

144. Ibid., pp. 40–41.

145. Ibid., p. 38.

146. Kitchen, *Reliability*, pp. 287–288.

147. George E. Mendenhall and Gary A. Herion, 'Covenant', *ABD* 1:1182. So too Weinfeld, *Deuteronomy 1 – 11*, pp. 7–8.

148. Mendenhall and Herion, *ABD* 1:1182.

chapters do not fit easily within any treaty document or law code.[149] Further, the book is about Yhwh's relationship with his people – it is not a political treaty. Nonetheless, the closer connections with Hittite treaties demand a satisfactory explanation.

Summary and conclusions

This chapter has outlined the main pieces of evidence usually adduced in discussing the composition of the book of Deuteronomy. To draw the different strands together, I propose the following seven propositions.

(1) The question of the composition of Deuteronomy is very complex. To adapt from the scientist J. B. S. Haldane, the book's composition is not only stranger than we imagine, but stranger than we can imagine. The difficulty is that the evidence points in different directions. Some evidence points towards an earlier date, in some cases towards an origin in the second millennium: the explicit testimony, the testimony of tradition, the presence of diverse traditions within one book, parallels with Hittite treaties and language of immediate destruction. However, other evidence points to a final date of production significantly later: the shift in rhetorical perspective, the relationship with the rest of the Pentateuch (different language, formulations, law codes) and connections with other Old Testament works. Evidence of material from a later date sits less comfortably with an overall early dating than vice versa.

(2) The relationship between explicit and implicit evidence needs careful reflection. To regard some statements as self-evident and determinative for the interpretation of all other data is ultimately inconsistent. Not that such claims should be scorned or ignored, but rather the whole book – its explicit statements and its implicit evidence – needs to be interpreted historically. At the same time, it is a mistake to reduce explicit claims of authorship or origin to the ideology of one faction or another, particularly if the values espoused *in* the text would then run counter to the values involved in the production *of* the text.

(3) The case for dating needs to be a cumulative and coherent one that accounts for all the evidence. It is a mistake to assert Mosaic authorship as an unexamined default, then take components of an alternative view in isolation and identify possible flaws in each component and assume that a compelling

---

149. Mayes, *Deuteronomy*, p. 34.

view has been expressed. It is equally a mistake to assume Josianic provenance as a default and to ignore awkward evidence.

(4) The book of Deuteronomy has genuinely Mosaic origin, but discerning what Moses *did* say as opposed to what later writers have reframed or thought Moses would have wanted to say in their situation is not straightforward. Two modern analogies may help. Both Gray's *Anatomy*, originally published in 1858 and now in its fortieth edition, and Davidson's *Hebrew Grammar*, now in its twenty-seventh edition, originated in the people whose names the books bear. However, discerning what precisely they wrote would be extremely difficult if one only had access to the most recent edition.

(5) We would do well to heed the warning of Weinfeld:

> The concept of 'composition of a book' is meaningless with regard to the Israel of ancient times . . . Today when we speak of a book, we mean a composition written by a certain person at a specific place and time: every line is impressed with the personality of the author and the period and milieu in which it was written. Such was not the case in Israel or in the ancient East . . . The author of ancient times was generally a collector and compiler of traditions rather than a creator of literature, and was certainly not an author in the modern sense of the term. Even if the book of Deuteronomy had been put into writing in the days of Hezekiah–Josiah, that does not mean to say that all of its contents reflect that period, for in the book of Deuteronomy there have been preserved for us very ancient laws . . .[150]

(6) Attention to the composition of Deuteronomy has value for the scholarly enterprise and beyond. For the world behind the text, the world of the authors, events and production of its text, it stands at the heart of so many debates and discussions that it cannot be neglected. Beyond the concerns of historical-critical scholarship, such attention can also illuminate aspects of hermeneutics, given Deuteronomy's existence alongside other law codes which deal with the same situations.

(7) Notwithstanding the above, complexity of composition should not paralyse the reader. The book of Deuteronomy demands to be read against (at least) two main backgrounds. First, it should be read standing with Moses and the people on the edge of the Promised Land, the rhetorical situation *in* the book. Second, it should be read in the context of the exile, the likely rhetorical situation *of* the book. The people of God find themselves a second time outside

---

150. Weinfeld, *Deuteronomy 1 – 11*, p. 83.

the land, looking in, waiting to enter (cf. 30:5). For the Christian reading the book, the circumcision of the heart (cf. 30:6) has come with Jesus Christ, and entering the land is both a past and a future reality.

2. CONTEMPORARY THEOLOGICAL INTERPRETATION OF DEUTERONOMY[1]

Paul A. Barker

Setting the scene

In 1995, Mark O'Brien published a survey of what was then current scholarship on Deuteronomy.[2] Much of the research to which he referred was written in German and the predominant emphasis throughout his paper was historical-critical. Indeed, the section that most directly deals with theology also includes language and style, altogether taking just over one page at the very end of his article. While theological issues do surface here and there, this reflects the main emphasis of scholarship at the time, as well as perhaps O'Brien's own interests.

In the decade and a half since he wrote, publications relating to Deuteronomy have continued to abound. Among longer commentaries in English alone are those by Merrill (1995), Tigay (1996), Wright (1996), Brueggemann (2001), Harman (2001), Christensen (2001–2), McConville (2002), Nelson (2002), Sherwood (2002), Biddle (2003), Currid (2006) and Work (2009). More are in the pipeline. Sadly Weinfeld did not live to complete his Anchor Bible commentary, the first volume of which has been so notable, and Hermeneia

---

1. I am grateful for comments from Dr Jerry Hwang on this chapter.
2. M. A. O'Brien, 'The Book of Deuteronomy', in *Currents in Research: Biblical Studies* 3 (1995), pp. 95–128.

has apparently withdrawn from the long-awaited English commentary by Braulik and Lohfink, though they are still working on this and we hope it will be published somewhere eventually. To this list can be added several popular-level commentaries and expositions, a multitude of monographs and various collections of essays and journal articles.

With regard to theology, O'Brien's main comments relate to the relationship between law and grace in Deuteronomy. He cites Braulik, Janzen and Perlitt, who all argue that God's establishment of the relationship with Israel elicits a response of obedience, rather than obedience being the requisite for that relationship.[3] Braulik argued that the law is a pledge of God's grace, and that the theology of Deuteronomy presumes a 'justification' that enables one to obey God's law. Janzen focused on love, arguing that the essence of Deuteronomy is found in God's love for his people and their response to that love. Perlitt argued that obedience to the law is based on the prior love that God expresses for his people, noting in particular 6:20–24 and 7:6–8.

O'Brien's lack of focus on theology may be illustrated by his omission of McConville's *Law and Theology* (1984) from this discussion of law and grace. It is cited only with reference to dating and the overall purpose of Deuteronomy. However, McConville's thesis contributes a great deal to the theological issues of grace and law, as does his later *Grace in the End*.[4]

The only other theological topic that O'Brien briefly surveys is the attitude of Deuteronomy to the poor. Here he summarizes Kessler's conclusion, in critique of Braulik, that conduct towards a neighbour is a constitutive element of righteousness, not just its fruit.[5]

---

3. O'Brien, 'Deuteronomy', p. 116; G. Braulik, 'Law as Gospel: Justification and Pardon According to the Deuteronomic Torah', *Int* 38 (1984), pp. 5–14; J. G. Janzen, 'The Yoke that Gives Rest', *Int* 41 (1987), pp. 256–268; L. Perlitt, '"Evangelium" und Gesetz im Deuteronomium', in T. Veijola (ed.), *The Law in the Bible and Its Environment* (Helsinki: Finnish Exegetical Society), pp. 23–28.

4. J. G. McConville, *Law and Theology in Deuteronomy*, JSOTSup 33 (Sheffield: JSOT Press, 1984); idem, *Grace in the End: A Study in Deuteronomic Theology*, SOTBT (Grand Rapids: Zondervan, 1993). The latter is listed in O'Brien's bibliography, but unmentioned in his text.

5. O'Brien, 'Deuteronomy', pp. 116–117; R. Kessler, 'Die Rolle des Armen für Gerechtigkeit und Sünde des Reichen. Hintergrund und Bedeutung von Dtn 15,9; 24,13.15', in F. Crüsemann et al. (eds.), *Was Ist der Mensch? Beiträge zur Anthropologie des Alten Testaments: Hans Walter Wolff zum 80. Geburtstag* (Munich: Chr. Kaiser Verlag, 1992), pp. 153–163.

Elsewhere O'Brien avoids opportunity for theological comment. For example, he only discusses cultic centralization in relation to historical-critical matters and the Josianic reforms, and not in relation to its theology. Identification of the 'fathers' in Deuteronomy is another potentially theological matter. O'Brien mentions Römer's position that 'fathers' refers to the exodus generation and Lohfink's critique (with Römer's subsequent response) that 'fathers' refers to the patriarchs as well as the exodus generation.[6]

O'Brien spends some time discussing views on the overall purpose of Deuteronomy. Significant among these is McBride's argument that the book is a constitution or polity for Israel. Specifically, he argues that Deuteronomy is not a theological treatise but a practical or catechetical manual.[7] However, this issue is a theological one and, as McConville says (quoted by O'Brien), 'the purpose of the laws is primarily theological and hortatory'.[8] This relates to the theology of leadership in the laws of 16:18 – 18:22, which O'Brien also addresses.[9]

In his survey of the different sections of Deuteronomy, O'Brien's main focus remains historical-critical. However, from time to time theological themes arise. He notes the 'flurry of activity' about 6:4, the *Shema*, with comments on its translation and meaning, the theme of love and the issue of monotheism.[10] That flurry has continued, as we shall see below.

The past fifteen years have arguably produced much more theological fruit than the previous fifteen, and we may speculate why this is so. While some theology arises from purely academic interest, much is no doubt prompted by major social issues. Deuteronomy proves to be a fertile dialogue partner, not least on the issues of war, election, community and ethics generally.

Since O'Brien's article, 11 September 2001 looms large. That act of terrorism has caused a surge of writing about the theology of war and politics. Looking

---

6. O'Brien, 'Deuteronomy', pp. 104–105; T. Römer, *Israels Väter: Untersuchungen zur Väterthematik im Deuteronomium und in der deuteronomistischen Tradition*, OBO 99 (Göttingen: Vandenhoeck & Ruprecht, 1990); N. Lohfink, *Die Väter Israel sim Deuteronomium: Mit einer Stellungnahme von Thomas Römer*, OBO 111 (Göttingen: Vandenhoeck & Ruprecht, 1991).

7. O'Brien, 'Deuteronomy', p. 107; S. D. McBride, 'Polity of the Covenant People: The Book of Deuteronomy', *Int* 41 (1987), pp. 229–244.

8. McConville, *Law and Theology*, p. 55, quoted in O'Brien, 'Deuteronomy', p. 106.

9. See the chapter in this volume on Deut. 16:18 – 18:22 by Philip S. Johnston (pp. 139–156).

10. O'Brien, 'Deuteronomy', p. 109.

back, it is striking that this was not a major issue in 1995. The election of Israel and the theology of other nations are clearly relevant to current world politics.

This interest in Deuteronomy's theology or ideology is a healthy trend, not least since it is 'the most important book in the Old Testament for writing an Old Testament theology'.[11] Indeed, '[t]he theological significance of Deuteronomy can scarcely be overestimated. Inasmuch as this book offers the most systematic presentation of truth in the entire OT, we may compare it to Romans in the NT.'[12]

This chapter is a survey of the study of the theology of Deuteronomy. We are not considering the more philosophical question of what is theology or theological interpretation. Rather we will survey the study of Deuteronomy's theology under the following themes: mission, election, war (*ḥērem*), politics, community, monotheism, name theology and grace. The literature is increasingly vast, and of necessity we will be selective.[13]

Mission

Christopher Wright's 1996 commentary explicitly raised what he called a 'missional hermeneutic' for reading Deuteronomy.[14] In the preface he wrote, 'If there is anything fresh in the presentation offered here, it will mainly be due to my concern to engage with the *missiological* relevance of Deuteronomy.'[15] While recent biblical criticism has entertained feminist, vegetarian, homosexual and materialist hermeneutics among others, a missiological reading does not share the same standing. As Wright goes on to say, 'the whole Bible is related to mission'. So reading Deuteronomy through missiological eyes is not an esoteric exercise, but rather a central biblical perspective.

Deuteronomy presents a God of 'sovereign and worldwide purpose' and it 'bends every rhetorical, literary, emotional and moral skill to the task of

---

11. B. K. Waltke with C. Yu, *An Old Testament Theology: An Exegetical, Canonical and Thematic Approach* (Grand Rapids: Zondervan, 2007), p. 479.

12. D. I. Block, 'Deuteronomy', in K. J. Vanhoozer (ed.), *Theological Interpretation of the Old Testament: A Book-by-Book Survey* (Grand Rapids: Baker, 2008), p. 67.

13. For issues of dating, see James Robson, 'The literary composition of Deuteronomy', in this volume, pp. 19–59.

14. See also C. J. H. Wright, *The Mission of God: Unlocking the Bible's Grand Narrative* (Downers Grove: InterVarsity Press, 2006), pp. 33–69, on a missional hermeneutic.

15. C. J. H. Wright, *Deuteronomy*, NIBCOT (Peabody: Hendrickson, 1996), p. xi.

equipping and motivating God's people to live for the purposes of God in each generation'.[16] In particular, in Deuteronomy Israel faces a future in a new cultural context of polytheistic and pagan Canaan. Such a culture challenges its loyalty to Yhwh. So, 'inasmuch as the relationship between the gospel and human cultures is a central missiological issue, the story of Israel's engagement with Canaanite culture is a rich vein for cross-cultural missiological reflection'.[17] One could respond that Deuteronomy's message is to exterminate Canaanite culture rather than engage with it. However, the context of entry into Canaan is still significant, and some laws in the book indicate that idolatry will be a huge temptation and threat.

In Deuteronomy, Israel is to be a paradigm for the nations. Wright takes his cue here from the promises to Abram in Genesis 12:3 that, through his descendants, all nations of the world will be blessed. Wright correctly reads Israel's election as missionary and not as implying rejection of the other nations in general.

The nations in Deuteronomy are not, therefore, viewed all in the same light. Those in Canaan itself stand under Yhwh's judgment for their immorality and idolatry. Other nations are depicted as an audience and Israel's performance becomes critical for determining their response to Yhwh. The main text is 4:6–8, which for Wright most clearly combines ethics and mission.[18] In the event of Israel's obedience to Torah, the nations will not just perceive that Israel is a great and wise nation, but will also recognize the nearness of Israel's God and the righteousness of its law.[19] Israel will be incomparable among the nations as Yhwh himself is incomparable among the gods, points made through the rhetorical questions of 4:7–8 and 4:32–35 respectively. The conclusion Wright draws is that 'the ethical quality of life of the people of God (their obedience to the law in this context) is a vital factor in the attraction of the nations to the living God'.[20]

Elsewhere the nations are also important for the long-term strategy of Yhwh. After the golden calf idolatry (9:16, 28), one reason for Moses' intercession is

---

16. Ibid., p. 8.

17. Ibid., p. 9.

18. Ibid., pp. 12–13.

19. See R. P. O'Dowd, *The Wisdom of Torah: Epistemology in Deuteronomy and the Wisdom Literature*, FRLANT 225 (Göttingen: Vandenhoeck & Ruprecht, 2009), pp. 39–40, on the wisdom theme in these verses. He later argues that the Decalogue and *Shema* are also missional. See pp. 171–173.

20. Wright, *Deuteronomy*, p. 49.

the reputation of Yhwh in the eyes of Egypt if he were to destroy Israel. In the blessings of the covenant (28:10), a blessed Israel will result in the nations seeing and fearing Israel.

Deuteronomy 26:16–19, which concludes the legal section and leads into the covenant curses and blessings, is a paradigm for mission in the book. Dan Block focuses on verse 19: 'for him to set you high above all nations that he has made, in praise and in fame and in honour'.[21] Like Wright, Block argues persuasively that this refers to the praise, fame and honour of Yhwh, not Israel. So this expression encapsulates the missiological paradigm in Deuteronomy: obedient Israel will be blessed by Yhwh, which culminates in being lifted above other nations (at least economically and politically, as in 15:6), and results in the nations bringing praise and honour to Yhwh. A similar idea is found in 28:1 where, contingent on obedience to the law, 'the LORD your God will set you high above all the nations of the earth'. Thus Deuteronomy's missionary direction is centripetal. Block summarizes the formula thus: 'demonstrate gratitude for divine grace through loyal living and experience the Lord's blessings, thereby attracting the attention of the nations, who would give praise and glory to the Lord and would join Israel in their covenant relationship with Him.'[22]

Block also highlights the ethical connection with mission. In 26:19, Israel is to be 'a people holy to the LORD'. Israel is not separated from the nations simply to receive Yhwh's attention, but rather to be a mediator between Yhwh and the world.[23]

Election

Deuteronomy is replete with references to the related theme of Yhwh's election of Israel. As MacDonald notes, 'The prominence of election in Deuteronomy is something of a truism . . . it belongs to the nature of election that no description of the relationship between Yhwh and Israel is complete without reference to the non-elect.'[24] The *locus classicus* is: 'For you are a people holy to the LORD

---

21. Unless otherwise identified, Scripture quotations in this chapter are from NRSV.

22. D. I. Block, 'The Privilege of Calling: The Mosaic Paradigm for Missions (Deut. 26:16–19)', *Bibliotheca Sacra* 162 (2005), p. 404. Similarly Wright, *Deuteronomy*, p. 273.

23. Block, 'Privilege', p. 401.

24. N. MacDonald, 'The Literary Criticism and Rhetorical Logic of Deuteronomy I – IV', *VT* 56 (2006), p. 218.

your God; the LORD your God has chosen you out of all the peoples on earth
to be his people, his treasured possession' (7:6; see also 10:14–15; 14:2, 21). The
emphasis here and elsewhere is on Yhwh's sovereign choice, for no explicable
reason, of Israel as his chosen people. Israel was not chosen because it was
numerous (7:7–8), nor because it was righteous (9:4–6). Rather, Israel was chosen
because of Yhwh's promise to and love of Abraham (4:37; 7:8; 10:15). The
divine election of Israel is thus an act of pure grace. Yhwh has acted uniquely
for Israel in rescuing them from slavery in Egypt and in speaking to them at
Horeb from the fire (4:32–39).[25]

Israel is elected out of all the nations of the world: 'chosen you out of all
the peoples on earth' (7:6); 'chose you, their descendants after them, out of
all the peoples' (10:15); 'it is you the LORD has chosen out of all the peoples
on earth' (14:2). The goal is that Israel will be lifted high above the nations, as
seen above. Thus the election of Israel by Yhwh is not an end in itself but a
means of bringing the nations to Yhwh. Election thus serves the missional
purpose of Yhwh.

There has been a growing discussion of this issue in recent years, occasioned
in part by the increasing debate about the Old Testament's laws concerning
warfare, on which see further below. For some, the election of Israel implies
the rejection and condemnation of other nations and is a theology to be itself
rejected. For others, the missional hermeneutic of Wright cautions against such
a conclusion. The election of Israel is in fact for the sake of the other nations.
It is through Israel, the descendants of Abraham, that the nations of the world
will be blessed.

In discussing Deuteronomy 7, McConville notes the 'rejectionist hermeneutic', that the election of Israel implies the rejection of other nations, but
argues that 'the particular is a necessary precondition of the universal'. Israel is
to be subject to Torah and thus a paradigm for the other nations. In fact, the
later judgment of Israel followed by salvation is also paradigmatic and the basis
of hope for the nations.[26]

Lohr's recent thesis deals in depth with these contesting views of election.[27]
He pays significant attention to Kaminsky's categorization of nations as elect,

---

25. Block, 'Deuteronomy', p. 78.

26. J. G. McConville, *Deuteronomy*, AOTC (Leicester: Apollos; Downers Grove:
    InterVarsity Press, 2002), pp. 163–164 (163).

27. J. N. Lohr, *Chosen and Unchosen: Conceptions of Election in the Pentateuch and Jewish-
    Christian Interpretation*, Siphrut: *Literature and Theology of the Hebrew Scriptures* 2
    (Winona Lake: Eisenbrauns, 2009).

anti-elect or non-elect.[28] The anti-elect are those deemed to be enemies of God. This includes the Canaanites in the land, as well as people like Achan, who by his sinful actions in Joshua 7 becomes part of this group. On the whole he argues that the anti-elect incur this position by their actions. In contrast, the non-elect are not damned or condemned. This category is ambiguous, in that such Gentiles are able to serve God in their own way. Election carries responsibility, rather than privilege, and the elect are to be a medium of blessing to the nations.[29] In many ways, the group of non-elect in Kaminsky's terminology fits Wright's observation that many nations are Israel's audience and that their destiny depends to an extent on Israel's behaviour which they will observe.

Lohr discusses at length three passages from Deuteronomy regarding election, starting with 4:15–20. The problematic text is verse 19 which refers to the sun, moon and stars, the host of heaven, being allotted to peoples everywhere. Following MacDonald, Lohr agrees that they are allotted to non-Israelite nations for worship.[30] Lohr then goes on to ask why, and whether this action by Yhwh is for good or ill, redemption or destruction. Several scholars consider the action to be punishment, i.e. the nations are handed over for idolatry to celestial deities as Yhwh's punishment of them. Others such as Miller, Tigay and Weinfeld see this verse positively, arguing that Deuteronomy prohibits Israel's worship of other gods but allows other nations to do so.[31] Still others regard the verse as ambiguous, neither clearly redemptive nor punitive, or as provisional, anticipating a future, fuller worship of Yhwh. Such was the view of Clement of Alexandria and Origen, for example.[32] Goldingay expresses this

---

28. J. S. Kaminsky, 'The Concept of Election and Second Isaiah: Recent Literature', *Biblical Theology Bulletin* 31 (Winter 2001), pp. 135–144; idem, 'Did Election Imply the Mistreatment of Non-Israelites?', *HTR* 96 (2003), pp. 397–425.

29. See Lohr, *Chosen*, pp. 33–46, for a fuller discussion and evaluation of Kaminsky.

30. Ibid., p. 155; N. MacDonald, *Deuteronomy and the Meaning of 'Monotheism'*, FAT 2/1 (Tübingen: Mohr Siebeck, 2003), pp. 172–173 n. 91. This is the majority view of commentators. MacDonald links this allocation to the land given to Edom, Moab and Ammon by Yhwh in 2:1–19. See MacDonald, 'Literary Criticism', p. 219.

31. P. D. Miller, 'God's Other Stories: On the Margins of Deuteronomistic Theology', in *Israelite Religion and Biblical Theology: Collected Essays*, JSOTSup 267 (Sheffield: Sheffield Academic Press, 2000), pp. 593–602; M. Weinfeld, *Deuteronomy 1 – 11*, AB 5 (New York: Doubleday, 1991), p. 206; J. H. Tigay, *Deuteronomy*, JPS Torah Commentary (Jerusalem: Jewish Publication Society, 1996), p. 50.

32. Lohr, *Chosen*, pp. 158–159.

position simply: 'For the time being, God has left them (the other nations) with just those religious resources (sun, moon, stars). Only as God uses Israel to enable them to see there are bigger things to be said about God can they be introduced to a bigger picture.'[33] McConville acknowledges that 4:19 is 'surprising' and notes like many its parallel with 32:8–9, where similar language is used ('allotted' and 'inheritance' as a word pair). That other nations had their own particular deities is found elsewhere (Ps. 82; Dan. 10; *Jubilees* 15:31–32). However, McConville is uncommitted regarding the text's intent: on the one hand, 'Deuteronomy may give formal assent' to the idea that other nations have their own deities; on the other, '[m]ore probably it is meant to contrast with the statement of Israel's special status in the next verse'. Then he concludes, 'It may even imply criticism; the exegesis of Gen. 1:14–27 in vv. 16–19 supports this view, because that text also implies criticism of ANE polytheism.'[34] Currid also regards the verse as critical of the worship of the heavenly bodies by other nations, arguing that the positive reading is hard to reconcile with the 'radical monotheism' of Deuteronomy. While noting the 'verbal gymnastics' of various Jewish Targums to deal with the text, he concludes simply by saying that the heavenly host was given 'to all the peoples to give order to the universe, to adorn the skies and in so doing display his handiwork to all peoples'.[35]

Lohr's own conclusion is that Deuteronomy, 'a book that is often deemed the most exclusive and xenophobic text of the canon, leaves the nations in an ambiguous light'. He goes on to propose that it 'does *permit* and not extinguish our larger thesis that the unchosen, whether an individual or a nation, can operate appropriately in relation to God, perhaps showing "fear" of him'.[36]

Lohr's second text is Deuteronomy 7. We shall return below to a wider discussion of ḥērem, which features strongly in this passage. At this stage, however, we note his emphasis on election carrying responsibility and obligation in general allegiance to Yhwh.

His third text, often overlooked in discussion, is 10:12–22. Here, Israel's election is grounded in creation and carries clear responsibilities of total devotion to Yhwh, expressed in terms of five largely synonymous verbs in verses 12–13. No explicit comment is made in the passage about other nations. However, part of the obligation placed on the chosen people, Israel, is a care for the aliens in their midst. Lohr argues that this may imply that the destruction

---

33. J. Goldingay, *Numbers and Deuteronomy for Everyone* (London: SPCK, 2010), p. 105.

34. McConville, *Deuteronomy*, p. 108.

35. J. D. Currid, *Deuteronomy* (Darlington: Evangelical Press, 2006), p. 105.

36. Lohr, *Chosen*, p. 160.

of the Canaanite nations is limited to the conquest only and that subsequently Israel is to love the aliens and strangers.[37]

Lohr concludes that election in Deuteronomy carries the clear responsibility for Israel of allegiance to Yhwh. The focus is on Israel's obedience, and not the other nations. However, with respect to the nations, Deuteronomy makes a clear distinction between the seven Canaanite nations and others, which are regarded with at least neutrality. The seven nations of 7:1 are clearly anti-elect, 'beyond recovery, beyond a second chance and are to be obliterated, liquidated, scattered'.[38] However, the other non-elect nations may even receive benefit from Israel's obedience, suggested by the commands to Israel to care for the alien in 10:19.[39] Lohr therefore reinforces Kaminsky's tripartite categorization of elect, anti-elect and non-elect.

War (ḥērem)

Christian responses to divinely commanded genocide are discussed much more fully elsewhere in this book.[40] However, it is still important to survey here various approaches to and interpretations of warfare and ḥērem in Deuteronomy, especially in connection with election.

Although Deuteronomy is primarily a legal text with respect to warfare, it also includes a brief narrative of the defeat of Sihon and Og in chapters 2 – 3, a war fought to a degree according to ḥērem principles. The territories of Sihon and Og become part of the tribal allocations of land, suggesting that this Transjordanian land is regarded as part of the Promised Land.

In his discussion of election in Deuteronomy 7, Lohr interacts with Chris Wright, Gordon McConville and, to a lesser degree, John Goldingay on the theme of mission.[41] All three argue that the ultimate redemption of other nations is important in Deuteronomy, as seen above. To differing degrees, all three argue that the promises of Genesis 12:1–3 are seen in Deuteronomy as fulfilled by Israel's settlement in the land, and separation from other nations is

---

37. Ibid., p. 192.

38. Ibid.

39. See also Jenny Corcoran, 'The alien in Deuteronomy 29 and today', in this volume, pp. 229–239, on Deuteronomy's inclusion of the aliens in Israel.

40. Christian Hofreiter, 'Genocide in Deuteronomy and Christian interpretation', in this volume, pp. 240–262.

41. Lohr, *Chosen*, pp. 176–183.

a necessary step towards that fulfilment.[42] All three regard *ḥērem* as a temporary measure to bring about a greater good for the nations. In response, Lohr regards this argument as 'peculiar' and accuses them of reading Deuteronomy through the skewed lenses of universal salvation and missional interest. This is an intriguing accusation. Lohr claims that

> the ultimate purpose of the call was to bless Abraham, though this clearly had wider implications. His descendants are of utmost importance (they too will be blessed and possess a land); the nations feature secondarily. Verse 3 contains a blessing for the nations, though this is obtained through an act that blesses Abraham (and his people). The idea of blessing the nations by all contextual indications, is there to show Abraham precisely how blessed he is – even the nations, all of them, will find blessing, depending on their treatment of him.[43]

Lohr's downplaying of the missional emphasis of Wright and McConville may come from his indebtedness to Jewish writers, not least Kaminsky, but perhaps also via his *Doktorvater* Moberly, who reads Genesis 12:2–3 similarly.[44]

Following MacDonald, Lohr argues that *ḥērem* demonstrates that Yhwh is the 'ultimate oath-keeper', especially with regard to land.[45] For Lohr, therefore, *ḥērem* is secondary, serving the primary purpose of the promises of Yhwh to Abraham. In this he agrees with Goldingay, Wright and McConville. However, they differ in their reading of Genesis 12:2–3. Here I suggest Lohr is wrong in his assessment of the focus of the Abrahamic promises. The promise of blessing for the nations in verse 3 serves not so much to show how blessed Abraham is, but rather is the climax of the promises in those verses. That all the nations of the world will be blessed is not for the glory of Abraham but for the benefit of the nations and the glory of God. This also fits better contextually in the narrative of Genesis 1 – 11.[46]

---

42. J. Goldingay, *Theological Diversity and the Authority of the Old Testament* (Grand Rapids: Eerdmans, 1987), p. 152; Wright, *Deuteronomy*, pp. 11–12; McConville, *Grace in the End*.

43. Lohr, *Chosen*, pp. 179–180.

44. See the review of Lohr by D. Patrick, *RBL* 09 (2010), p. 4; R. W. L. Moberly, *The Theology of the Book of Genesis*, Old Testament Theology (Cambridge: Cambridge University Press, 2009), pp. 141–161.

45. MacDonald, *Meaning*, p. 159; Lohr, *Chosen*, p. 181.

46. See R. Bauckham, *Bible and Mission: Christian Witness in a Postmodern World* (Milton Keynes: Paternoster; Grand Rapids: Baker, 2003), pp. 28–31. 'In Abraham's case he is singled out precisely so that blessing may come to all the nations' (p. 28).

Goldingay, Wright and Lohr all regard the command to destroy the Canaan-ites as demanding real battle and real conquest. In their arguments, the ethical questions raised by this are mitigated by drawing in the nations (Goldingay, Wright) or by serving the oath-keeping God (Lohr). McConville is more ambiguous regarding whether the command is to be taken literally, as we shall see below.

This leads us into a wider discussion of the interpretation of *ḥērem* in Deuter-onomy in recent years. The prominent atheist Richard Dawkins, for example, has written that 'the killing of the Canaanites was an act of ethnic cleansing in which "bloodthirsty massacres" were carried out with "xenophobic relish"'.[47] Without doubt, the events of 11 September 2001 provoked an escalation of interest in 'holy war' in the Old Testament, and in how to understand the command to exterminate the Canaanites in Deuteronomy 7 and elsewhere. Trimm's exhaustive bibliography gives some three hundred articles and books, the vast majority of which were written after 1990.[48]

Several who argue that the warfare laws demanded real conquest seek to alleviate Dawkins's 'bloodthirsty massacres'. Among these are Richard Hess, who provides a helpful overview of wars in the Old Testament and argues that the *ḥērem* law is limited to the actual conquest generation, it does not advocate war in order to extend the boundaries of the Promised Land and, by contrast to ANE laws, it refrains from bloodthirsty delight in seeing enemies killed. Jericho and Ai were probably military forts, and the general language used is probably stereotypical.[49]

The other main avenue of interpretation is that the language of *ḥērem* and warfare in general is idealistic or propagandist. Nelson argues that the language of *ḥērem* does not concern sacrifice or warfare, but is a 'culture map category', parallel to 'holy' and 'unclean'. Following Moberly, MacDonald argues that *ḥērem* is a metaphor for religious fidelity: people are not killed, but religious paraphernalia is destroyed. Earl argues that *ḥērem* is about separation from other nations, not killing, and that the destruction of the Canaanites

---

47. P. Copan, *Is God a Moral Monster? Making Sense of the Old Testament God* (Grand Rapids: Baker, 2011), p. 163.

48. C. Trimm, 'Recent Research on Warfare in the Old Testament', *Currents in Biblical Research*, forthcoming.

49. R. S. Hess, 'War in the Hebrew Bible: An Overview', in R. S. Hess and E. A. Martens (eds.), *War in the Bible and Terrorism in the Twenty-First Century*, BBR Sup 2 (Winona Lake: Eisenbrauns, 2008), pp. 19–32. Also Copan, *Moral Monster*, pp. 158–206.

is a myth.[50] Hofreiter deals more fully with Earl's mythological reading, MacDonald's metaphorical reading and Hess and Copan's hyperbolic readings of *ḥērem*.[51]

The gap between those who take the command for war literally and those who see it as metaphor is not wide. McConville and Wright see the *ḥērem* command in Deuteronomy 7 as intended literally, yet McConville writes that '*ḥērem* draws a "culture map" in which Israel occupies a different religious and social space . . . This is not far from C. J. H. Wright's . . . concept of Deuteronomy as a critique of Canaanite culture.'[52] For Moberly, this 'seems to imply that √*ḥrm* is to be understood metaphorically'.[53] McConville responded by acknowledging that metaphor 'is an indispensable tool in the interpretation of Deuteronomy'.[54]

Turner summarizes the 'standard critical position' (exemplified by Tigay) as follows: '(T)he authors of Deuteronomy – writing much later – inferred from common ANE practice that the disappearance of Canaanites was due to this policy (*ḥērem*). Thus, the policy was purely theoretical and did not exist when Israel entered the land.'[55] Brueggemann comments on 7:1–5: 'because the seven nations are long gone, the rhetoric in this text is now to be understood *symbolically and not literally*; Israel has long since given up its readiness to undertake such

---

50. R. D. Nelson, '*Ḥērem* and the Deuteronomic Social Conscience', in J. Lust and M. Vervenne (eds.), *Deuteronomy and the Deuteronomic Literature: FS for C. H. W. Brekelmans*, BETL 133 (Leuven: Leuven University Press, 1997), pp. 39–54; MacDonald, *Meaning*, pp. 108–122; R. W. L. Moberly, 'Toward an Interpretation of the Shema', in C. Seitz and K. Greene-McGreight (eds.), *Theological Exegesis: Essays in Honour of Brevard S. Childs* (Grand Rapids: Eerdmans, 1999), pp. 133–137; D. S. Earl, 'The Christian Understanding of Deuteronomy 7', *Journal of Theological Interpretation* 3 (2009), pp. 41–62; idem, *The Joshua Delusion? Rethinking Genocide in the Bible* (Eugene: Cascade Books, 2010).

51. Hofreiter, 'Genocide'.

52. McConville, *Deuteronomy*, p. 90.

53. R. W. L. Moberly, 'Theological Interpretation of an OT Book: A Response to Gordon McConville's *Deuteronomy*', in R. E. Clements, R. W. L. Moberly and J. G. McConville, 'A Dialogue with Gordon McConville on Deuteronomy', *SJT* 56 (2003), pp. 523–524, quoting McConville, *Deuteronomy*, p. 90.

54. J. G. McConville, 'A Response from Gordon McConville', in Clements et al., 'Dialogue', p. 530.

55. K. J. Turner, *The Death of Deaths in the Death of Israel: Deuteronomy's Theology of Exile* (Eugene: Wipf & Stock, 2011), p. 192 n. 46.

barbaric actions.'[56] Similarly, Stern argues that Deuteronomy 20 dates from the time of Jeroboam II. Rather than a command to fight, its extraordinary purpose was to prevent retaliation against Moab.[57] In general, these views seek to downplay the violence of the law by reinterpreting it in later historical situations.

Nelson and Rowlett argue that the wars describe the ideal warrior and are in effect a literary fantasy. Hess responds, 'This theory fails to convince anyone who has studied the ancient Near Eastern evidence.'[58] The ANE sources show that warfare and destruction were real, delighted in and described in substantially more bloody detail than the Old Testament ever even hints at. Trimm also notes a growing consensus concerning connections between the biblical material regarding warfare and ANE material, something that von Rad's seminal work had discounted.[59] Thus the argument runs against those who regard the laws of warfare as fantasy, literary fiction or mere idealism.

However, it has also been shown that the language of warfare in ANE is hyperbolic and exaggerated. Younger has argued this most persuasively, followed by Copan.[60] So the language of complete extermination fits the ANE pattern of language and need not be taken absolutely literally.

This discussion about warfare and ḥērem takes us beyond Deuteronomy, but certainly includes its theological interpretation, not least of chapters 7 and 20. With regard to the latter, there is discussion over the distinction in 20:10–18

---

56. W. Brueggemann, *Deuteronomy*, Abingdon OTC (Nashville: Abingdon, 2001), p. 95.

57. P. D. Stern, *The Biblical* Herem: *A Window on Israel's Religious Experience*, BJS 211 (Atlanta: Scholars Press, 1991).

58. Hess, 'War', p. 28. See R. D. Nelson, 'Josiah in the Book of Joshua', *JBL* 100 (1981), pp. 531–540; L. L. Rowlett, *Joshua and the Rhetoric of Violence*, JSOTSup 226 (Sheffield: Sheffield Academic Press, 1996); R. D. Nelson, 'Divine Warrior Theology in Deuteronomy', in B. A. Strawn and N. R. Bowen (eds.), *A God So Near: Essays on Old Testament Theology in Honor of Patrick D. Miller* (Winona Lake: Eisenbrauns, 2003), pp. 241–259.

59. Trimm, 'Research', pp. 18–19. On Deuteronomy 20:19–20 and Assyrian background with regard to siege and destroying fruit trees, see J. L. Wright, 'Warfare and Wanton Destruction: A Reexamination of Deuteronomy 20:19–20 in Relation to Ancient Siegecraft', *JBL* 127 (2008), pp. 423–458.

60. K. L. Younger, *Ancient Conquest Accounts: A Study in Ancient Near Eastern and Biblical History Writing*, JSOTSup 98 (Sheffield: JSOT Press, 1990); Copan, *Moral Monster*, pp. 170–173.

between nations near and those far away. The standard interpretation is that terms of peace are to be offered only to those nations 'far from you'. However, some argue that the instruction to offer terms of peace applies to all nations near and far, and that the difference between these nations is what happens to the spoils of war.

Copan argues that the language of 'driving out' the enemy (e.g. in 9:1) shows that the main concern is not killing but expulsion, and that even the language of annihilation and destruction is equivalent to exile from the land. Turner develops this argument at length, cautioning against 'an overly literalistic reading'. Exile is the death of the nation and the expulsion of the Canaanites from the land is their destruction.[61]

On Deuteronomy 7, Turner comments that the 'language of absoluteness and triumph in this passage is tempered by two significant issues. First, the destruction of the nations will not be punctiliar. God will clear them away "little by little" ... Second, the fate of the nations can become Israel's fate.'[62] Several writers argue that the command in verse 3 not to intermarry is nonsensical if the *ḥērem* is to be taken literally.[63] While acknowledging that the sequence is strictly illogical and that the command 'preserves an unexpected compromise between rigour and practicality', McConville suggests that this sequence 'corresponds to the course of the history that would follow Israel's entry to the land'.[64] McConville later comments that the *ḥērem* is an ideal, in effect a metaphor, 'symbolizing the need for radical loyalty to Yahweh on the part of Israel'.[65] Lohr cleverly shows that the rhetorical force of verse 3 does not demand a metaphorical interpretation of verses 1–2: '[it] is not completely illogical to command the destruction of something and then to add negative alternatives that should not take place.' So the alternative of intermarriage indicates a temptation that awaits Israel and may underline the command of *ḥērem*.[66] This rhetorical argument is compelling. Deuteronomy is full of powerful rhetoric and this argument fits its style well. Others consider verses 1–2 to be exaggerated, in line with hyperbolic ANE warfare language. Since the coexistence of Israelites with Canaanites is assumed in verse 22, we ought not read verses 1–2 as literally demanding a complete extermination of Canaanites. Turner distinguishes between reading

61. Copan, *Moral Monster*, p. 181; Turner, *Death*, pp. 58–61.

62. Turner, *Death*, pp. 56–57.

63. MacDonald, *Meaning*, pp. 108–123.

64. McConville, *Deuteronomy*, p. 153.

65. Ibid., p. 161.

66. Lohr, *Chosen*, pp. 167–169.

the command as hyperbole and as metaphor, though his explanation appears far from clear.[67] ANE hyperbolic language for warfare is clearly not a metaphor.

In conclusion, the debate about warfare is strongly motivated by ethical concerns about the nature of God. We need to remember that the sins of the Canaanites are highlighted, notably idolatry but also child sacrifice (12:31). Deuteronomy portrays the Canaanites as generally wicked (9:4–6) and a temptation or snare to Israel if not exterminated (12:30; 20:18).[68] It is Yhwh's right to punish sins, and Deuteronomy is clear that an idolatrous Israelite is treated in much the same way as an idolatrous Canaanite. So the warfare commanded is not ethnically driven, but morally. It is also strictly limited geographically. For nations beyond the Promised Land, Deuteronomy has at least a neutral attitude in general and an ultimate missional aim for the role of Israel. While there is likely hyperbolic language in the commands for *ḥērem*, the warfare was to be understood literally and not as a literary fiction.[69]

Politics

The discussion of *ḥērem* leads us into a brief note on political theology and Deuteronomy. McConville's recent and well-received monograph on this topic deals with Genesis to Kings, but Deuteronomy figures prominently in his thinking. One of his arguments is that the political theology espoused by Deuteronomy, along with Genesis to Kings, promotes not violence but rather justice and righteousness.

McConville rightly takes issue with those like Schwartz who argue that monotheism is a driving cause for violence and aggressive nationalism. For Schwartz, 'Whether as singleness (this God against the others) or totality (this is all the God there is), monotheism abhors, reviles, rejects, and ejects whatever it defines

---

67. Turner, *Death*, p. 193 n. 48.

68. E. A. Martens, 'Toward Shalom: Absorbing the Violence', in Hess and Martens (eds.), *War in the Bible*, p. 47.

69. See also, C. J. H. Wright, *The God I Don't Understand: Reflections on Tough Questions of Faith* (Grand Rapids: Zondervan, 2008), pp. 86–108; E. H. Merrill, 'The Case for Moderate Discontinuity', and T. Longman, 'The Case for Spiritual Continuity', in S. N. Gundry (ed.), *Show Them No Mercy: Four Views on God and Canaanite Genocide* (Grand Rapids: Zondervan, 2003), pp. 63–94, 161–187; McConville, *Grace in the End*, pp. 139–144.

as outside its compass.'[70] In response, McConville argues that Deuteronomy sees Yahwism as a 'critique of oppression'. McConville argues that biblical monotheism is far from promoting violence and that violence is more inherent in polytheism, as seen in Assyrian policy. Rather, Yahwism critiques its culture and, as Yhwh is the Creator, there is ultimately a vision of universal peace.[71] Volf also questions Schwartz's logic: 'Does not a monotheistic claim to universal truth also work against the tendency to divide people into "us" and "them"?'[72] He goes on to argue that 'neither the character of the Christian faith (its being a religion of a monotheistic type) nor its most fundamental convictions (such as that God created the world and is engaged in redeeming it) are violence inducing'.[73]

A second major part of McConville's argument is that Deuteronomy promotes politics of justice and righteousness. Undoubtedly this is a clear theme in Deuteronomy's ethics. Yhwh is himself righteous (32:4) and executes justice for the widow and orphan (10:18). Covenant keeping will produce a society that practises justice and righteousness (6:24–25). The laws themselves are righteous (4:8). Judges are to reflect the same just and righteous character that Yhwh himself is (16:18–20).[74]

McConville also draws attention to Deuteronomy's view of nationhood, arguing that it conceives a 'trans-tribal people', transcending kin relationships, incorporating non-Israelites and not conceived as an empire.[75]

Finally, 16:18 – 18:22 demonstrates a balance of power between the various leading offices and thus a clear delimiting of the authority of the king. McConville suggests that this law 'even anticipates the modern constitutional principle that the executive "neither makes the law of the land nor stands above it"'. Thus Deuteronomy's king is 'self-effacing'.[76] Clements agrees with regard to the monarchy's limitations in Deuteronomy: 'the Deuteronomic "law of the king" . . . has abandoned the primary claims regarding kingship as an institution which Israel has shared with, and derived from, the many monarchies of the

---

70. R. M. Schwartz, *The Curse of Cain: the Violent Legacy of Monotheism* (Chicago and London: University of Chicago Press, 1997), p. 63; J. G. McConville, *God and Earthly Power: An Old Testament Political Theology* (London: T&T Clark, 2006), pp. 12–13.

71. McConville, *Power*, pp. 19–29.

72. M. Volf, 'Christianity and Violence', in Hess and Martens (eds), *War in the Bible*, p. 8.

73. Ibid., p. 15.

74. McConville, *Power*, pp. 78–81.

75. Ibid., pp. 92–93. See also Corcoran, 'The alien', on Deuteronomy 29:10–15.

76. McConville, *Power*, pp. 86, 144.

ancient Near East. In its place Deuteronomy sets a *torah*-focused charter for a new Israel . . . '[77]

Mann also highlights the book as a political theology. Like McConville, though not in as developed a way, he argues that Deuteronomy adapts a political model from ANE treaty forms and applies it to the relationship between Yhwh and Israel. Deuteronomy borrows not only the structure of such documents but also much of the content. 'It models its understanding of God in terms of a political treaty.'[78]

Barrett focuses on God's threats against Israel if they turn to idolatry, and on the similarities between Yhwh's threats of destruction and those of a modern state against traitors.[79] Although the differences between these appear significant, he sees sufficient similarity to support his case. So Barrett traces parallels between idolatry and modern treason, between Yhwh's coercion of Israel to covenant loyalty and the coercion of other nations by modern states like the USA, between the harsh punishments meted out against idolaters and those meted out in the war on terror, and between the brutality of the covenant curses culminating in exile and that of modern atrocities. However, Hwang notes weaknesses in Barrett's thesis, not least the question of the use of suzerain–vassal language, which arguably 'is oriented more toward the familial than the political realm'.[80]

Community

The discussion about Deuteronomy's political theology raises the issue of its theology of community. While this is not a theme that has occasioned significant writing in recent years, a few comments are in order here.

Deuteronomy's ethic is primarily social. Mann cites as evidence the law of an unsolved murder in 21:1–9 where the community as a whole will be infected with blood-guilt if the prescribed ritual does not occur, the frequent expression 'purge the evil from your midst', and 29:18–28 which anticipates a similar spread of sin from an individual to the entire community.[81]

---

77. R. E. Clements, 'The Origins of Deuteronomy: What Are the Clues?', in Clements et al., 'Dialogue', p. 516.

78. T. W. Mann, *Deuteronomy*, WBC (Louisville: Westminster John Knox, 1995), p. 9.

79. R. Barrett, *Disloyalty and Destruction: Religion and Politics in Deuteronomy and the Modern World*, LHB/OTS 511 (New York: T&T Clark, 2009).

80. J. Hwang, 'Review of Barrett', *RBL* 01 (2011), p. 5.

81. Mann, *Deuteronomy*, p. 12.

We would also note the book's rhetoric which draws together various generations as if they were one. So in recounting the incident of the spies, Moses
consistently uses the second person, though many of his audience were not yet
born when Israel first arrived at Kadesh. The same technique occurs in 5:2,
where Moses insists that Yhwh's covenant at Horeb was made with his immediate
audience in Moab.

Deuteronomy addresses itself to 'all Israel' (1:1), largely subsuming tribal
identifications. Fellow Israelites are 'brothers', language that reflects the strength
of community desired in the book, the Transjordanian tribes must help their
'brothers' in conquering Cisjordan, and the king must be from among the
'brothers' and not a foreigner.[82]

The concern for society as a whole is reflected in many other ethical demands
of the book, not least those regarding debts and slavery and the sabbatical year
in 15:1–18, which show that Deuteronomy's 'primary concern is for the public
good, not private gain'.[83] These laws highlight a special concern for the landless
groups vulnerable to poverty, namely the widow, orphan, Levite and alien.

A notable feature regarding community is Deuteronomy's emphasis on
justice. Yhwh himself is righteous (32:4), as are his laws in general (4:8). The
judges appointed locally are to administer justice without partiality (16:18–20),
modelling themselves on Yhwh's own character (10:17–18). However, the
responsibility for justice also belongs to the people as a whole (16:18).[84]

The promotion of community in Deuteronomy is supported in its focus on
proper worship. For Firth, 'worship's primary goal is the creation of community
in response to Yahweh'.[85] The emphasis on corporate worship is important. For
example, special mention is made of including the landless groups (mentioned
above) in festivals and feasts (e.g. 12:18; 16:11). Tithes are normally taken to the
central place of worship (14:23) and used for a celebration which must include
the landless (14:26–27). However, in the third year the tithe (or, as some suggest,
additional tithe) is stored locally for the special support of the poor (14:28–29).
Firth also notes that the laws regarding debt release and slavery in 15:1–18, being
tied to a sabbatical year, are thus also tied to a context of worship.[86]

---

82. McConville, *Power*, pp. 92–93.

83. Mann, *Deuteronomy*, p. 13.

84. McConville, *Power*, p. 94.

85. D. G. Firth, 'Worship as Community Creation: Deuteronomy's Vision of Worship',
in D. J. Cohen and M. Parsons (eds.), *In Praise of Worship: An Exploration of Text and
Practice* (Eugene: Wipf and Stock, 2010), p. 7.

86. Ibid., p. 15.

Monotheism, *Shema*

In recent years there has been much discussion about the meaning of the *Shema* (6:4) and the nature of monotheism in Deuteronomy. The last four Hebrew words of the *Shema*, *yhwh 'ĕlohēnu yhwh 'eḥad*, are difficult to translate. This is not the place to engage in the details,[87] but translation inevitably influences theology, and in this case vice versa.

The key theological issue can be put simply: does the *Shema* teach Yhwh's unity (Yhwh is one) or his uniqueness (Yhwh alone)? The former view has three possible meanings, according to Block. That Yhwh is one could mean that the God of Abraham, Isaac and Jacob is one and the same God, Yhwh. Or it could be a statement against poly-Yahwism, that there are various forms of Yhwh. Or, third, it could argue for Yhwh's integrity.[88] Similarly, for McConville the use of *'eḥad* implies that 'oneness is essential to Yhwh's nature' and indicates unity or integrity.[89] Wright argues that the verse means either incomparability or singularity, though he also allows the possibility of integrity.[90]

In response to McConville and others, Moberly sees nothing in the text or context to support an emphasis on unity. Rather, the text clearly argues that Yhwh is to be the 'sole object of Israel's love'. The emphasis placed by others on unity, he claims, obscures this prime theological point of uniqueness. He rightly argues that verse 5 explicates verse 4, and makes more sense if verse 4 means that Yhwh is to be the object of exclusive worship.[91]

Block also argues cogently for uniqueness rather than 'oneness'. Following Weinfeld, he disagrees with those who think that *'eḥad* would not be used if the meaning were Yhwh 'alone', listing several texts where *'eḥad* means 'alone' or similar. To say Yhwh is 'one' is illogical, and to claim that the verse upholds the internal integrity of Yhwh is forced. Rather, it makes more sense grammatically and contextually for the translation to be 'Yhwh is the only one' or 'Yhwh is the one and only'. This connects much more obviously to the following command: 'Verse 5 confirms that the fundamental issue in the *Shema* is exclusive and total devotion to Yahweh, a sense scarcely reflected in the traditional

---

87. For a summary of translation views, see D. I. Block, 'How Many is God? An Investigation into the Meaning of Deuteronomy 6:4–5', *JETS* 47 (2004), pp. 193–212.

88. Ibid., p. 198.

89. McConville, *Deuteronomy*, p. 141.

90. Wright, *Deuteronomy*, pp. 96–97.

91. Moberly, 'Theological Interpretation', pp. 520–521. McConville does not respond to this directly.

translation of the verse.'[92] He supports this with an insightful observation of the parallels between 6:4–9 and 6:10–25, showing the connection between verse 4b, 'Yhwh alone', and verses 14–15, 'You shall not go after other gods . . .'[93] This underscores that the issue in the *Shema* is not Yhwh's 'oneness' or 'integrity', but rather that Yhwh *alone* is to be Israel's God. The issue here is allegiance. Block concludes:

> The *Shema* should not be taken out of context and interpreted as a great monotheistic confession . . . Nor is the issue in the broader context the nature of God in general or his integrity in particular – though the nature and integrity of his people is a very important concern. This is a cry of allegiance, an affirmation of covenant commitment in response to the question, 'Who is the God of Israel?'[94]

Although he argues for the same meaning, Moberly advocates the traditional translation of 'Yhwh our God, Yhwh is one', clarifying: 'To say that Yhwh is "one" is not to say something about God that is separable from its human counterpart of "love", but rather designates Yahweh as the appropriate recipient of unreserved "love".'[95] Block takes issue with this, saying that the translation 'Yhwh is one' does not communicate this and in fact 'misleads the reader'. Meaning in context ought to govern translation, not dictionary definition.[96]

On the related issue of monotheism, McConville offers a salutary caution:

> The discussion whether Deuteronomy is monotheistic in the strict sense is arid. The book always thinks of God's oneness in relational terms, that is, in the context of his relationship with Israel. It is this God, Yahweh, and not another, who is supreme in the affairs of Israel and of the nations – a point made in dialogue, explicitly and implicitly, with the polytheism of Canaan.[97]

However, Wright goes further: 'Deuteronomy is uncompromisingly, ruthlessly monotheistic. It affirms that Yahweh alone is God and there is no other.'[98] He

---

92. Block, 'How Many', p. 204.

93. Ibid., p. 205.

94. Ibid., p. 211.

95. Moberly, 'Towards an Interpretation', p. 133.

96. Block, 'How Many', p. 212.

97. McConville, *Grace in the End*, p. 124.

98. Wright, *Deuteronomy*, p. 10.

specifically rejects the view that Deuteronomy is mono-Yahwistic but not mono-theistic: 'if Israel had wanted to make an explicitly monotheistic declaration in absolute terms, what more could he (or she, cf. 1 Sam. 2:2) have said than Deut. 4:39 or 32:39?'[99] Wright concludes elsewhere: 'The reason why there is no other god *like* Yhwh is because there is no other god, period.'[100] For Wright, 'heartbeat' texts include the *Shema* (6:4) and 4:32–40, as well as those that show the universal nature of Yhwh.[101] Block persuasively argues that, while monotheism is found in 4:32–40, it is not in the *Shema*.

Does uniqueness deny the existence of other gods? Bauckham argues that Old Testament monotheism does not deny the existence of other gods, but rather that Yhwh is 'in a class of his own, a wholly different class from any other heavenly or supernatural beings, even if these are called "gods"'.[102] MacDonald takes a different stance: Deuteronomy 4:35, 39 advocates that Yhwh is the only god *for Israel*, in a context which acknowledges the existence of other gods.[103] For MacDonald, true monotheism denies the existence of other gods, something that Deuteronomy declines to do.[104] Bauckham challenges MacDonald at this point, arguing that Deuteronomy declares the uniqueness of Yhwh, and understands that does not simply consist in what Yhwh does for Israel (the point at which MacDonald stops) but also includes what Yhwh objectively is. Bauckham argues that 4:35, 39 states more than merely that Yhwh is the only god for Israel. Rather, from what Yhwh has done for Israel, Israel is to realize that Yhwh is God of gods and that the other gods are 'impotent nonentities'. Yhwh alone is the god of supreme power.[105]

The debate about monotheism is not merely academic. In the discussion above on *ḥērem*, we noted Schwartz's attack on monotheism as the root of all violence, along with the responses from Copan, Hess and Volf.

---

99. Ibid., p. 18 n. 24.

100. Wright, *Mission*, p. 82. See also O'Dowd, *Epistemology*, p. 173, who links the *Shema* to what he calls 'missional monotheism'.

101. Also O'Dowd, *Epistemology*, p. 47.

102. R. Bauckham, 'Biblical Theology and the Problems of Monotheism', in C. G. Bartholomew et al. (eds.), *Out of Egypt: Biblical Theology and Biblical Interpretation* (Carlisle: Paternoster, 2004), p. 211; Wright, *Mission*, pp. 81–82.

103. MacDonald, *Meaning*, pp. 79–85.

104. Ibid., p. 215.

105. Bauckham, 'Biblical Theology', pp. 193–196.

Name theology

Ever since von Rad's influential article, it has been widely accepted that Deuteronomy reflects a distinctive 'name theology' in which Yhwh is transcendent and his presence on earth is manifest through his 'name' dwelling in the place he chooses.[106] This compares with the Priestly writer's understanding of the immanence of God represented in the tabernacle, temple and glory. So Deuteronomy is regarded as demythologizing a priestly concept.

Wilson challenges this. Comparing Deuteronomy 1 – 5 and 9 – 10 with their counterparts in Exodus and Numbers, he concludes that there is no lesser idea of the presence of Yhwh in Deuteronomy than in the other books. Indeed, in some cases there is a heightened awareness of Yhwh's presence. For example, in 4:36, a passage often used to advocate a transcendence view, Yhwh is present in both heaven and earth. MacDonald supports this, and adds that the presence of Yhwh on earth is fundamental to the conquest theme in Deuteronomy 4 as well as chapters 1 – 3.[107] Further, Wilson concludes that the occurrences of '*lipne Yhwh* (before Yhwh) in Deut. 12 – 26 should be understood in the literal sense and thus that they point to the localized Presence of the Deity at the "chosen place"'.[108] His argument also counters the traditional view that *lipnē yhwh* refers to Yhwh's real presence in the Priestly writing but cannot be so in Deuteronomy.[109]

In a different way, Richter has also argued against the consensus view. For her, name theology in Deuteronomy suggests ownership of the location, since 'to place one's name' is borrowed from an Akkadian idiom associated with inscriptions claiming ownership. Further, she identifies the chosen place in Deuteronomy with Mount Ebal and the inscription of a monument there claiming Yhwh's presence and hence ownership.[110] However, her argument for

---

106. G. von Rad, 'Deuteronomy's "Name" Theology and the Priestly Document's "Kabod" Theology', in G. von Rad, *Studies in Deuteronomy*, trans. D. Stalker, SBT 9 (London: SCM Press, 1953), pp. 37–44; German original, 1948.

107. MacDonald, 'Literary Criticism', pp. 215–216.

108. I. Wilson, *Out of the Midst of Fire: Divine Presence in Deuteronomy*, SBLDS 151 (Atlanta: Scholars Press, 1995), p. 204.

109. See also J. G. McConville and J. G. Millar, *Time and Place in Deuteronomy*, JSOTSup 179 (Sheffield: Sheffield Academic Press, 1994), pp. 114–115.

110. S. L. Richter, *The Deuteronomistic History and the Name Theology: lᵉšakkēn šᵉmô šām in the Bible and the Ancient Near East*, BZAW 318 (Berlin: de Gruyter, 2002); idem, 'The Place of the Name in Deuteronomy', *VT* (2007), pp. 342–366.

Ebal as Yhwh's chosen place is unconvincing. Deuteronomy identifies Ebal with curse, not blessing. Ebal is the site for a particular ceremony acknowledging fulfilment of the land promise, not a site for regular and central sacrifice. Tying 'the place' to any one site clashes with the later location at Shiloh and then Jerusalem. In addition, the association of 'place his name there' with monuments and inscriptions is not as clear as Richter suggests.[111]

Hundley proposes a mediating position: Deuteronomy does not absent Yhwh from earth, but name theology leaves the nature of his presence on earth ambiguous.

> The Deuteronomist's principal contribution lies not in moving God to heaven but in leaving undefined God's presence on earth. Rather than being a substitute presence or merely a descriptor of hegemony, the name serves to simultaneously guarantee Yhwh's practical presence and to abstract the nature of that presence.[112]

Hundley also argues that, in the ANE, name constitutes a person and can denote presence; in the Hebrew Bible as well, the name 'is inextricably linked to the named' and 'the name is often used interchangeably with Yhwh'.[113] The 'name' can therefore be understood as fully personal and not an abstraction. This resonates with Wilson's refutation of name theology as a demythologization.

Hwang extends Wilson's thesis by arguing that 'Israel's entire journey towards the land takes place before the divine presence' and thus *lipnē yhwh* applies not only in the central sanctuary but also at times in Kadesh, Horeb, Moab and Ebal. He goes on to say that 'the juxtaposition of the "name" with Israel's posture *lipnē yhwh* presupposes a concrete (though not necessarily corporeal) rather than abstract understanding of the presence of Yhwh'.[114]

In conclusion, Deuteronomy does use distinctive language to denote the presence of Yhwh on earth, in his chosen place. Wilson's thesis and Hwang's development show convincingly that Deuteronomy does not perceive of Yhwh as any less present on earth than the Priestly texts.

---

111. M. Hundley, 'To Be or Not To Be: A Reexamination of Name Language in Deuteronomy and the Deuteronomistic History', *VT* 59 (2009), pp. 541–543.

112. Ibid., p. 552.

113. Ibid., p. 550.

114. J. Hwang, *Rhetoric of Remembrance: An Investigation of the "Fathers" in Deuteronomy*, Siphrut: *Literature and Theology of the Hebrew Scriptures* 8 (Winona Lake: Eisenbrauns, 2012), pp. 133–134.

Grace

Scholars have traditionally separated texts within Deuteronomy that reflect optimism for the future from those that express pessimism. The usual approach is to posit two or more redactions to the Deuteronomistic History, developing Noth's influential thesis.

Synchronic readings have provided a richer and more satisfactory theological understanding of Deuteronomy's outlook for Israel's future. In his 1993 monograph, McConville noted that Deuteronomy 29 – 30 'takes for granted that the people will indeed fail', an unsurprising expectation given the assessment of Israel in 9:4–6. This is then resolved in 30:2–3 by anticipating Israel's exilic repentance. However, the 'crucial point' is the promise of Yhwh to circumcise the heart in 30:6, which proposes an answer to Israel's inability to obey.[115]

This theme of grace has been developed in recent years. Millar cogently reviews the theme of pessimism in Deuteronomy 4 – 11, and summarizes:

> Deuteronomy displays an ambivalent attitude to the possibility of Israel's being willing or able to fulfil her covenantal obligations. Resounding calls to obedience sit alongside dismissive scepticism which denies that such revolutionary obedience will ever become reality.[116]

Similarly, Boda comments that the ubiquity of the appeals to obedience in Deuteronomy 'may suggest pessimism over Israel's ability to obey God's word'. He goes on to observe that there is little by way of forgiveness or sacrifice in Deuteronomy, that repentance is only envisaged after the 'drastic discipline' of exile and that, although

> Yahweh's covenant with Israel is based solely on God's grace, the book of Deuteronomy expresses little hope in Israel's ability to maintain this covenant. The deuteronomic theology of the two ways and their outcomes suggests that sin will ultimately be remedied through the disciplinary action of Yahweh by covenant curses ending in exile. But the penitential theology of Deuteronomy expressed in chaps. 4, 10, and 30 reveals that Yahweh will effect directly an inner transformation

---

115. McConville, *Grace in the End*, pp. 134–138.
116. J. G. Millar, *Now Choose Life: Theology and Ethics in Deuteronomy*, NSBT 6 (Leicester: Apollos, 1998), p. 170.

of Israel's heart, circumcising hearts and producing repentance to bring an end to exile.[117]

This priority of grace is the central theme in my own thesis, in which I analyse three sections of Deuteronomy that deal with Israel falling into serious sin, two in the past and one in the future.[118] Deuteronomy recounts the sins at Kadesh following the spies' report (1:19–46) and at Horeb concerning the golden calf (9:7–29). On both occasions, Yhwh extends his grace to Israel, as he will do in response to the sin anticipated in Deuteronomy 29 – 30.

That Deuteronomy fully expects Israel to fail is clear, especially in its later chapters. The Ebal ceremony and proclamation of curses without blessings in chapter 27 presupposes future failure.[119] The length of curses compared to blessings in chapter 28 and the language from 28:45 (curses as certain, not merely hypothetical) underline this.[120] Deuteronomy 29 – 30 clearly expect future failure in the land, as does 31:16–29 and Moses' song in chapter 32. Turner summarizes that in Deuteronomy 'exile is predicted as an eventual fact in Israel's future. The major texts on exile strongly suggest this inevitability'.[121] Deuteronomy is clear that this is due to Israel's corrupt or uncircumcised heart (see, for example, 10:16; 29:4). However, it is equally clear that Israel's failure is not the final word. Just as Yhwh extended grace at Kadesh and Horeb, so will he do climactically in exile.

In discussing 29:4, Grisanti concludes, 'Individual Israelites received this spiritual perception when they genuinely entered into the covenant relationship with God by faith. This view does not place the initiative or total responsibility on the Israelites. Rather, it integrally links the reception of the ability to discern with a faith relationship with Yahweh.'[122] Essentially he is attempting to steer a middle course through the initiative of Israel and that of God. 'Individual Israelites *who have a faith relationship with God* have the ability to perceive the larger significance of God's actions on the nation's behalf.'[123] While there is a degree

---

117. M. J. Boda, *A Severe Mercy: Sin and Its Remedy in the Old Testament*, Siphrut 1 (Winona Lake: Eisenbrauns, 2009), pp. 111–112.

118. P. A. Barker, *The Triumph of Grace in Deuteronomy: Faithless Israel, Faithful Yahweh in Deuteronomy*, Paternoster Biblical Monographs (Carlisle: Paternoster, 2004).

119. P. A. Barker, 'The Theology of Deuteronomy 27', *TynB* 49 (1998), pp. 277–303.

120. Turner, *Death*, pp. 134–135.

121. Ibid., pp. 226–227.

122. M. A. Grisanti, 'Was Israel Unable to Respond to God? A Study of Deuteronomy 29:2–4', *Bibliotheca Sacra* 163 (2006), p. 188.

123. Ibid., p. 195.

of mutuality between what Israel must do and what Yhwh will do, Grisanti fails to resolve how an Israelite would come to a 'faith relationship' with Yhwh and the initiative seems again to rest with Israel, and not Yhwh.

The same issue is especially focused in interpretation of 30:1–10. What prompts the return from exile predicted in 30:1–10? Several writers place the initiative with Israel, as Turner notes.[124] O'Dowd, for example, argues for 'an inherent ambiguity to this mutual turning' and regards Deuteronomy's position on the present genera-tion as 'even hopeful'.[125] However, this does not fit what Deuteronomy shows of Israel's poor record of responding to Yhwh. The initiative must, and does, come from Yhwh. This is the climax of grace in Deuteronomy.

However, there are two positions on the precise nature of this act of Yhwh. Following Vanoni and Braulik, I argue that 30:1–10 is chiastic, with the circum-cision of the heart in verse 6 at the centre. Yhwh circumcising the heart of Israel in the future, in exile (30:6), is what prompts Israel to repent and turn again to Yhwh (vv. 1–2). The effect of circumcision of the heart in verse 6 results in obedience (šûb) in verse 8, the same verb used of repentance in verse 2.[126]

A number of writers hold to a different order of events expected in these verses, in effect placing the circumcision of the heart as the climax of Yhwh's actions for Israel rather than as the precipitating action. That is McConville's reading of 30:1–10, though he comments that both models 'highlight the careful structuring of the passage to achieve a balance between Israel's obligation to repent and Yahweh's willingness to restore them'.[127]

Turner argues that the succession of verbs in 30:1–10 takes precedence over the chiastic structure. Thus 'divine circumcision is held off until Israel is back in the land', and 'it is plausible to posit a divine work of grace in the heart prior to the circumcision'.[128] I remain unconvinced that two separate works of grace in Israel's heart are envisaged and place more weight than Turner on the chiastic centrality of circumcision in 30:1–10. Nonetheless, along with McConville, we conclude that Yhwh's grace is definitive for Israel's future.

Related to this is the theological interpretation of 30:11–14. Most commonly this paragraph is understood as Moses reverting to the present rather than continuing the future orientation of 30:1–10. This places priority on Israel's

124. Turner, *Death*, p. 169 n. 300.

125. O'Dowd, *Epistemology*, pp. 96–97.

126. Barker, *Triumph*, pp. 163–168, 197.

127. McConville, *Deuteronomy*, p. 424.

128. Turner, *Death*, pp. 174–175.

ability to follow God's word, something that sits uneasily with the theology of the book as a whole. I have argued instead that the paragraph ought to be interpreted as a continuation of the future expectation of 30:1–10.[129] Coxhead presses this even more strongly, and thus strengthens the case for the priority of grace for Israel's future.[130] In contrast, O'Dowd argues that 'the rhetoric demands an understanding of circumcision that is present and continual and not merely eschatological'.[131] While the rhetoric employs the expectation of heart-circumcision and return from exile in directing Israel to choose life in 30:15–20, that does not imply that circumcision is 'present and continual' as O'Dowd says. The clear future orientation of 30:1–5 must be taken seriously and not collapsed under a rubric of rhetoric.

The grace extended to Israel derives from the Abrahamic promises. This is clear for the recollection of sins at Kadesh and Horeb (1:35; 9:27). On 1:35, Hwang comments that the reference to the patriarchs 'provides a theological backdrop of promise and covenant that frames the entire narrative of Deuteronomy 1'.[132] Similarly with the sin anticipated in Deuteronomy 29 – 30, Yhwh's grace is derived from the promises to Abraham. Thus Yhwh will bring Israel back to the land 'that your ancestors possessed' and make them 'more ... numerous than your ancestors' (30:5, similarly v. 7). In fact there are numerous allusions to the Abrahamic promises in 30:1–10.[133] While Hwang suggests that 'ancestors' in 30:5 refers not to the patriarchs but to the 'populous generation at Moab',[134] he argues (as we will see below) that Deuteronomy sees the 'fathers' as a timeless symbol of Yhwh's faithfulness. It is not inappropriate to see the grace of Yhwh in bringing Israel back from exile as deriving ultimately from the Abrahamic promises.

Covenant

This raises the issue of the nature of covenant in Deuteronomy and its relationship to grace. Turner argues that the Moab covenant, being a renewal of the

---

129. Barker, *Triumph*, pp. 182–193.

130. S. R. Coxhead, 'Deuteronomy 30:11–14 as a Prophecy of the New Covenant in Christ', *WTJ* (2006), pp. 305–311.

131. O'Dowd, *Epistemology*, p. 97.

132. Hwang, *Rhetoric*, p. 49.

133. Barker, *Triumph*, pp. 169–175; Turner, *Death*, p. 176.

134. Hwang, *Rhetoric*, p. 76.

Sinai covenant, is thus 'a symbol of divine grace and commitment to the people. This fundamental stance of grace must be kept in mind.'[135]

Following ANE covenant treaty parallels, scholars have typically distinguished between conditional and unconditional treaties, the former presenting promises from Yhwh and the latter placing obligation on Israel. This language has been used to contrast the Abrahamic covenant as primarily unconditional with the Sinai/Horeb covenant as conditional.[136] Both Turner and Hwang have challenged this distinction with respect to Deuteronomy, though in different ways.

Turner argues that the covenants with Abraham and at Horeb are both unconditional and conditional in different senses. Horeb is conditional in the demands of fidelity placed on Israel, but unconditional since 'the covenant itself will be fulfilled in one way or the other', in blessing or curse. The patriarchal covenant in Deuteronomy is conditional in having conditions attached to blessings (7:12; 8:18), but unconditional in the land having being sworn by Yhwh to the fathers. While Deuteronomy allows some continuity between the Abrahamic and Horeb covenants, for example, 'fathers' can relate to the patriarchs as well as the exodus generation, ultimately the book maintains a distinction between the two covenants.[137]

Using speech-act theory to analyse Deuteronomy's rhetoric, Hwang argues that the book deliberately conflates generations and 'fathers'. This counters the common redactional approach championed differently by Römer, who argues that 'fathers' refers to the exodus generation and the patriarchal references are late, and by Lohfink, who argues the reverse.[138] Hwang notes, from 4:37 for example, that the term 'fathers' becomes 'more of a timeless symbol of divine faithfulness than a concrete generation in Israel's history'.[139] He suggests that 'Moses' citation of the "covenant of the fathers" in Deut 4:31 extends outside the narrative world of Deuteronomy to encompass all of Yhwh's past and future dealings with Israel, from the patriarchal promises to the return from exile, under a singular and all-encompassing covenant that is simultaneously "unconditional" and "conditional"'.[140] Thus Deuteronomy reflects a 'theological balance' or 'symbiosis' between grace and law. Despite

---

135. Turner, *Death*, p. 236.

136. See Hwang, *Rhetoric*, pp. 156–168, for a summary of scholarship.

137. Turner, *Death*, pp. 239–241.

138. Hwang, *Rhetoric*, pp. 4–5, 33, 206.

139. Ibid., p. 203.

140. Ibid., p. 202.

this balance, there remains 'a primacy to divine grace in Israel's history'.[141] Hwang summarizes:

> divine grace always entails human obedience, while human obedience is never demanded without a prior act of divine grace. The theological interplay between grace and law suggests that Deuteronomy cannot be separated so readily into unconditional and conditional strands of covenant theology as held by redaction critics.[142]

Deuteronomy 6:20–25 is also important for understanding the relationship between grace and law. In answer to the son's question about the meaning of the laws, four elements are listed which 'present the foundation of the Lord's covenant relationship with Israel'. These are the rescue from Egypt with a mighty hand, the signs and wonders in Egypt, the bringing of Israel out from Egypt and Yhwh's speaking with Israel at Sinai; the 'giving of the Law was thus a climactic moment of divine grace'.[143] Along similar lines, Fretheim states that the 'law is a gracious gift of God', all the more so 'because it is episodically integrated with the story of God's other gracious activities. God's actions in the narrative show that the law is not arbitrarily laid upon the people, but is given "for our good always, that God might preserve us alive" (Deut. 6:24).'[144]

Epilogue

Deuteronomy is a central book in the growing study of the New Testament's understanding of the Old Testament, not least concerning the end-of-exile theme and Paul's use of the Old Testament. It is beyond the scope of this chapter to address such issues. Suffice it to note that Deuteronomy is one of the most important books for biblical theology, it lies at the centre of the debate on the question of perfect obedience (see Gal. 3:10 and Deut. 27:26),

---

141. Ibid., p. 213.

142. Ibid., p. 232.

143. D. I. Block, 'The Grace of Torah: The Mosaic Prescription for Life (Deut. 4:1–8; 6:20–25)', *Bibliotheca Sacra* 162 (2005), p. 13.

144. T. E. Fretheim, 'Law in the Service of Life: A Dynamic Understanding of Law in Deuteronomy', in Strawn and Bowen (eds.), *A God So Near*, p. 192.

and the restoration text of 30:1–10 was significant in the intertestamental period.[145]

Deuteronomy is a rich mine of theology, and this chapter has merely surveyed the most topical contemporary themes; much recent theological interpretation has not been addressed. What is most encouraging is the growing interest in the book's theology, alongside its dating, origins and suggested redactions. While study of these other issues has its place, it often sidelines theological concern and undervalues the book's rich nuances and subtleties.

© Paul A. Barker, 2012

---

145. K. J. Turner, 'Moses on the New Perspective: Does Deuteronomy Teach Covenant Nomism?', unpublished paper presented to Evangelical Theology Society (2008). Among the numerous books and articles, see G. Waters, *The End of Deuteronomy in the Epistles of Paul*, WUNT 2/221 (Tübingen: Mohr Siebeck, 2006); S. Moyise and M. J. J. Menken (eds.), *Deuteronomy in the New Testament: The New Testament and the Scriptures of Israel*, LNTS (London: T&T Clark, 2007); Coxhead, 'Deuteronomy 30:11–14', pp. 305–320; D. M. Allen, *Deuteronomy and Exhortation in Hebrews: A Study in Narrative Re-presentation*, WUNT 2/238 (Tübingen: Mohr Siebeck, 2008); D. Lincicum, *Paul and the Early Jewish Encounter with Deuteronomy*, WUNT 2/284 (Tübingen: Mohr Siebeck, 2010).

PART 2

ISSUES IN DEUTERONOMY

3. THE DECALOGUE STRUCTURE OF THE DEUTERONOMIC LAW

John H. Walton

Introduction: backstory

In 1977 I was in the midst of the coursework for my doctorate at Hebrew Union College and enrolled in a class on Deuteronomy offered by Stephen Kaufman. Only three or four of us were in the class, and we soon learned that Kaufman had discovered what he believed to be the organizing principle of the Deuteronomic Laws (DL). Throughout the course we moved through the book section by section, hammering out the details of the theory that DL grouped its laws according to the sequence of the Decalogue.[1] I was fascinated by the approach and convinced that it could lead to productive understanding of both the Decalogue and DL. In the aftermath of the class I continued to think and study, and in 1987 followed this with my own variation on the theme.[2]

---

1. S. A. Kaufman, 'The Structure of the Deuteronomic Law', *Maarav* 1/2 (1978–9), pp. 105–158.
2. J. H. Walton, 'Deuteronomy: An Exposition of the Spirit of the Law', *Grace Theological Journal* 8 (1987), pp. 213–225. Few commentators have found this article and it has therefore received little direct critique, though it has been accepted by J. Currid, *Deuteronomy* (Auburn: Evangelical Press, 2006). Walter Kaiser, *Toward Old Testament Ethics* (Grand Rapids: Zondervan, 1983), embraces Kaufman's position, though he notes that Deut. 5 – 11 pertain to Commandment One (p. 131), a suggestion that I formalized in my paper.

'Word'[3]	Kaufman division 1979	Walton division 1987
1	Deut. 12[4]	Deut. 6 – 11
2		Deut. 12
3	Deut. 13:1 – 14:27	Deut. 13:1 – 14:21
4	Deut. 14:28 – 16:17	Deut. 14:22 – 16:17
5	Deut. 16:18 – 18:22	Deut. 16:18 – 18:22
6	Deut. 19:1 – 22:8	Deut. 19:1 – 21:23
7	Deut. 22:9 – 23:19	Deut. 22:1 – 23:14
8	Deut. 23:20 – 24:7	Deut. 23:15 – 24:7
9	Deut. 24:8 – 25:4	Deut. 24:8 – 24:16
10	Deut. 25:5–16	Deut. 24:17 – 26:15

My article proposed one major departure from Kaufman's view, and one major elaboration. I suggested that only Word 2 is addressed in Deuteronomy 12, not Words 1 and 2. The section of Deuteronomy addressing Word 1 is not in DL, but in the parenetic introduction to DL in Deuteronomy 6 – 11.[5] While portfolios of legal sayings are capable of elaborating the other Words of the Decalogue, the first Word requires more of a rhetorical elaboration. This idea is substantiated by the fact that the exposition of the Decalogue begins right after the reiteration of the Decalogue in Deuteronomy 5.

The major elaboration I offered to Kaufman's theory was the suggestion that Deuteronomy's exposition arranges the words of the Decalogue and DL into four major categories and addresses each of these categories at both the divine and the human level.

Category	Divine	Human
Authority	Word 1 / Deut. 6 – 11	Word 5 / Deut. 16:18 – 18:22
Dignity	Word 2 / Deut. 12	Words 6, 7, 8 / Deut. 19:1 – 24:7
Commitment	Word 3 / Deut. 13:1 – 14:21	Word 9 / Deut. 24:8 – 24:16
Rights and privileges	Word 4 / Deut. 14:22 – 16:17	Word 10 / 24:17 – 26:15

---

3. I will use 'word' as a reflection of the Hebrew designation of these as *děbarîm*, 'words', rather than as 'commandments'.

4. In this Kaufman follows the Catholic/Lutheran numbering of the Decalogue, 'Structure', p. 145; see further discussion below in n. 31.

5. Kaufman, 'Structure', p. 110, noted that earlier scholarship had indeed associated Deut. 6 – 11 with the first commandment, going all the way back to S. R. Driver, *Deuteronomy*, ICC (New York: T&T Clark, 1909), p. ii.

My article attempted to demonstrate that Deuteronomy presents the spirit of the law by associating portfolios of sayings with the ten Words, according to these four categories. Consequently I was inclined to see the book as a legal commentary on the ten Words. This was in direct contradiction to Kaufman, who insisted that 'Deuteronomic Law is not a commentary or sermon on the laws of the Decalogue. It contains instead covenant stipulations, a collection of "statutes and judgments" designed to provide a divine authority for the religious and social reforms it proclaims.'[6]

Response to the theory over the last thirty years

Georg Braulik offered one of the more extensive treatments of DL structured by the Decalogue.[7] Although he differs in how he attributes sections of DL to Words of the Decalogue, his conclusion indicates a general agreement with the theory proposed by Kaufman.

> In the intention of the final redaction, the system of the whole body of laws is to be interpreted on the basis of the order of the Ten Commandments. The individual laws thus appear as concretizations of the Decalogue ... The double expression 'statutes and ordinances' (*ḥuqqîm ûmišpaṭîm*) in fact signals a commentary of the Decalogue through the Deuteronomic legal corpus, since its structure, at the level of final redaction, is oriented to the order of the commandments of the Decalogue.[8]

Other commentators follow Braulik's inclination to differ from Kaufman at selected points, whether they follow Braulik's modified scheme or not.[9] Richard

---

6. Kaufman, 'Structure', p. 125.
7. G. Braulik, 'The Sequence of the Laws in Deuteronomy 12 – 26 and in the Decalogue', in Duane L. Christensen (ed.), *A Song of Power and the Power of Song: Essays on the Book of Deuteronomy*, SBTS (Winona Lake: Eisenbrauns, 1993), pp. 313–335; German original, 'Die Abfolge der Gesetze in Deuteronomium 12 – 26 und der Dekalog', in N. Lohfink (ed.), *Das Deuteronomium: Entstehung, Gestalt und Botschaft*, BETL 68 (Louvain: Louvain University Press, 1985), pp. 252–272.
8. Braulik, 'Sequence', p. 334.
9. E.g. Mark E. Biddle, *Deuteronomy*, SHBC (Macon: Smyth & Helwys, 2003), pp. 197–203; Eugene H. Merrill, *Deuteronomy*, NAC (Nashville: Broadman & Holman Publishers, 1994); J. G. Millar, *Now Choose Life: Theology and Ethics in Deuteronomy* (Grand Rapids: Eerdmans, 1998); Dennis T. Olson, *Deuteronomy and the*

Nelson remains unconvinced that DL's treatment of authorities should be associated with the Decalogue Word about parents and instead he proposes a number of other associative principles that connect the sections of DL.[10] Following Cassuto and others, Rofé observes associative links as one of several structuring principles analogous to those detected in ANE legal compilations.[11] At times, he rearranges the Deuteronomic material so that it is more conducive to this analysis.

Patrick Miller recognizes the association of DL with the Decalogue, but is not persuaded that this accounts for all of the material in DL.[12] Several other commentators accept a relationship between some of the Decalogue and DL, but demonstrate similar reservations that the case cannot be sustained throughout DL without special pleading.[13]

Besides the direct interaction with Kaufman's theory, additional avenues have opened up in connection with ANE comparative studies on the one hand, and literary analysis using speech-act theory on the other.

Contribution of ANE comparative studies

Scholars continue to refine our understanding of ancient legal compilations. It is no longer feasible to think of ANE law as revealed by deity, nor as codified

---

Death of Moses (Minneapolis: Fortress Press, 1994), p. 65. For a summary of the categories of response, see B. Levinson, *'The Right Chorale': Studies in Biblical Law and Interpretation* (Winona Lake: Eisenbrauns, 2011), pp. 231–232.

10. R. Nelson, *Deuteronomy*, OTL (Louisville: Westminster John Knox, 2002).

11. A. Rofé, *Deuteronomy: Issues and Interpretation* (Edinburgh: T&T Clark, 2002), pp. 61–70, categorized the links as the associate, the topical, the chronological, the ending with consolation, and the arrangement by length of the literary units. He describes these principles more thoroughly on pp. 55–59. This approach is generally adopted in Jeffrey H. Tigay, *Deuteronomy*, JPS Torah Commentary (Philadelphia: Jewish Publication Society, 1996), p. 451. For the work on the ANE compilations, most depend on H. Petschow, 'Zur Systematik und Gesetzestechnik im Codex Hammurabi', *ZA* 23 (1965), pp. 146–172; cf. idem, 'Zur "Systematik" in den Gesetzen von Eschnunna', in *Symbolae Iuridicae et Historicae Martino David Dedicatae*, 2 (Leiden: Brill, 1968), pp. 131–143.

12. Patrick D. Miller, *The Ten Commandments* (Louisville: Westminster John Knox, 2009), p. 5; for his reservations, see his *Deuteronomy*, Interpretation (Louisville: John Knox, 1990), pp. 128–129, 160.

13. E.g. Frank Crüsemann, *The Torah* (Minneapolis: Fortress, 2007), pp. 205–207.

law, actual rulings, legal reform, or even anthology of best practice, though each of these has served as a theory. It is now more common to hear legal collections described neutrally as 'compilations',[14] or more specifically as treatises, as proposed by Bottéro for Hammurabi's Law Code:

> In the eyes of its author the 'Code' was not at all intended to exercise by itself a univocal normative value in the legislative order. But it did have value as a model; it was instructive and educative in the judicial order. A law applies to details; a model inspires – which is entirely different. In conclusion, we have here not a law code, nor the charter of a legal reform, but above all, in its own way, a treatise, with examples, on the exercise of judicial power.[15]

Viewed as treatises, these compilations may now be considered alongside the medical treatises and the astrological treatises of divination literature. All these treatises correspond to the list form, so common in ancient Mesopotamia,[16] and instruct practitioners in the applied wisdom of the relevant field by providing examples. In the case of the legal texts, judges could be nurtured in wise decision making through study of the collected cases. That also explains why such lists were sometimes used secondarily as evidence for the wisdom and justice of the king in his report to the gods. Consequently, these compilations are not formally legislative stipulations serving as prescriptive decrees of the law of the land; rather, they are descriptive illustrations of some of the forms that wise justice would take.

B. S. Jackson has coined the neologism 'wisdom-laws' to describe this genre. Such legal sayings have the benefit of helping people to resolve their differences without resort to the formal judicial system.

> We encounter approval and discouragement, as well as permission, prescription and prohibition. We move from popular teaching through approval and disapproval of behaviour patterns, proverbs and narrative, to royal appropriation

---

14. See, for example, D. Charpin, *Reading and Writing in Babylon* (Chicago: University of Chicago Press, 2010), p. 183.

15. J. Bottéro, 'The "Code" of Hammurabi', in *Mesopotamia* (Chicago: University of Chicago Press, 1992), pp. 156–184 (167).

16. See further J. Walton, *Ancient Near Eastern Thought and the Old Testament* (Grand Rapids: Baker, 2006), pp. 289–291.

and sponsorship of the ideal of domestic teaching, as clothed in the Deuteronomic endorsement of wisdom, and ultimately to the priestly ideal of teaching through a written text.[17]

We face some limitations in applying this understanding of ANE legal compilations to Deuteronomy, and must make some adjustments. For example, the treatise form is typically and necessarily casuistic.[18] Casuistic law is not something that people would be asked to obey, though judges may be asked to 'observe' it so that its principles might be emulated.[19]

Despite its formal similarity with ANE legal compilations, the fact that DL is presented in Deuteronomy as the stipulations of a covenant gives it a far different function. We might postulate that at some time in the prehistory of some of the legal sayings they belonged to an ANE-style list, but that would be speculation and would not help to decipher the structure of DL. Nevertheless, the idea of offering wisdom for holiness has some attractiveness and is pursued further below. The overall benefit of this analysis here is to show that offering wisdom was one of the primary purposes driving such organizational enterprises in the ancient world.

Further information can be derived from a study of the Decalogue against an ANE backdrop. In the first Word it is important that the preposition *'al pěnê* ('before [the face of]') is typically spatial as opposed to representing priorities. With this reading, the Word evokes the image of the divine council chamber, in which other gods are absent.[20] Although Yahweh is seen as acting

---

17. B. S. Jackson, *Wisdom-Laws: A Study of the Mishpatim of Exodus 21:1 – 22:16* (Oxford: Oxford University Press, 2006), p. 477.

18. This is true of the Mesopotamian divination and medical treatises as well.

19. Deuteronomy has thirty-one examples of casuistic formulation in DL, a relatively small percentage of the total.

20. B. Levine also accepts that the preposition indicates spatiality, but proposes that the focus is the terrestrial sacred spaces where the images of other gods must not be brought into the presence of Yahweh in sacred space dedicated to him. In part this conclusion is predicated on Levine's belief that this prohibition is one with the ban on making images, which he views as an elaboration of the command not to have other gods in the presence of Yahweh. B. Levine, 'The Cultic Scene in Biblical Religion: Hebrew *'al panai* and the Ban on Divine Images', in *In Pursuit of Meaning: Collected Studies of Baruch A. Levine* (Winona Lake: Eisenbrauns, 2011), vol. 1, pp. 283–299. This would be an acceptable alternative to the one I have offered.

in council (e.g. 1 Kgs 22:19–22), the 'sons of God' that populate the council are not other gods. The point of the Word would be that divine authority is not distributed among many gods; Yahweh rules alone, though he can choose to delegate responsibility. Consequently, Word 1 indicates how Yahweh operates in the heavenly realm, and DL's treatment concerns how Israel should respond to him. Since the other gods have been disenfranchised and have no authority or status worthy of worship, Yahweh is to be the sole focus of Israel's attention.

Word 2 must be understood in light of how images worked in the ancient world. They are not simply works of art. Images embody the essence of deity and thereby serve a mediatorial role at three levels: they mediate the presence of the deity, the revelation of the deity (through oracles) and the worship of the deity from the people (offerings presented before the image). In contrast, for Israel the only mediatorial image is the image of God given to humans. As Word 1 describes how God operates in the heavenly realm, Word 2 describes how God operates in the earthly realm. Therefore DL treats the location of the Presence of Yahweh, twice making the point that Israel are not to worship Yahweh as the nations before them worshipped other gods (Deut. 12:4, 30–31). The Decalogue says what they are *not* to do; DL in contrast responds with what they *are* to do.

When examined in light of the ANE environment, Word 3 involves the abuse of the divine name in magic or rhetoric associated with authority.[21] It is in many ways the equivalent of modern identity theft, which exploits the authority (in the modern case, economic) associated with an individual. The more power an entity has, the more that power is subject to abuse. If we follow the pattern now established in Words 1 and 2, we would expect to find that, where the Decalogue tells what not to do, DL would offer Israel's response to the prohibition and tell them what they should do instead.

In Deuteronomy 13, DL addresses various situations in which the Israelites are to respond with merciless force when someone is fomenting rebellion against Yahweh by enticing them to worship other gods. Here the connection to the third Word hangs by a mere thread. The false prophet's enticement is preceded by the announcement of a 'sign and wonder'. Since no other god would be

---

21. The Word does not suggest that Yahweh's name is being used as if it were powerless (in which case the preposition *k* would have been used), but that his name is being used *for* vain purposes (using the preposition *l*). It is thereby assumed that the name has power, not that it is powerless.

considered able to produce a sign or wonder,[22] this announcement implies that the prophet speaks in Yahweh's name. Thus the prophet is claiming Yahweh's power illegitimately by using it towards the ultimately vain pursuit of proposing the worship of other gods.[23] The second and third paragraphs (family members, citizens of a town) would then be tangential connections, describing those who might encourage Israelites to worship other gods. These are acts of sedition and violate oaths sworn in Yahweh's name.[24]

Thus, instead of the pattern we expected from Words 1 and 2, in which DL presents what Israel should do instead of what had been prohibited in the Decalogue, we find DL encouraging them to be proactive in how to act against someone who has violated the Word of the Decalogue. We do not expect the inter-relationship between the Decalogue and DL always to follow the same path, and this is certainly an acceptable option.

As Word 3 presents how God's authority should not be abused, Word 4 addresses how God's authority should be properly recognized. Admittedly, no comparable sabbath observance is known in the rest of the ancient world.[25] Nevertheless, since the premise of sabbath observance is divine rest, the nature of the Decalogue Word can be investigated against that background.

In the ANE divine rest is located in the temple. While examples exist in the literature that portray the resting deity as otiose and inattentive, the more significant aspect of divine rest pertains to divine rule. The temple is viewed as the hub of the cosmos and the place from where the deity rules in the cosmos. Since it is contrary to the nature of Yahweh to be viewed as otiose, and he is constantly portrayed as ruling, especially from his temple, we would conclude that we should equate rest to rule (see Ps. 132:13–14). Divine rest occurs when he has brought order to his realm, whether cosmic or terrestrial. These two

---

22. Cf. Deut. 4:34. No statements in the Old Testament specifically state that other gods cannot do signs and wonders, but none is ever portrayed doing so and Deuteronomy would hardly be willing to attribute this to other gods. The prophet in Deut. 13 would gain little by saying that some other god has given a sign or wonder, so people should go and worship him. However, it would be different if he offered a sign putatively from Yahweh that it was acceptable to worship other gods.

23. Note that the word from the saying, šaw', is sometimes used as a synonym for idols and the gods they represent (Ps. 24:4; Jer. 18:15; Jon. 2:8).

24. Scholars have noted the close relationship between Deut. 13 and the Vassal Treaties of Esarhaddon. See J. Berman, 'CTH 133 and the Hittite Provenance of Deuteronomy 13', *JBL* 130 (2011), pp. 25–44; Levinson, *'Right Chorale'*, pp. 184–192.

25. G. Hasel, 'Sabbath', *ABD* 5:849–856.

aspects are reflected in the two versions of the Decalogue: Israel is entreated to observe the sabbath because God has brought order to their cosmos (Exod. 20:11) and to their nation (Deut. 5:15).

The impact of this connection is that Yahweh's rest is equated to his reign, so Israel's rest is not commemoration through imitation, but commemoration through acknowledgment. Since their work represents their attempts to bring order and control to their world, to refrain from that work is one way they acknowledge that it is God who ultimately brings order, not themselves. Sabbath observance is a way to recognize the ownership of God over the earth, honouring him as the one in control.

Just as the Decalogue addresses what properly belongs to God, DL deals with other areas where people must release their claims on what they perceive as their possessions, for example tithes. To summarize thus far, Words 1 and 2 concern God's operations, Words 3 and 4 address in reverse order how people should and should not respond to God's power, control and authority. DL calls upon the Israelites to pursue doggedly those who violate the third Word as they take responsibility for the enforcement of the prohibition. DL calls on the Israelites to recognize the limitations of human ownership and control (what is yours and, more importantly, what is not), letting go of what is not ultimately yours in recognition of the fourth Word.

In the case of these first four Words, an understanding of the Decalogue in light of its ANE context has allowed us to see some ways that DL relates to the Decalogue.

Speech-act theory and law

Another tool that may be able to aid us in thinking through the Decalogue and DL can be found in the categories of speech-act theory.[26] In the language of speech-act theory, the 'locution' refers to the words used in the communication, i.e. in DL the actual wording of the saying. The 'illocution' refers to the speech-act that the communicator is undertaking through the mechanism of the locution. It is at this level that much of the discussion about the nature of ANE and biblical law takes place. Is the communicator intending to legislate? To reveal deity? To stipulate the terms of a covenant? To instruct those making legal decisions? To document the wisdom or justice of the king for propagandistic

---

26. I am not an advocate of speech-act theory as a whole, but I find its terminology useful.

purposes? Further, whatever the original illocution, it can shift when re-contextualizing takes place. For example, the illocution would inevitably change if a simple listing of legal sayings is incorporated with prologue and epilogue into a report to the deity.

The third element in speech-act theory is 'perlocution', referring to the response that the communicator expects from the audience to which he/she is communicating. If the illocution is to legislate, the perlocution would be obedience; if the illocution is to provide stipulations for a covenant, the perlocution would be faithfulness, and so on. Communicators anticipate a particular perlocution even when they may believe the desired response to be unlikely. The fact that the response deviates from the expectation does not mean that the perlocution is variable, only that it may be idealistic.[27]

When we consider biblical law, from the same set of locutions we can identify a variety of potential illocutions and therefore perlocutions. For example, we are probably right to assume that some of the legal locutions that appear in the Pentateuch would have served the illocution of legislation in Israelite society (whether formal and written or informal and orally transmitted). None of the collections in the Pentateuch, however, is legislative in nature.[28] They have been preserved in the Pentateuch in a literary context more closely connected to covenant than to law.[29] In this second illocution they serve as stipulations to a relationship by agreement.

In the legislative illocution they do not apply to modern-day Christians because we are not Israelites living in the land and in their society. In the covenantal illocution they do not apply to us because we are not related to God through the covenant that he made with Israel. We could, however, identify a third illocution that derives from the fact that these laws are included in the

---

27. Understanding of perlocution varies from one theorist to the next, so not all would accept these statements.

28. They do not constitute a formal legal code that would have been preserved and referenced as a comprehensive law of the land.

29. For the most obvious of differences between the two, law is imposed without the agreement of those for whom it functions, whereas covenant is established through the volitional agreement of the parties involved. For comparison on numerous levels, see G. Mendenhall, 'The Conflict Between Value Systems and Social Control', in H. Goedicke and J. J. M. Roberts (eds.), *Unity and Diversity: Essays in the History, Literature and Religion of the Ancient Near East* (Baltimore: Johns Hopkins University Press, 1975); summarized in chart form in Walton, *Ancient Near Eastern Thought*, pp. 299–301.

canon of Scripture. In canonical context they are presented as God's revelation of himself to provide wisdom to be holy as he is holy.[30] This illocution of wisdom for holiness remains intact and relevant to all believers, whether or not they are part of Israel's society and Israel's covenant. With this variety of illocutions (from the same locution) comes a variety of perlocutions. Christians today are not required to organize society by Israel's legislation or to maintain the stipulations of the covenant. But we are asked to be holy.

The next step is to see whether the terminology of speech-act theory can help us to understand the relationship between DL and the Decalogue. Rather than assuming that all of DL is to be related to the Decalogue, we will approach DL below with the question of which sections can be easily related to the Decalogue. Most scholars who have interacted with Kaufman have been willing to concede that certain sections of DL do appear to match up with the Words of the Decalogue. Their reservations about Kaufman's view concern those sections of DL that cannot be easily related.

Decalogue connections

DL is introduced in chapter 5 with the well-known locutions of the Decalogue. These, their associated illocutions and their range of meanings would be well recognized by the audience. Deuteronomy 6 – 26 offers an extensive set of elaborative locutions. The illocutions would generally relate to stipulations of the covenant articulated in Deuteronomy, and each would have its range of meaning. Nevertheless, we could inquire further into what role these speech-acts have in the book. For example, the speech-acts in the sections with parallels in other Pentateuchal books are generally reiterations of those legal locutions with Deuteronomic language attached to adapt them to the needs of the book.

Those passages that easily correlate to the Decalogue would have a different role in the book. I propose to view them as specifying sample perlocutions related to the Words of the Decalogue – expansive examples of how the Israelites should respond to the Decalogue's Words. This view retains the per-spective emphasized in my 1987 article, that DL takes steps to capture the spirit of the law.

---

30. This fits well with the understanding that the legal compilations from the ancient world also have wisdom as the main goal, but there it is legislative wisdom for those who are part of the judicial enterprise.

Decalogue sections

Word 1: other gods

Scholars both before and after Kaufman have maintained that Deuteronomy 6 – 11 ought to be included as part of the Decalogue exposition. The major objection to this is that DL is a markedly different genre to Deuteronomy 6 – 11 and has its own introduction. This objection can be alleviated somewhat if one follows the Catholic/Lutheran numbering system.[31] Whatever way one would approach it, there is no question that Deuteronomy 6 – 11 can appropriately serve as commentary on 5:6–7. Word 1 disqualifies other gods in favour of Yahweh's exclusive authority. The parenetic discourse of Deuteronomy 6 – 11 correlates admirably with this concept, and its proximity to the presentation of the Decalogue supports this reading.

Deuteronomy 6 begins with an introductory formula that marks a new section. The chapter moves immediately to the *Shema*, which addresses both the uniqueness of God as sole divine authority (6:4; 10:14–19) and the expected response of the Israelites (6:5–9; 10:20–22). This sets the stage for the topics addressed in the remainder of Deuteronomy 6 – 11, including not forgetting the Lord (6:10–12; 8:1–5), fearing him (6:13; 10:12–13), not following other gods (6:14–16), keeping his commands (6:17–25; 7:7–11; 8:6–9), driving out nations so as not to be drawn to other gods (7:1–4), and destroying their worship places (7:5–6). This section also includes description of how Yahweh alone fulfils the role typically expected of deity in the ANE – protection and provision for his people (7:12–16; 8:10–20). As Yahweh has shown himself to be the sole possessor of divine authority over the Egyptian gods, he will do the same with regard to Canaanite deities in giving Israel the land (7:17–24; 9:1–6). Yahweh will not share divine authority with others (6:14–15; 9:7–21).[32] The images of their gods are to be destroyed so that the Israelites do not look to them for

---

31. This was proposed by Augustine and eventually adopted officially at the Council of Trent. This numbering combines 'no other gods' and 'no idols' into one Word, and divides coveting into two sections (wife; tangible property). This might be feasible if Deuteronomy were the only Decalogue text, but in Exodus it is much more difficult to divide the prohibition of coveting. If one considers the phrase 'I am the Lord … slavery' as an introduction to Word 1, then Deut. 6 – 11 could be viewed analogously as an introduction to the exposition of the Decalogue in the DL. As the focus of Word 1, the prohibition of idols would begin the actual legal section of the Decalogue and would likewise begin the DL (Deut. 12).

32. This section could easily be attached to Word 2.

benefits (7:25–36). After a return to discussion of the ten Words (given on Sinai again, 10:1–11), the text addresses the necessity of faithfulness to the covenant relationship (11:1–32, reiterating many previous points). The content of Deuteronomy 6 – 11 can therefore be seen to relate specifically to the first Word, as it indicates how Israel should respond to the idea that they have no other God before Yahweh. As suggested above, this is due to Yahweh's sole possession of divine authority. With the possible exception of the verses about the golden calf, these chapters have no point of contact with any of the other Words.

Word 2: images

If this ultimately concerns how Yahweh operates in the human world, and Deuteronomy addresses how Israel is to respond to the Word, one could hardly imagine a more important issue to address than the temple. No image mediators are allowed by the Word, but Deuteronomy does not offer more detail about the prohibition. Instead it turns to positive instruction: Israelites are to destroy all of the accoutrements of Canaanite worship (12:2) because they are not to imitate the way that the people of the land worshipped (12:4, 29–31, inclusio verses framing the section).

The alternative to icon mediation is found in Deuteronomy's 'name theology'. Gifts and sacrifices are to be brought before the 'name' (12:11). This chapter carefully distinguishes between eating meat (anywhere) and giving offerings (only at the central sanctuary). Thus mediation of presence and worship take place aniconically at the central shrine. In this way the passage that is parallel to the second Word shows how worship should take place, whereas the Decalogue Word itself indicates how worship should *not* take place.

Word 3: God's name

In Deuteronomy 13, the first paragraph addresses the classic case of God's name being used in vain. The most dangerous scenario and most egregious violation occurs when a prophet (presumably one claiming to speak in the name of Yahweh) encourages the worship of other gods. Logically a prophet speaking in Yahweh's name would not suggest that other gods should be worshipped in place of Yahweh, but could conceivably suggest that they could be worshipped alongside him. For example, some prophets must have been supportive of the deviant theology that considered Asherah to be a consort of Yahweh.

Deuteronomy 13 does not elaborate on the prohibition of Word 3, but conveys to the Israelites how to respond when someone violates it: they are to have a zero tolerance policy. This is a different level of perlocution from that found in relation to the first two Words. Rather than alternative behaviour, the reflection on Word 3 addresses reaction to those who are guilty of the violation.

Deuteronomy 13 then transitions to others who might commend the worship of other gods (relatives, 13:6–11; an entire town, 13:12–16). Since these are not prophets, the scenarios no longer involve taking Yahweh's name in vain, though they might conceivably be acting on the words of prophets. While these might seem better suited to a section on Word 1, in reality they are several steps removed. The second scenario does not explicitly focus on the actual worship of other gods, or on what should be done when relatives worship other gods, but specifically on what should be done when they try to persuade *you* to worship other gods. The third scenario involves a whole town that has succumbed to the worship of other gods.

The common denominator in these three scenarios is the enticement to worship other gods. The second and third scenarios may be tangential as they move away from the involvement of a prophet, but they follow the course set by the first. Just as the Word itself indicates that Yahweh does not hold guiltless those who misuse his name, so the Israelites are to give no quarter to those who issue or succumb to the invitation to do so.[33] Any sedition against the covenant represents a misuse of God's name, especially since the covenant was established by oath.

Deuteronomy 14:1–21 does not transparently relate to either Word 3 or Word 4, so is not a simple transition passage. It possibly functions as a summary statement for the treatment of the first three Words in Deuteronomy 6 – 13. That is, if the people are truly to follow these three Words, then they will distinguish themselves from the people around them in the ways this section delineates.

Deuteronomy 14:21 contains the first of about twenty-five sentence sayings scattered throughout DL.[34] Nearly two thirds of the anomalous sections (i.e.

---

33. The combination of seditious words by prophets, relatives and towns is paralleled in the Vassal Treaty of Esarhaddon as well as in a Hittite treaty, see Berman, 'CTH 133 and the Hittite Provenance of Deuteronomy 13', pp. 25–44.

34. 14:21, kid in mother's milk; 16:21–22, Asherah, standing stones; 17:1, defective animals; 19:14, boundary stone; 19:21, *lex talionis*; 22:4, fallen animal; 22:5, gender clothing; 22:6–7, bird and young; 22:8, parapet; 22:9, two kinds of seed; 22:10, yoking ox and donkey; 22:11, wool and linen; 22:12, tassels; 22:30, incest with father's wife; 23:1, emasculation; 23:2, child of forbidden marriage; 23:15–16, slave taking refuge; 23:17–18, prostitution; 24:6, millstones; 24:7, kidnapping; 24:8–9, skin disease; 24:16, fathers and children; 24:17–18, cloak of widow; 25:4, muzzled ox; 25:11–12, wife intervening. The number of sentence sayings may vary depending on how they are defined.

not connected to the Decalogue) in my identification system contain sentence sayings (twelve out of nineteen anomalous sections, with the remaining seven being relatively short, but having multiple segments). Furthermore, half of the sentence sayings are currently designated as anomalous and, more importantly, few of the sentence sayings fit solidly into the Decalogue core.[35]

Word 4: sabbath

Deuteronomy 14:22 – 15:11 addresses goods that cannot be considered possessions (tithes belonging to God and to Levites, 14:22–29) and goods that, though they belong to you, should be generously shared with the needy (not through charity but through periodically cancelled debts, 15:1–11). These relate to the Decalogue because honouring the sabbath entails (in my assessment) acknowledging that Yahweh is the one who brings order to our world, which we accomplish by honouring him as the rest-giver and ruler. Since he is ruler, we give to him that which we owe. Since he is the one who brings order to the chaos of our world (cosmic, social and spiritual), so we who are in his image can provide order to the chaos of another's world (one weighed down by debt, especially not of their own making). These paragraphs offer additional ways to live in response to the issues addressed in the sabbath Word. They are not additional ways to honour the sabbath, but ways to reflect the worldview that sabbath observance entails.

The next two sections (freeing servants, 15:12–18; firstborn animals, 15:19–23) can be seen as at least tangentially related to cancelling debts and tithing respectively, and therefore are considered to be in the Decalogue exposition. The treatment of the festivals in 16:1–17 can also be seen as loosely connected with Word 4, since festival observance is similar to sabbath observance. This section includes rest from work (16:8), giving freewill offerings (16:10) and generally acknowledging that Yahweh is responsible for ordering their existence (16:11–15).[36]

Word 5: parents

The fifth Word pertains to honouring parents who are the most basic link in the authority structure of ancient Israel. Several options are available for exploring Israelite responses to such a Word. We note from the start that this

---

35. The reason why some of them are included in the Decalogue core is because they are surrounded by other sections that *do* belong to the core. Nevertheless, most could be omitted without effect. See table on p. 115.

36. I am grateful to Aubrey Buster for observing these connections.

Word already tells Israel something positive they *should* be doing rather than issuing a prohibition, and includes the motivation clause 'that you may live long in the land'. This might suggest that the particular honouring of parents that is enjoined includes receiving the traditional teaching of the Torah so it can continue to be passed on from generation to generation, thereby ensuring the prosperity. We could conclude, therefore, that Word 5 is concerned with the authority structures in the land that preserve faithfulness to the covenant from generation to generation.

The Deuteronomic reflection on this Word begins with the brief paragraph concerning judges doing justice and not taking bribes (16:18–20, an expansion of Exodus 23:8). It is tangentially related to Word 5 in so far as it concerns authority structures in Israel, but more essentially related as a condition for continuing to live in the land.[37]

The next section pertains to violation of the Decalogue of the highest order, and appropriately these cases of worshipping other gods are identified as capital crimes (16:21 – 17:7).[38] This behaviour comes of not honouring parents and the instruction in the covenant that they have tried to convey. Such violations would cause the people to be expelled from the land, as Word 5 of the Decalogue warned.

Other authorities besides parents are responsible for the upkeep of the covenant in society, especially the central court (with its senior judge and priest, 17:8–13) and the king (17:14–20). The connection between parents and the court is seen in the injunction to 'Be careful to do everything they direct you to do. Act according to the law they teach you and the decisions they give you. Do not turn aside from what they tell you, to the right or to the left' (17:10–11).[39] Contempt is the opposite of honour, and here it is punished with death.

The king is also to act appropriately in his position of authority. Central to the Deuteronomic paragraph about the king is his responsibility to be immersed in the law so he upholds the covenant in the land (17:18–20). There is also a

---

37. This section could easily have been placed in connection with Word 9, but the combination of appointing authorities (judges) and the idea of living (long) in the land commend this placement. In fact, a close variation of this is also found in connection to the ninth Word (25:15), but there pertains to weights, not authorities. These two verses are the only ones in DL where a condition is placed on continuing to live in the land as in the fifth saying of the Decalogue.

38. As is true with most of the sentence laws, these fit uncomfortably in this section.

39. Scripture quotations in this chapter are from NIV.

correlation between those who honour parents living long in the land and the king who rules in light of the covenant reigning a long time over Israel (18:20).

The next section, 18:1–8, deals with priests and Levites, another segment of Israelite society holding authority. They have primary responsibility for instruction in the covenant and maintaining covenant observance. That said, we notice that the three paragraphs deal not with priestly authority but instead with their living circumstances: the fact that they have no land allotment, the support they receive from the people, and the rights of the itinerant Levites. They are not to accumulate lands (as temples and priests routinely did in the rest of the ancient world), just as the king was not to accumulate wealth (17:16–17). Acquisition of wealth corrupts. At the same time they are to be honoured by the people whom they serve.

Attention is next turned to other specialists who could potentially carry authority in society, but these are ones who stand in violation of the covenant (18:9–13). Sorcerers, divination experts, witches and mediums are *not* to be honoured, *not* to be given authority and *not* to be tolerated. Indeed, their practices are abhorrent and must be eradicated.

The discussion of the role of the prophet concludes this section. The prophet's station and status in the ANE was comparable to the divinatory personnel just excoriated. Not only is prophecy legitimate, but prophets are established by God as a means of authority. Thus, as with parents and courts, 'you must listen to[them]' (18:15); the people are obligated to submit to prophetic authority (18:19). As with other authorities, the prophet is bound to the covenant (18:18).

Word 6: murder
The discussion of the cities of refuge (19:1–13) provides a loose introduction to the section of Deuteronomy that involves taking life by addressing a situation in which life is taken inadvertently. It can easily be defended as part of the Decalogue exposition pertaining to the sixth Word, but it is separated from the following section dealing with murder by three short paragraphs: the sentence saying against moving a boundary stone (19:14), the section on witnesses (19:15–20), and the *lex talionis* (paralleled in Exod. 21:24 and Lev. 24:20). These three apparently anomalous paragraphs could be considered in a number of ways. One possibility is that they are displaced passages. The boundary stone saying would fit comfortably with Word 8 on theft, while the witnesses section and the *lex talionis* would fit comfortably with Word 9 on false witness. Such displacement cannot be ruled out, but it should be an analysis of last resort. A second possibility is that they are tangents that relate obliquely to their surroundings. For instance, moving a boundary stone might lead to

false witnesses or to murder. Furthermore, false witnesses in capital crimes would lead to those witnesses being put to death by the courts (though capital punishment is not specified). These solutions require significant creativity and are vulnerable to the charge of special pleading. The third possibility, equally unsatisfying, is to consider these simply as anomalies inserted at some later period by a scribe with no understanding of the structure.

I propose that the witnesses section concludes the cities of refuge paragraphs. This is supported by the parallel in Numbers 35:30 where regulations about two witnesses are associated with the cities of refuge and connected to capital punishment. Thus the boundary stone saying would be the only unexplained interruption (typical of the sentence sayings). If Deuteronomy 19 in its entirety reiterates Numbers 35 (with the suitable addition of the *lex talionis*), the boundary stone saying in Deuteronomy 19:14 occurs in the place of Numbers 35:26–28, which indicates that the accused may never safely go beyond the boundary of the city of refuge until the high priest dies, and then return home. Either of these aspects in Numbers 35 could relate to moving a boundary stone. So the avenger of blood could feasibly move the boundary stone of the city of refuge to catch the accused unexpectedly outside the limit. Alternatively, and more plausibly, in the long absence of the accused, the avenger of blood or some other interested party might move the boundary stone to reduce the landholding of the accused. While these explanations are highly speculative, they could explain the presence of the boundary stone saying within the contiguous segment in Deuteronomy dealing with the cities of refuge.

The next sections related to Word 6 include the regulations for warfare and the procedure for an unsolved murder. The former effectively clarifies the Decalogue prohibition by implying that the taking of life through warfare is not a violation of the Decalogue, provided Israel is fighting at Yahweh's behest (20:3–4). The chapter contains a variety of instructions about warfare, but highlights the treatment of cities that have been attacked. It provides the conditions in which people must not be put to death needlessly, but also those in which they must be obliterated. The section on procedures for an unsolved murder is likewise intimately related to the Decalogue as it indicates how seriously the loss of life must be taken. The emphasis is on establishing innocence from blood-guilt and providing for the ritual treatment of bloodshed.

What does it look like to be faithful to the sixth Word? It does not require pacifism, but does require warfare to be conducted under the direction of Yahweh and for his purposes. Warfare is Yahweh's mechanism for punishing wickedness and establishing order when it is threatened by injustice and tyranny. Observance of the sixth Word also requires that corporate responsibility be assumed when blood has been shed, even when no perpetrator can be identified. Life is precious.

The transitional section (21:10 – 22:12) between Words 6 and 7 is the most complicated and opaque. It is comprised of five paragraph sayings (21:10 – 22:3)[40] and eight sentence sayings (22:3–12). Family relationships are involved in the paragraphs concerning marriage to a captive woman (21:10–14) and the rights of the firstborn son of the unloved wife (21:15–17). Yet they do not offer a smooth transition into the Deuteronomic reflection on Word 7 because of the diversity of sayings in 21:18 – 22:12. Alternatively, the sayings on the woman captured in war (21:10–14), the rebellious son (21:18–21) and corpse exposure (21:22–23) could be associated with the previous section about death and war, but we would expect the captive woman saying to be adjacent to the warfare section. Further, the saying on the rights of the firstborn interrupts this series and has no transparent connection to death and war.

The sentence sayings in 22:3–12 have posed the most intractable problems for those trying to unravel the structure of DL. Some of the sayings could be broadly related to sparing life (e.g. the bird and its young, 22:6–7; the need for a parapet on the roof, 22:8). Others would more conveniently relate to coupling, and thus to marriage (e.g. two kinds of seed, 22:9; yoking ox and donkey, 22:10). Others show no identifiable relationship to either.

Word 7: adultery

However one interprets Deuteronomy 21:18 – 22:12, when we get to 22:13 it is obvious that attention has turned to issues involving integrity in marriage. The Decalogue Word pertained specifically to adultery, whereas the Deuteronomic reflection expands to questions concerning a new bride's virginity and sexual relationships outside marriage. The core of this section is the elaborated expression of the Decalogue Word itself in 22:22, as one of a series of casuistic formulations in this section.

The isolated statement against one type of incest (22:30) could certainly fit in a section on sexual behaviour, though it is odd that only this one variation is presented. This leads into a series of legal paragraphs (as opposed to sentence sayings) in 23:1–18 that have no apparent relationship to the Decalogue, to the sections surrounding them, or to one another. A very general common denominator could be that these deal with that which is appropriate or allowed in the assembly or camp of Israel – one category of semi-sacred space. Along

---

40. Aside from the two apparently anomalous paragraph sayings in 23:3–14, these are the only anomalous paragraph sayings in DL.

those lines, the emasculated, the offspring of forbidden marriages and certain foreigners are not to be counted in the assembly (23:1–7), nocturnal emissions banish one from the camp (23:9–11), excrement is inappropriate to the camp (23:12–14), and slaves taking refuge are given free run in the camp (23:15–16), while neither prostitutes nor their revenues are allowed. These pertain directly to neither sexual ethics nor theft, so their presence here does not offer any connection to the Decalogue.

Word 8: theft

The next paragraphs all concern what properly belongs to someone and therefore could be associated with the eighth Word, though the nature of what belongs to a person is wide ranging. Deuteronomy 23:19–20 on charging interest to an Israelite could plausibly be seen as taking something which does not rightfully belong to you, though the text certainly does not put it in these terms. In 23:21–23, delay in giving to God what was vowed to him is also a matter of keeping in your possession what belongs to another – in this case God. And 23:24–25 specifies when taking produce from your neighbour becomes theft.

The paragraphs in 24:1–7 transition from theft of tangible property to that of intangibles. Deuteronomy 24:1–4 prohibits a man from taking advantage of a woman's status in a way that robs her of her self-respect.[41] The recently married man in 24:5 and his wife could be robbed of their chance to have descendants if he is immediately sent off to war. A man's livelihood is stolen if the upper millstone is taken in pledge (24:6). The section ends with a legal saying that addresses not just kidnapping, but selling into slavery, which steals freedom and self-respect. As with the other sentence sayings in DL, these fit only loosely into the Decalogue structure.

Word 9: false witness

The integrity of the justice system is the focus of the ninth Word of the Decalogue, since false witnesses were the biggest obstacle to justice, especially

---

41. Note that she has committed no offence – that which is indecent would be a condition, not an action – and the prohibition is on the first husband, not on the woman. Most strikingly, the explanatory verb in 24:4 (the very rare *hutqattel* form) describes the situation in terms of the husband's offence: 'Because he has caused her to declare/consider herself to be unclean.' See J. Walton, 'The Place of the *Hutqattel* within the D-stem Group and its Implications in Deuteronomy 24:4', *Hebrew Studies* 32 (1991), pp. 7–17.

when the ability to gather forensic evidence was limited. The integrity of the justice system is then addressed in a variety of ways (24:7 – 25:19). The opening verse seems at first anomalous – what does skin disease have to do with anything? The key is found in the reference to Miriam, whose slander of Moses brought the punishment of skin disease (24:8–9; cf. Num. 12:1–2, 10).[42] This suggests that such oblique connections are not foreign to Deuteronomy's style, and similar explanations could be adopted for the sentence sayings.

From there the paragraphs concern abuses of the justice system. The paragraphs concerning the pledge (24:10–13) and treatment of the hired man (24:14–15) move beyond the Decalogue to address the just treatment of vulnerable classes on issues that would not typically end up in court.[43] The final saying concerning fathers and children (24:16) returns to the judicial assessment of penalties.

Justice can be aborted in the evidence-gathering process; it can also be undermined if verdicts are premised on faulty principles. In ANE law, one principle held that if a man caused the death of someone of lower status in another man's family, justice would be served by having someone of comparable status in the perpetrator's family put to death.[44] God allows no such principle to govern Israel's understanding of justice.

The paragraphs from 24:17 to 25:19 also concern treating the vulnerable with justice. The convicted criminal is protected from excessive beating and even the ox treading grain is treated fairly. The widow who desires to have a son for her deceased husband is vulnerable and the brother responsible for levirate duties might refuse, thus denying her justice. A man engaged in a fight is vulnerable to his opponent's wife intervening while he is occupied, and his ability to produce children is protected. Different-sized weights take advantage of customers who would be victimized by such deception.

These paragraphs are concerned with doing justice, whether in the courts or outside them. Literarily, they are bound together by anecdotes forming an inclusio. The section that started with the exhortation to remember

---

42. This was noted by Kaufman, and, as indicated in his footnote, was suggested in class by me.

43. That they occasionally may be brought to the courts for legal rulings is evidenced in the ninth-century Yabneh Yam inscription (*mesad hashavyahu*) on an ostracon on which a complaint is filed concerning the unjust seizing of a worker's garment.

44. Hammurabi, paragraphs 230–232, *COS* 2.131, p. 349.

Miriam now concludes with the exhortation to remember the Amalekites (25:17–19). The Amalekites are doomed to destruction because of their unjust treatment of the most vulnerable, i.e. those lagging behind. Consequently, this is a tight section that transparently relates to the Decalogue's Word about false witness.

Word 10: coveting

The Decalogue Word against coveting exhorts the Israelites to resist the desire to possess what belongs to others. In DL's exposition of Word 8, that which was 'stolen' was either in an ambiguous state regarding possession,[45] or not subsequently owned by the thief (e.g. dignity, freedom, self-respect). This helps show the distinction between withholding that which has been vowed (23:21–23) and withholding firstfruits and tithes (26:1–15), applying Word 10. The former has been assigned to the Lord by the action of vowing one's own possession, and the transfer must still be completed. The latter intrinsically belongs to Yahweh, therefore coveting is the appropriate description of the attitude which leads to withholding these contributions. The Decalogue Word pertains to not taking (or desiring to take) into your possession property that belongs to someone else. This complementary section in Deuteronomy pertains to not taking into your possession what belongs to Yahweh (26:13, 'sacred portion').

We might also wonder why we have a section on tithes in 14:22–29 (associated with Word 4) as well as in 26:1–15. The most significant overlap is between 14:28–29 and 26:12. Deuteronomy 14:28–29 requires the tithes as God's due (i.e. such gifts recognize God's provision and the order he brings, appropriate to the fourth Word). In contrast, 26:12 focuses on the declarations to be made when the donation is given (26:3–10, 13–15) as an indication of the appropriate attitude towards the donations. By focusing attention on one's attitude towards that which belongs to the Lord, the section parallels the tenth Word, which prescribes the correct attitude towards other people's belongings.

---

45. The paragraphs in Deut. 23:19–25 associated with the eighth Word concern tangibles in a grey zone of possession (interest, vowed property and produce at the edges). These do not strictly pertain to another's possessions.

Decalogue and Deuteronomy

Decalogue	Deuteronomy references	Deuteronomy focus
1: No other God	6 – 11	Drive out others; remember; love, fear, obey Yahweh alone
2: No images	12	One place of worship; do not worship as they do
3: Honour name	13	Eradicate those who speak falsely about God or abuse his name
Appendix: 14:1–21		Clean and unclean food
4: Sabbath	14:22 – 16:17	Releasing what is ultimately not yours and celebrating God's order
Appendix: 16:1–17		Festival observance
5: Honour parents	16:18 – 18:22	Authorities should be worthy of respect and traditions must be followed to remain in land
6: Murder	19:1 – 21:9	Cities of refuge, warfare and unsolved murder
Anomalies: 21:10 – 22:12		(Five paragraph sayings; eight sentence sayings)
7: Adultery	22:13–30	Preserve sexual integrity
Anomalies: 23:1–18		Regulations for the camp (two paragraph sayings; four sentence sayings)
8: Theft	23:19 – 24:7	Preserve inviolate that which belongs to another
9: False witness	24:8 – 25:19	Avoid slander and any abuse of the justice system
10: Coveting	26:1–15	Give to God what is his

Conclusion

As I began this study, I was mentally prepared to set aside the Decalogue structure entirely, considering its existence as possibly the result of wishful thinking and forced associations. Nevertheless, it is evident that scholars over the last thirty years have largely agreed that at least parts of DL should be associated with the Decalogue's ten Words. In this re-evaluation it was evident that nearly all of the Decalogue Words were reflected in undeniable ways,[46] and they were present in order. This being the case, it is logical to work with the sections that did *not* transparently relate to the Decalogue to see if some pattern or common denominators occurred.

If all ten Words of the Decalogue are represented in DL and in order, it is difficult to deny that the Decalogue stands as one of the ordering principles of DL. If a high percentage of the legal paragraphs of DL can be associated at least loosely with the Decalogue, then the Decalogue becomes *the* primary ordering principle of DL.[47]

Nevertheless, this still leaves us with a few sections that appear anomalous, particularly 21:10 – 22:12 and 23:1–18. A number of options could theoretically explain these.

1. These sections could be later additions by scribes who were unaware of the Decalogue structure. But we would still have to ask: why these sayings and why in these places?[48]
2. These sections do relate to the Decalogue core, but we simply do not understand how or why. We have seen that some of the connections that can be made are oblique, so it would be no surprise if other connections might escape us.
3. These sections might relate to expanded or variant lists of foundational Words that include the Decalogue along with other Words. For example,

---

46. The most arguable is the association between Word 10 and Deut. 26:1–15, which would never have brought coveting to mind on its own. Nevertheless, if nine are present, one cannot help but look for number 10 and with that in mind, 26:1–15 can be viewed in that way.

47. By my count, 287 verses in Deut. 12 – 26 out of a total of 331 verses (over 85%) fit as Decalogue exposition. The percentage is much higher when Deuteronomy 6 – 11 is included. Different counts and percentages would be arrived at if some of the sections that I have explained as fitting tangentially were included in the 'anomalies' count.

48. Although I consider it possible, and even likely, that compositional layering could be present, I am much more sceptical of our ability to identify which sections belong to which layers or to identify such layers with particular time periods or ideological factions. Such epistemological positivism is insufficiently sceptical of our own critical faculties.

Exodus 34:10–26 includes a collection of foundational Words similar to the Decalogue, and several of these correspond to sections in DL (though not to the anomalies). However, it would be difficult to explain how this could be, since the Decalogue is presented at the beginning of Deuteronomy 5. We would appropriately assume that DL is working from that form of the Decalogue.

4. Some of the 'anomalous' sayings may fit with multiple Decalogue Words and their positioning reflects relatedness to the sections on either side.

Of these, options 2 and 4 appear most defensible, but more study could well be productive. Nevertheless, this study confirms that the Decalogue is the primary organizing principle of DL. That being the case, the material gathered in DL helps us to understand the spirit of the law. It also demonstrates that the Decalogue suffused Israelite life and that a hermeneutical process was in place from earliest times.

© John H. Walton, 2012

4. CENTRALIZATION AND DECENTRALIZATION IN DEUTERONOMY

Peter T. Vogt

The consensus view: centralization

Since the early 1970s and the publication of Moshe Weinfeld's seminal work *Deuteronomy and the Deuteronomic School*,[1] one of the few areas of consensus in modern Deuteronomy scholarship is the view that at the heart of the book is a revolutionary programme of reform marked by centralization, secularization and demythologization.[2] Even prior to Weinfeld, however, centralization was identified as an important aspect of Deuteronomy's programme. Both Driver and von Rad, for example, maintained that centralization was an important

---

1. Moshe Weinfeld, *Deuteronomy and the Deuteronomic School* (Oxford: Clarendon Press, 1972; repr. Winona Lake: Eisenbrauns, 1992), pp. 191–243.
2. Similar views are held by, for example, R. E. Clements, 'The Book of Deuteronomy: Introduction, Commentary, and Reflection', in Leander Keck et al. (eds.), *The New Interpreter's Bible* (Abingdon: Nashville, 1998), vol. 2, pp. 271–287; idem, *Deuteronomy*, OTG (Sheffield: Sheffield Academic Press, 1989); J. H. Tigay, *Deuteronomy* דברים: *The Traditional Hebrew Text with the New JPS Translation* (Philadelphia: Jewish Publication Society, 1996), pp. xvii–xviii; A. D. H. Mayes, *Deuteronomy*, NCB (London: Marshall, Morgan & Scott, 1979), pp. 57–60.

goal of the authors of Deuteronomy and that the book sought to advance that aim.[3]

Questions may be raised, however, about this view. Is this the best understanding of the textual data? What exactly does centralization mean? What are the implications of Deuteronomy's centralization? In this chapter, I argue that Deuteronomy centralizes *sacrifice* to the 'place that Yahweh will choose', but that *worship* is, in fact, decentralized and extended to the people throughout the land. This represents a very different understanding of Deuteronomy's purposes from how it is often understood.[4]

The nature of centralization

Centralization, as usually understood, involved the elimination of local shrines that were thought to have existed throughout Israel prior to the Deuteronomic reforms. Although interpreters differ in their views as to the date and provenance of Deuteronomy, many hold that it is in large part a product of the seventh century BC and was advanced by Josiah's court in an effort to obtain and maintain independence from Assyria and unify the people.[5] The proliferation of local shrines and pagan altars extended in Manasseh's day to the building of altars to pagan gods and the construction of an Asherah pole in the temple itself (2 Kgs 21:1–9). Josiah's reforms were designed to re-establish proper worship of Yahweh, both in the temple and throughout the land.

The motivations of the rulers who were responsible for Deuteronomy (not all agree that it is a product of Josiah's court) are disputed. Steinberg maintains that Deuteronomic centralization served to advance the interests of the monarchy and exercise greater control over the people.[6] Others see

---

3. S. R. Driver, *A Critical and Exegetical Commentary on Deuteronomy*, 3rd ed. (Edinburgh: T&T Clark, 1901), pp. xxvii–lvii; G. von Rad, *Deuteronomy: A Commentary* (London: SCM, 1966), pp. 88–89. Note, however, that von Rad saw centralization as a later development in the process that he believed led to the final form of the book. See below.

4. The arguments presented here build on and advance those presented in Peter T. Vogt, *Deuteronomic Theology and the Significance of Torah: A Reappraisal* (Winona Lake: Eisenbrauns, 2006).

5. See M. Weinfeld, *Deuteronomy 1 – 11: A New Translation with Introduction and Commentary*, AB 5 (New York: Doubleday, 1991), pp. 65–77.

6. N. Steinberg, 'The Deuteronomic Law Code and the Politics of State Centralization', in N. K. Gottwald and R. A. Horsley (eds.), *The Bible and Liberation: Political and Social Hermeneutics*, rev. ed. (London: SPCK, 1993), pp. 365–375.

centralization more benignly, as a means of ensuring that covenant loyalty is lived out.[7]

A key part of that reform was the elimination of the local altars (whether dedicated to Yahweh or to other gods). Driver maintains that 'the law of [Deuteronomy] thus marks an epoch in the history of Israelitish religion: it springs from an age when the old law . . . sanctioning an indefinite number of local sanctuaries had been proved to be incompatible with purity of worship; it marks the final, and most systematic, effort made by the prophets to free the public worship of Jehovah from heathen accretions'.[8] Levinson similarly sees Exodus 20:24–25 as permitting a multiplicity of altars, permission which is later rescinded or countermanded.[9]

Accordingly, Deuteronomy 12:2–4 commands,

> Destroy completely all the places on the high mountains, on the hills and under every
> spreading tree, where the nations you are dispossessing worship their gods. Break
> down their altars, smash their sacred stones and burn their Asherah poles in the fire;
> cut down the idols of their gods and wipe out their names from those places. You
> must not worship the LORD your God in their way.[10]

This is followed by the exhortation to seek 'the place' that Yahweh will choose, and to offer sacrifices there (and only there). For those who see Deuteronomy as the product of the monarchic period, 'the place' must be Jerusalem, due to the presence of the ark of the covenant there beginning in David's reign (2 Sam. 6). Through centralization, in this view, cultic life was under better control, thus allowing for loyalty to Yahweh to be lived out more effectively. Moreover, the monarchy was strengthened and the institutions associated with the central administration were elevated. However, centralization also necessitated further changes, which we will now examine.

The effect of centralization: secularization

The elimination of local sanctuaries represented a rather drastic transformation of religious life for the Israelites. In this view, all slaughter of animals prior to

---

7. R. D. Nelson, *Deuteronomy: A Commentary*, OTL (Louisville: Westminster John Knox, 2002), p. 149.

8. Driver, *Deuteronomy*, p. 138.

9. B. M. Levinson, *Deuteronomy and the Hermeneutics of Legal Innovation* (Oxford: Oxford University Press, 1997), pp. 31–34.

10. Unless otherwise indicated, Scripture translations in this chapter are from the NIV (2011).

the Deuteronomic reform was carried out at local altars and was considered sacrificial, even if the slaughter was solely for the purpose of consuming meat. But when the local altars were eliminated in the altar law of Deuteronomy 12, how were people to be able to eat meat lawfully? It would be untenable to expect the people to slaughter their animals for food on the altar at the central sanctuary, since this could represent a long journey for a significant number of people (cf. 12:21).

The answer, in the view of many interpreters, is found later in chapter 12, where permission is given to slaughter and eat meat in the towns throughout the land. Deuteronomy 12:15–16 says:

> Nevertheless, you may slaughter your animals in any of your towns and eat as much of the meat as you want, as if it were gazelle or deer, according to the blessing the LORD your God gives you. Both the ceremonially unclean and the clean may eat it. But you must not eat the blood; pour it out on the ground like water.

Subsequent verses note that this is distinct from sacrifices, which, along with the tithe of grain and other offerings, were only to be consumed at the central sanctuary (12:17–18).

This is understood as a concession to practical reality that was necessitated by centralization and is often seen as an example of secularization. An aspect of daily life that was formerly a part of the cult was now freed from its cultic moorings.[11]

Secularization is further seen in the reference to the blood. Leviticus 17:6 requires that the blood of all slain non-game animals be brought to the Tent of Meeting and the blood sprinkled on the altar. This has been understood as necessary due to the fact that spilled blood demands 'vengeance and satisfaction', and the blood manipulation atones for the shedding of that blood.[12] Weinfeld sees in Deuteronomy 12 a transformation – and even rejection – of that understanding such that the blood is simply poured out 'like water' (12:16, 24). He concludes that as a result of Deuteronomy's reforms, the blood 'has no more sacral value than water has'.[13]

In this way, 'profane slaughter' results from centralization. There are, however, other examples of secularization that are seen as stemming from centralization. They include a secularized, professional judiciary necessitated by the elimination

---

11. Weinfeld, *Deuteronomic School*, p. 214.

12. Ibid.

13. Ibid.

of the judicial role played by priests at the local altars (16:18); establishment
of cities of refuge because of the abolition of local altars that could have
served as refuges (4:41–43; 19:1–10); transformation of the feast of Passover/
Unleavened Bread to a largely humanitarian, secular celebration (16:1–8).[14]

An alternative understanding: centralization and decentralization

Although the view just described has been accepted by many Old Testament
interpreters, there are problems with it. We will examine the problems associated with this view and then present an alternative understanding of what
Deuteronomy is attempting to accomplish.

The altar law in Exodus

First, we should note that it is not at all clear that the altar law in Exodus 20:24–25
envisions multiple altars, as usually understood. This is an important consideration because this understanding is often used to support the idea that the
altar law in Deuteronomy is not only different from the one in Exodus, but is
also a rejection or repudiation of earlier thinking and practice.

Exodus 20:24 says, 'Make an altar of earth for me and sacrifice on it your
burnt offerings and fellowship offerings, your sheep and goats and your cattle.
Wherever I cause my name to be honoured, I will come to you and bless you.'
The specific provision here is singular ('*an* altar of earth', rather than '*altars* of
earth'), which raises the question as to whether multiple altars are in view.
Moreover, as Cassuto has noted, the setting of this law in the narrative of
Exodus suggests that the emphasis is on Yahweh's continuing presence with
the people. In the narrative world of Exodus, the people are receiving the law
at Sinai, where Yahweh's presence was experienced in dramatic and profound
ways. Yet the people were not to stay at Sinai, but would instead move on to
the land Yahweh had promised to their ancestors. The Israelites may have felt
that in leaving Sinai they were also leaving Yahweh behind. The altar law in
Exodus 20:24 stresses that Yahweh will be with his people in every *place* (*māqôm*
– not *places*) at which he causes his name to be remembered, not only at Sinai.[15]

Of greater importance, however, is the fact that in the narrative context of
Exodus 20, the focus is not on the number of altars. In the verses immediately

---

14. The limited scope of this chapter does not allow for detailed examination of these
    examples of secularization. They are discussed in Vogt, *Deuteronomic Theology*.

15. U. Cassuto, *A Commentary on the Book of Exodus* (Jerusalem: Magnes, 1967), pp. 256–257.

prior to the altar law, Exodus 20:22–23, the author[16] draws a contrast between iconic worship and proper worship of Yahweh. The focus is clearly on proper worship of Yahweh in contrast to idols, not on the number of altars.

In light of this, I conclude that the differences between the altar law in Exodus 20 and Deuteronomy 12 have often been overstated. Both laws assert that a legitimate site is one that is associated with Yahweh's name. Furthermore, both laws associate legitimacy with Yahweh's choice of it. In Exodus 20:24 that is indicated through the fact that a legitimate site is one chosen by Yahweh to have his name remembered there. The use of the causative stem here with the first person (*'azkîr*) highlights that it is Yahweh who chooses where to cause his name to be remembered. Similarly, a legitimate site in Deuteronomy 12 is one chosen by Yahweh as a habitation for his name.

The altar law in Deuteronomy

There is also good reason to question whether Deuteronomy 12 is directed primarily against multiple altars dedicated to Yahweh worship, as often maintained. Rather, the focus is explicitly on eliminating the influence of Canaanite religion and, like the altar law in Exodus, drawing a contrast with the worship of the nations.

The opening verses of chapter 12 highlight this:

> *Destroy completely* all the places on the high mountains, on the hills and under every spreading tree, where the nations you are dispossessing worship their gods. *Break down* their altars, *smash* their sacred stones and burn their Asherah poles in the fire; cut down the idols of their gods and wipe out their names from those places. (12:2–3, my italics)

The language used here is emphatic, beginning with the opening command (using a Hebrew construction that intensifies the verbal idea[17]) and then followed by intensive forms of the verbs 'break down' (*nātaṣ*) and 'smash' (*šābar*).

---

16. The issue of the authorship of the Pentateuch (including Deuteronomy) is a complex one that is beyond the scope of this chapter. I am using the term 'author' here in the sense of 'implied author' as understood in literary criticism. That is, it refers to the presentation of the 'real' (empirical) author within the text. For more on the construct of the implied author, see J. K. Brown, *Scripture as Communication: Introducing Biblical Hermeneutics* (Grand Rapids: Baker, 2007), pp. 41–42.

17. On the use of the infinitive absolute with a finite verb, see B. K. Waltke and M. O'Connor, *An Introduction to Biblical Hebrew Syntax* (Winona Lake: Eisenbrauns, 1990), p. 586.

There is, moreover, a polemical element in this text. The worship of the Canaanites is said to take place on the high mountains, the hills and 'under every spreading tree'. This is different from proper sacrifice to Yahweh, which is to occur at the place that he chooses. The contrast being drawn is between the indiscriminate worship of the Canaanites and the very particular requirements established by Yahweh.[18] The sense is that the Canaanites worship their gods in any place and every place; Israelites are to offer sacrifices to Yahweh *only* where and in the manner he chooses.

The structure of the chapter further demonstrates the author's priorities. Deuteronomy 12 highlights through the use of a chiastic structure the need for proper worship of Yahweh in contrast to the ways in which Canaanite worship is described, as seen in the following illustration:[19]

A			Introductory statement: these are the laws you shall observe	12:1
	B		No God but Yahweh: destroy worship centres of false gods	12:2–4
		X	Demonstrate loyalty to Yahweh alone in all aspects of worship	12:5–28
	B'		No God but Yahweh: do not imitate worship of false gods	12:29–31
A'			Closing statement: observe all that is commanded	12:32[20]

At the centre of the chiasm is the call to demonstrate loyalty to Yahweh alone, in contrast to the ways in which the Canaanites are said to have worshipped their gods. This is clearly an important priority of the author.

The nature of centralization in Deuteronomy

In drawing a contrast between worship depicted as Canaanite and proper Yahweh worship, particular rhetorical emphasis is put on the 'place' (*māqôm*) at which sacrifices to Yahweh will be offered. As we have noted, verse 2 calls

---

18. M. Greenberg, 'Religion: Stability and Ferment', in A. Malamat (ed.), *The World History of the Jewish People*, vol. 4, 2, *The Age of the Monarchies: Culture and Society* (Jerusalem: Massada, 1979), p. 199, maintains that worship at multiple sites is considered to be inherently pagan in Deut. 12. Therefore, it is to be avoided.

19. Cf. D. L. Christensen, *Deuteronomy 1:1 – 21:9*, WBC 6A (Nashville: Thomas Nelson, 2001), pp. 234–235.

20. Deut. 13:1 in the Hebrew text.

for the destruction of all the 'places' (*mĕqômôt*) of Canaanite worship. In contrast, the Israelites are commanded to bring their sacrifices and offerings *only* to the place (*māqôm*) of Yahweh's choosing. The juxtaposition of 'places' and 'place' helps highlight the unique demands placed on the Israelites and draws a contrast between legitimate worship of Yahweh and that of the gods of the nations.

Similarly, 12:3–5 calls for the elimination of the 'names' (*šēmôt*) of the gods from their holy sites and the establishment of the 'name' (*šēm*) of Yahweh at his chosen place. This emphasizes the uniqueness of Yahweh's claims and establishes a striking difference between the practices of his people and that of the nations.

This is all the more significant when we consider the ANE setting of this text. In the ANE world, the gods were thought to have a particular relationship with the land, such that the inhabitants of that land were the people of that god, regardless of nationality, prior relationship, and so on.[21] Indeed, the gods were thought to be uniquely powerful in their territory. So the elimination of the very 'names' of the gods from their worship sites implies eradication of *all* their claims of legitimacy over the people of the land (including the Israelites). This is a radical stance for the Israelites to take, but one that is necessary from the standpoint of being free of pagan influence (12:30–31) and consistent with the theology of Yahweh's supremacy as the one true God (4:39).

The call for the elimination of the 'names' of the gods of the nations and the establishment of Yahweh's 'name' in the place of his choosing powerfully demonstrates Yahweh's right to establish his place, by virtue of his sovereignty and ownership of the land. Wright notes that 'to remove the names of Canaan's gods was to remove *their* presence and *their* power, just as the putting of Yahweh's name in a place was to fill it with *his* availability and *his* nearness'.[22]

As we have seen, Weinfeld and others see in this chapter a programme of centralization in order to solidify the monarchy and the claims of Jerusalem, as well as a repudiation of the multiple altars they see permitted in the altar law in Exodus. Contrary to that view, the author's intent here is, rather, to highlight Yahweh's supremacy and sovereignty. The location of the place is not specified, primarily because it is unimportant compared with the importance

---

21. For more on the ANE conceptions of the relationship between gods, people and land, see D. I. Block, *The Gods of the Nations: Studies in Ancient Near Eastern National Theology*, 2nd ed. (Leicester: Apollos, 2000).

22. C. J. H. Wright, *Deuteronomy*, NIBC 4 (Peabody: Hendrickson; Carlisle: Paternoster, 1996), p. 159.

of worshipping Yahweh in accordance with his desires.[23] And in contrast to the thinking of the ANE world, there is nothing inherently sacred about the place; its sanctity and legitimacy derive from Yahweh's choice of it. Moreover, the sacred sites at which the nations worshipped their gods can safely be destroyed since there is nothing inherently sacred about them, either. Their sanctity is derived from the association with the gods, who do not exist in the view of Deuteronomy.

I argued above that the focus of Deuteronomy 12 is on the contrast between proper worship of Yahweh and false worship of gods, as seen in the very structure of the chapter. Central to proper worship is the demonstration of loyalty to Yahweh, as that is the bulk of the chapter (vv. 5–28). Allegiance to Yahweh is lived out, first, through bringing sacrifices and offering to Yahweh *only* at the place he designates (12:5–7, 11–14). According to verse 12, worship at 'the place' is to be marked by inclusion of all Israelites (male and female, slaves as well as free, and the Levites), as well as rejoicing.

There is also an important element of choice on the part of the Israelites. Deuteronomy 12:5 says, 'But you are to seek the place the LORD your God will choose from among all your tribes to put his Name there for his dwelling. To that place you must go.' The use of the verb 'seek' (*dāraš*) together with the preposition 'to' (*'el*) has the sense of 'turning to' or 'choosing' and often involves the choosing of either God or 'false religious intermediaries'.[24] The intent is not to have the Israelites simply *identify* the place that Yahweh has chosen, but rather to choose to *worship* joyfully at the place he has chosen and to consciously and intentionally reject the places and names of the gods of Canaan.

The altar law in Deuteronomy thus serves to highlight the supremacy of Yahweh and emphasizes the need for the people of Israel to dedicate themselves wholeheartedly to serving Yahweh. This complete and total devotion to Yahweh

---

23. Similarly unaddressed is the issue of how many sites are permitted. Much scholarly attention has centred on the issue of whether Deut. 12 permits a central sanctuary but allows for other legitimate Yahweh-altars, or whether the altar law in chapter 12 envisions a sole sanctuary (although perhaps fulfilled in a succession of places). As with the question of the location, this does not seem to be the focus of the chapter. I think the most likely explanation that fits the data of both Deut. 12 and the historical books is that the altar law in Deut. 12 envisions a single sanctuary chosen by Yahweh, but that this requirement could be and was met in a series of places in succession. For more on this, see Vogt, *Deuteronomic Theology*, pp. 177–179.

24. J. G. McConville, *Deuteronomy*, AOTC (Leicester: Apollos; Downers Grove: InterVarsity Press, 2002), p. 219.

must begin with a rejection of all other competing gods and ideologies. No half-hearted measures are to be permitted; the people are called to worship Yahweh in the manner and at the place of his choosing.

Deuteronomy's demand for acknowledging the supremacy of Yahweh is central to its vision. It envisions the people gathered on the plains of Moab, at the 'back door' of the Promised Land. The previous generation had failed when perched similarly on the cusp of realizing the promises made to the patriarchs. In Deuteronomy, the people are exhorted to reject the example of the previous generation and instead commit themselves to total devotion to Yahweh, the God who made promises to the patriarchs and who had demonstrated his ability to keep those promises. Acknowledging the supremacy of Yahweh first in proper worship is a necessary requirement for the people to live out their calling of being the people of God and a means by which Yahweh would bless all nations (Gen. 12:1–3).

The vision of Deuteronomy: the supremacy of Yahweh lived out in worship

This understanding of centralization underscores the supremacy of Yahweh in the ways we have seen. Clearly, Deuteronomy 12 mandates that sacrifice be carried out only at the place of Yahweh's choosing. But, as we have seen, there is in Deuteronomy 12 also the permission to eat meat in all the towns. As noted above, this is often seen as secularization that results from Deuteronomy's programme of centralization. In my estimation, however, the author's intention is something rather different and profound. We will now turn our attention to the issue of non-sacrificial slaughter and how it contributes to the development of Deuteronomy's vision.

The case for 'profane' slaughter

We must first consider the evidence for the alternative view described above. As we have seen, many interpreters maintain that all slaughter was carried out at an altar prior to Deuteronomy 12 and was, therefore, considered sacrificial. The primary evidence for this view is the fact that 1 Samuel 14:32–35 describes the people as eating meat with the blood, a situation to which Saul responds by bringing a large stone and commanding the people to slaughter the animals on the stone. The final verse states that Saul built an altar to Yahweh. In this view, the stone Saul brought is an altar reminiscent of the altar law of Exodus 20:25. The people sinned in not sacrificing the animals properly, including the sprinkling of the blood on the altar and giving Yahweh his portion, as the Torah requires. Saul's provision of an altar rectifies the situation. This is seen as evidence that all slaughter was understood as sacrificial.[25]

The problem with this view is that the text is explicit in noting that the people sinned not by failing to sprinkle the altar with blood or give Yahweh his portion, but rather by eating the meat with the blood. That this sin is noted three times in these four verses demonstrates that the author has this particular offence in mind. The prohibition on eating meat with the blood appears in Genesis 9:4, Leviticus 17:10–14 and Leviticus 19:26. Each of these instances is a general prohibition of eating blood; there is no apparent connection with sacrifice.[26] It is not necessary to conclude that the sin in 1 Samuel 14:32–35 is a failure to sacrifice properly to Yahweh. It seems more likely that the sin is the consumption of the meat with the blood, a serious offence on its own terms.

Likewise, the stone Saul brought need not be understood as an altar. Verse 35 says that Saul built an altar. But if the stone brought by Saul in verse 33 is understood as an altar suitable for sacrifice, thus resolving the sin of the people, it is unclear why a second altar would need to be built.[27] Verse 35 uses a form of the verb (*wayyiben*) that points to the building of the altar as subsequent to the slaughter of the animals. The most likely reading is that Saul brought a stone on which the people slaughtered their animals, thus properly draining the blood in accordance with the commands against eating the meat with the blood. He then built an altar at the location. The fact that 1 Samuel 14:32–35 may be read plausibly as dealing with blood manipulation rather than sacrifice suggests that slaughter was *not* always considered sacrificial. This renders unlikely the view that Deuteronomy 12 is an example of secularization such that something previously considered sacral is radically altered and rendered religiously insignificant.

---

25. M. J. Evans, *1 and 2 Samuel*, NIBC 6 (Carlisle: Paternoster, 2000), pp. 69–70; R. W. Klein, *1 Samuel*, WBC 10 (Waco: Word, 1983), p. 139. See also Weinfeld, *Deuteronomic School*, pp. 213–214.

26. Weinfeld, *Deuteronomic School*, p. 187, maintains that the phrase 'with the blood' is a circumlocution for eating without first sprinkling the blood on the altar, based on Lev. 19:26. But, as noted above, there is nothing in Lev. 19:26 that suggests a sacrificial context and the prohibition on eating meat with the blood is a general prohibition, as may be seen by its presence in Gen. 9:4.

27. H. W. Hertzberg, *I and II Samuel*, OTL (Philadelphia: Westminster, 1964), p. 116, argues that the stone brought in v. 33 was incorporated into the altar constructed in v. 25, but this is purely speculative.

At the same time, we must address what *is* happening in Deuteronomy 12 and the discussion of slaughtering animals for food. If secularization is not the best understanding of the textual data, what is a better alternative?

Non-sacrificial slaughter in imitation of sacrifice

Deuteronomy 12 may be better understood as expanding the realm of the sacred, not narrowing it. According to 12:15, people are permitted to slaughter and eat meat: 'Nevertheless, you may slaughter your animals in any of your towns and eat as much of the meat as you want, as if it were gazelle or deer, according to the blessing the LORD your God gives you.' This command is repeated in verse 21, where it is specified that this is for those living far away from the central sanctuary: 'If the place where the LORD your God chooses to put his Name is too far away from you, you may slaughter animals from the herds and flocks . . . '

The wording here is striking. In both verses 15 and 21, the word normally translated 'sacrifice' (*zābaḥ*) is used, despite the fact that this is ostensibly 'profane' slaughter. This word appears 134 times in the Old Testament, and in all but eight of those uses it unquestionably relates to sacrifice and so has sacral connotations.[28] Of the eight remaining instances, all but the two here in Deuteronomy 12 can plausibly be understood as having sacral connotations or as emulating a sacrificial sense.[29] Thus only these two verses are seen as possibly using the term 'sacrifice' (*zābaḥ*) to mean non-sacrificial slaughter.

Given the overwhelming sacral connotations of the word 'sacrifice' (*zābaḥ*) throughout the Old Testament, it seems rather unlikely that the author would employ that word here in Deuteronomy 12 to convey the idea of non-sacral slaughter. Moreover, there is another Hebrew term, *ṭābaḥ*, that has the sense of slaughter of animals that is not considered sacrificial. If the author wanted to communicate that the killing of animals in 12:15, 21 was religiously insignificant, the word 'slaughter' (*ṭābaḥ*) would convey exactly that sense, yet it was not used in favour of the word 'sacrifice' (*zābaḥ*). The fact that the word 'slaughter' (*ṭābaḥ*) is used in 28:31 to convey the killing of animals by the nations (which would certainly be a non-sacrificial act from the perspective of the author)

---

28. The eight are: Num. 22:40; Deut. 12:15, 21; 1 Sam. 28:24; 1 Kgs 19:16, 21; Ezek. 34:3; 2 Chr. 18:2.

29. See J. Milgrom, 'Profane Slaughter and a Formulaic Key to the Composition of Deuteronomy', *HUCA* 47 (1976), p. 2; Levinson, *Legal Innovation*, p. 28 n. 29.

demonstrates that the word was known to the author and could have been used if that were the communicative intention.[30]

The use of 'sacrifice' (*zābaḥ*) in this context, coupled with a more general expansion of the idea of holiness in Deuteronomy (see below), serves to highlight the religious significance of the killing of animals away from the chosen place. Deuteronomy creates a non-sacrificial ritual that highlights the religious significance of life lived in the land in allegiance to Yahweh.[31] It is, to be sure, not a sacrifice, as both clean and unclean may eat of it (12:15, 22). Indeed, the author is at pains to make clear the distinction between sacrifice and non-sacrificial slaughter in verses 25–26. But in my estimation, the author is also trying to highlight the religious significance of non-sacrificial slaughter.

This may be seen more readily when noting the specifications in Deuteronomy 12 as to how the blood is to be handled. Verses 16 and 24 command, 'you must not eat the blood; pour it out on the ground like water'. The word for 'pour out' used here is *šāpak*. This command is stated in terms reminiscent of how the blood was to be handled in actual sacrifice. Deuteronomy 12:27 commands that 'the blood of your sacrifices shall be poured out on the altar of Yahweh your God' (my translation). The same verb, 'pour out' (*šāpak*), is used to describe how blood is to be handled in sacrifice.

Deuteronomy is clearly not attempting to present sacrifice exhaustively[32] and, indeed, likely assumes familiarity with the more detailed presentation of sacrifice found elsewhere in the Torah. Leviticus 4, in its presentation of the sin (or purification) offering, commands that after the animal has been killed the priest is to take some of the blood, sprinkle it before Yahweh and then apply some with his fingers to the horns of the altar. He is then to 'pour out' (*šāpak*) the rest of the blood onto the altar (Lev. 4:7, 18, 25, 30, 34). The sin offering is the only one in which blood manipulation is a part of the ritual, and is likely intended to purify the altar.[33]

---

30. Regardless of how one understands the composition of Deuteronomy, the fact that the word 'slaughter' (*ṭābaḥ*) appears in the final form in Deut. 28:31 means that a final redactor could have ensured that the word for non-sacrificial killing be used in Deut. 12:15, 21, if that is, in fact, what was intended there.

31. Cf. Levinson, *Legal Innovation*, p. 49.

32. McConville, *Deuteronomy*, pp. 222–223.

33. See J. Milgrom, *Leviticus 1 – 16: A New Translation with Introduction and Commentary*, AB 3 (New York: Doubleday, 1991), pp. 254–261. This may also contribute to a sense of the holiness of the whole land (see below).

By commanding that blood be poured out in the practice of non-sacrificial slaughter, utilizing the very term used in connection with sacrifice, a parallel between sacrifice and non-sacrificial slaughter is established. In the case of non-sacrificial slaughter, the Israelites are to imitate or mimic that which is done in sacrifice. This, then, is a means by which even those living far from the central sanctuary and the visible reminders of Yahweh's presence are able to demonstrate loyalty to Yahweh on a regular basis, be mindful of his sovereignty and presence, and be reminded of Israel's calling to be a paradigm to the nations of what it means to be in relationship with Yahweh.

There is, moreover, a connection between the non-sacrificial ritual and Yahweh's blessing. Deuteronomy 12:15 says that the people are allowed to eat meat in their towns 'according to the blessing the LORD your God gives you'. Thus both the provision of the meat itself and the permission to eat it in a non-sacrificial manner are seen as part of Yahweh's blessing of the people and the land. This is entirely in keeping with Deuteronomy's unapologetic presentation of abundant material blessing of the people by Yahweh (cf. 6:10–11; 8:7–13; 28:1–14), as well as the sense, in Deuteronomy and throughout the Old Testament, that the instructions of Torah are a gracious gift.[34] Reverent slaughter marked by blood manipulation and abstinence from consuming it are part of the worshipful response of the people to the blessings of Yahweh, just as is the consumption of the tithe, sacrifices and offerings at the central sanctuary.

This suggests that Deuteronomy 12 centralizes *sacrifice* to the central sanctuary, but *worship* is decentralized. Wherever the people slaughter animals for food and engage in the manipulation of the blood, they (however briefly) are demonstrating their allegiance to Yahweh and his purposes and plans for Israel, the nations and the whole of creation. This further suggests that the claims of the central sanctuary are exclusive only with respect to sacrifice. This decentralization stresses the importance of constantly living out relationship with Yahweh, in matters great and small. It further highlights the fact that in Deuteronomy's vision there is no part of life that is outside Yahweh's interest or purview. Rather, all of life is religiously significant and matters to Yahweh and, therefore, has an impact on the nation as a whole.

---

34. See, for example, Deut. 10:12–13. On the idea of Torah as a whole as a gracious gift from Yahweh, see Peter T. Vogt, *Interpreting the Pentateuch: An Exegetical Handbook*, Handbooks for Old Testament Exegesis (Grand Rapids: Kregel, 2009), pp. 25–30.

Decentralization of holiness in Deuteronomy

Holiness of the people

The decentralization of worship noted in connection with non-sacrificial slaughter in Deuteronomy 12 is part of a broader programme of decentralization of holiness. Lohfink has demonstrated that in Deuteronomy there is a particular emphasis on the holiness of the people as a whole, not just the priests.[35] This may be seen in the way in which the holiness of the people is described. Consistently, the contrast is drawn between the people of Israel and the nations, not between the priests and the laity.[36] We see in 7:6, for example, a description of Israel as 'a people holy to the LORD your God. The LORD your God has chosen you out of all the peoples on the face of the earth to be his people, his treasured possession.' In Deuteronomy, the model of holiness is not priests or king, but the people as a whole, living out loyalty to Yahweh in every aspect of their lives.[37]

We should also note the reason for the people's holiness. Their holiness stems from the fact of Yahweh's election of them, as noted in the second half of 7:6: 'The LORD your God has chosen you out of all the peoples on the face of the earth to be his people, his treasured possession.'[38] This is immediately preceded by a call to eradicate all vestiges of pagan worship in the land: 'Break down their altars, smash their sacred stones, cut down their Asherah poles and burn their idols in the fire.'

Holiness of the land

It appears, furthermore, that Deuteronomy expands the concept of holiness to encompass the whole of the land, not just the sanctuary. We see this first in the command in 12:1–2 to destroy all Canaanite worship sites throughout the entire land. This points to the idea that the whole land is the realm of Yahweh, as he will not tolerate unauthorized or idolatrous worship sites anywhere. Since the whole of the land is Yahweh's realm, it is to be regarded as holy.

---

35. N. Lohfink, 'Opfer und Säkularisierung im Deuteronomium', in A. Schenker (ed.), *Studien zu Opfer und Kult im Alten Testament: mit einer Bibliographie 1969–1991 zum Opfer in der Bibel* (Tübingen: J. C. B. Mohr [Paul Siebeck], 1992), p. 35.

36. For more on this, see E. Regev, 'Priestly Dynamic Holiness and Deuteronomic Static Holiness', *VT* 51 (2001), pp. 246–247.

37. This is not to suggest that the holiness of the people in contrast to the nations is irrelevant in other parts of the Pentateuch, but rather to note that the idea is emphasized in Deuteronomy.

38. The same point is made in Deut. 14:2; 26:19; 28:9.

The reason for this is that such worship is incompatible with the presence of a holy God and his chosen people. In fact, such practices are described in 7:25–26 as 'detestable' (*tô'ēbâ*). This term is used to describe something that is contrary to someone's character and values or is innately evil.[39] The use of this term is significant for our discussion, as the presence of things designated as 'detestable' (*tô'ēbâ*) will result in expulsion from the land (v. 26). The argument being made is that the whole of the land is Yahweh's realm and he is giving it to the people he has chosen to set apart (make holy). The land is thus made holy by virtue of Yahweh's presence and ownership of it, as well as the presence of Yahweh's chosen people. Consequently, the presence of idolatrous worship must be eliminated, as that would be incompatible with the presence of the holy people of Yahweh. Here, again, the whole of the land, not just the sanctuary, must be free of any pagan worship.

We see something similar in the laws of warfare. Deuteronomy 20:13–15 says that when cities that are far away are conquered, the Israelites are to allow the women to live and may legitimately keep the spoils of war. In cities that are nearby, however, all conquered people and property are to be destroyed. Deuteronomy 20:18 provides the rationale for this: 'Otherwise, they will teach you to follow all the detestable [*tô'ēbâ*] things they do in worshipping their gods, and you will sin against the LORD your God.' There is likely more to this than meets the eye. Like the people condemned to destruction, the people in the cities 'far off' would be followers of other gods that Deuteronomy considers false. And the women and children who are kept as spoils of war (and the men, if the city being attacked surrendered) would equally be able to entice the Israelites to follow their false gods. Both the inhabitants of cities in the land and those far away represent a threat to the purity of Israel's worship. The only difference between the two groups is their proximity to the land of Canaan. This suggests that the land itself was considered holy. The use of 'detestable' (*tô'ēbâ*) once again in connection with the land further supports this conclusion.

Deuteronomy 24:1–4 is another instance in which the holiness of the entire land is demonstrated. This law forbids a man who has divorced his wife from remarrying her if she is later divorced or widowed by her second husband. Verse 4 states that such subsequent remarriage would be 'detestable' (*tô'ēbâ*) in the eyes of Yahweh. Significantly, the exhortation is to avoid bringing sin on

---

39. M. Grisanti, 'תעב', in *NIDOTTE*, 4:314. See also the discussion in Regev, 'Holiness', pp. 249–250; and Lohfink, 'Säkularisierung', pp. 36–37.

the *land*, not the people involved.[40] We might expect a call to avoid the defiling or degrading of the people, such as the rationale found in, for example, 25:3, which establishes a limitation on the number of lashes that can be meted out in corporal punishment so as to avoid degrading the perpetrator. This further points to a conception of the land as holy.

Other examples are found in Deuteronomy 21. In verse 23, it forbids leaving the corpse of an executed criminal exposed overnight, lest the land be defiled. Clearly, there is a sense in which the land is holy, and capable of being defiled. There is also the case of unsolved murder in verses 1–9. In the case where a body is found, a ceremony is held in which a heifer is killed and elders from the town nearest to where the body was discovered wash their hands over it and declare their innocence. At first glance, this text does not appear to have anything to do with the holiness of the land, as the atonement is said to be for the people, not the land (v. 8).[41] But we must note that the issue of the land frames the entire chapter, being referred to in verses 1 and 23. Moreover, verse 1 specifies that the law is applicable only when the people are in the land.[42] This suggests that there is something about the holiness of the land that renders such a ceremony necessary, which apparently would not be the case outside it. Finally, Milgrom maintains that the ceremony is 'incomprehensible without the assumption that the blood does contaminate the land on which it is spilt and that this ritual transfers the contamination to untillable land'.[43]

The laws concerning divorce and the two in Deuteronomy 21 are particularly important in considering Deuteronomy's perspective on the defilement of the land, as they represent three examples that are not found in other Pentateuchal sources. This lends further evidence for the view that Deuteronomy decentralizes the concept of holiness and that the entire land is holy, not just the sanctuary.

Passover and the third-year tithe: decentralized worship in the Holy Land

An additional area for consideration is the law concerning the feast of Passover/Unleavened Bread in 16:1–8.[44] Verse 2 says, 'Sacrifice as the Passover

---

40. Lohfink, 'Säkularisierung', p. 37. See also J. Milgrom, 'The Alleged "Demythologization and Secularization" in Deuteronomy (Review Article)', *Israel Exploration Journal* 23, 3 (1973), p. 157.

41. Weinfeld, *Deuteronomic School*, pp. 210–211.

42. Lohfink, 'Säkularisierung', p. 37.

43. Milgrom, 'Alleged "Demythologization and Secularization"', p. 157.

44. The issues surrounding the interpretation of this text have been dealt with extensively in J. G. McConville, 'Deuteronomy's Unification of Passover and *Maṣṣôt*:

to the LORD your God an animal from your flock or herd at the place the LORD will choose as a dwelling for his Name.' This law apparently centralizes the celebration of the feast, as Exodus 12 describes it as taking place in the home. This may suggest that the feast is entirely concentrated on the central sanctuary, and that is the locus of holiness and sanctity for this festival.

While it is certainly true that the primary focus of the feast is the central sanctuary, where the sacrifice is carried out, there are other features of this legislation that point to a more diffuse understanding of holiness. It is telling, in my estimation, that verse 4 commands that yeast be removed from the entire land[45] for the duration of the feast. This suggests that the whole of the land – as well as all the people, wherever they are found – is somehow understood as being within the realm of the feast.

Moreover, verse 7 commands the people to return to their 'tents' after the eating of the Passover meal. Interpreters are divided as to what is envisioned by the use of 'tent' ('ōhel). Some see it as referring to the homes of the people and conclude that Deuteronomy envisions that after the sacrifice the people return to their homes.[46] But Deuteronomy consistently uses the word 'tent' in reference to the Israelites' dwellings in the desert, and refers to the people as living in houses in the land. This has led others to conclude that 16:7 refers to temporary shelters erected in the environs of the central sanctuary, in which the people attending the feast would live for the duration of the festival.[47]

Deuteronomy 16:8 may help clarify what is intended. There it says, 'For six days eat unleavened bread and on the seventh day hold an assembly to the LORD your God and do no work.' But it is not clear just where this 'sacred assembly' ('ăṣeret) was to be held. If the tents of verse 7 are the homes of the people, then verse 8 would apparently require them to return to their homes at the end of the meal, but then make the trip back to the central sanctuary on the seventh day for the sacred assembly.[48] However, this seems very unlikely in practical terms. Some of the people would have lived quite far from the central sanctuary

---

A Response to Bernard M. Levinson', *JBL* 119 (2000), pp. 47–58; and the reply of B. M. Levinson, 'The Hermeneutics of Tradition in Deuteronomy: A Reply to J. G. McConville', *JBL* 119 (2000), pp. 269–286.

45. A literal translation of the Hebrew would be 'in all your border'.

46. Tigay, *Deuteronomy*, p. 155.

47. E. H. Merrill, *Deuteronomy*, NAC 4 (Nashville: Broadman & Holman, 1994), p. 253; P. C. Craigie, *The Book of Deuteronomy*, NICOT (Grand Rapids: Eerdmans, 1976), p. 244.

48. Levinson, *Legal Innovation*, pp. 79–80.

and it is unreasonable to think they would be expected to make a lengthy journey twice in the space of a week. This may support the idea that the people lived in tents at the central sanctuary, carried out a sacred assembly there on the seventh day and then returned to their homes. There is yet another possibility.

Given the tendency already noted in Deuteronomy towards the expansion of holiness, it is possible that what is envisioned here is an assembly held not just at the central sanctuary, but also in the towns throughout the land.[49] If so, the festival would be extended into the land through the elimination of yeast everywhere (not just the central sanctuary) and the holding of sacred assemblies in the towns. Sacrifice would only be carried out at the central sanctuary, but worship would be in the whole land.

The final clause of verse 8 lends support for this view, where it forbids work on the seventh day. This obviously applies to the pilgrims dwelling in tents temporarily at the sanctuary, but has greater relevance for those who did not make the journey to the sanctuary. Deuteronomy 16:16 makes clear that not everyone was required to go to the sanctuary. Only males are specifically required to go. Despite the fact that many women were likely to have participated in the pilgrimage feasts even though they were not required to (particularly given Deuteronomy's emphasis on the inclusion of women into the life of the nation, as seen in 12:12, 15; 15:12, 17; 16:11, 14), there were probably many women who remained behind. In addition, there were likely elderly men who did not make the trip, younger men who returned early and perhaps those who were unable to go for other reasons. Those who journeyed to the sanctuary were basically by definition unable to carry out their normal work.[50] Those who stayed behind, however, could carry out their normal work. They would participate in the festival through abstention from yeast and a nationwide cessation from work during the sacred assemblies in the towns. As with non-sacrificial slaughter, there is an extension of worship into the land as a whole, as people in the towns imitate what happens at the central sanctuary (while not engaging in sacrifice).

Finally, 14:28–29 points in the same direction. There, the Israelites are commanded to retain their tithe in the towns every three years. The significance of this may be seen in the fact that a later text, 26:12–15, highlights the importance of this practice as well as its fundamentally religious nature. Deuteronomy 26:13 refers to the portion retained as holy or sacred (*qōdeš*). So something that

---

49. Tigay, *Deuteronomy*, p. 156.

50. W. S. Morrow, *Scribing the Center: Organization and Redaction in Deuteronomy 14:1 – 17:13*, SBLMS 49 (Atlanta: Scholars Press, 1995), p. 145.

was inherently sacred and intimately associated with the central sanctuary is shared throughout the land as a religious observance. The dynamic inter-relationship between the sanctuary and the land may be seen in the fact that compliance with the law mandating that the tithe be kept in the towns in the third year must be declared before Yahweh at the central sanctuary (26:2, 13).[51]

Based on the data of these texts, it seems apparent that Deuteronomy envisions the whole of the land as holy, due to the presence of Yahweh in it as well as the Israelites, who were set apart to be his people. We have also noted a tendency to decentralize worship, extending worship throughout the land in a variety of ways, while centralizing sacrifice to the central sanctuary.

Conclusion: the vision of Deuteronomy

We have seen that the textual data point to seeing something in Deuteronomy that is very different from the programme envisioned by Weinfeld and others. Rather than representing a programme of centralization and secularization,[52] Deuteronomy instead centralizes sacrifice to the central sanctuary to highlight Yahweh's supremacy in being able to determine where and how he is worshipped while decentralizing other aspects of worship, extending it throughout the land. We will conclude this study with a discussion of how these tendencies contribute to Deuteronomy's vision.

In the narrative world of Deuteronomy, the people of Yahweh are gathered on the plains of Moab, on the verge of entry into the land promised to their ancestors. It is forty years since the Israelites experienced Yahweh's deliverance from Egypt. But it is just an eleven-day journey from Horeb (Sinai) to the 'front door' of the Promised Land (1:2). The delay was brought about by the rebellion of the people. They failed to trust Yahweh, and that generation was forbidden to enter into the land (1:34–35). Following the wilderness wanderings and the death of the previous generation, the second generation is once again on the verge of the land.

Moses then addresses Israel, though he will not be permitted to enter into the land with the people (3:23–29). Deuteronomy represents Moses' last, best chance to tell the people what they need to know in order to survive and thrive

---

51. McConville, *Deuteronomy*, p. 252.

52. Space does not permit discussion of demythologization, the third major element of Deuteronomy's programme as often conceived by Weinfeld and others. For a discussion and analysis of that element, see Vogt, *Deuteronomic Theology*.

in the land and in being the people of God. Accordingly, he sets out a vision for how the people are to live as the people of God in the land.

At the heart of that vision is the supremacy of Yahweh, as we have seen. Yahweh is the one true God (4:39; 6:4–5), and the Israelites are called to show total loyalty to him in every aspect of life. Failure to acknowledge and live out the supremacy of Yahweh will result in catastrophe for the nation (8:19–20).

Acknowledging Yahweh's supremacy consists, first, of worshipping him in the place and manner of his choosing, and in conscious and intentional rejection of other gods, worship practices and sites (Deut. 12). He alone is God and he alone can determine how he is to be worshipped.

Second, the people are called to live out their awareness of Yahweh's supremacy in every aspect of life. The legal material in Deuteronomy 12 – 26 highlights that all of life matters to God and there is no part of life that is unaffected by relationship with Yahweh. Every moment of every day offers the Israelites a choice: they can show loyalty to Yahweh or disloyalty to him. The regulations of Torah provide a constant reminder to the Israelites that they are the people of Yahweh, the one true God.

Torah adherence, then, is an important way in which the Israelites demonstrate their loyalty to Yahweh. We have noted that an important aspect of Torah in Deuteronomy is a life of worship, as aspects of worship are decentralized and extended to the people throughout the land. Just as the entire land is holy due to the presence of Yahweh in it, so, too, are the whole lives of the people to be filled with worship, because of Yahweh's presence and relationship with them. Accordingly, worship is not limited to those times at the central sanctuary where sacrifice is offered. Rather, through Torah adherence generally, and the practice of non-sacrificial slaughter, the celebration of Passover throughout the land and the third-year retention of the tithe in particular, the people worship Yahweh.

But there is an important purpose to worshipful living on the part of the people. Israel exists, according to the broader Pentateuchal narrative (Gen. 12:1–3), to be a blessing to the nations. It is the means by which Yahweh is working to restore creation to its intended glory and humanity to its proper place in relationship with him. Deuteronomy advances that idea by providing instruction as to how to live lives of worship that honour Yahweh's supremacy before a watching world (4:6–8). Centralization and decentralization in Deuteronomy, then, help advance God's 'restoration project'[53] in important ways.

© Peter T. Vogt, 2012

---

53. See Vogt, *Interpreting the Pentateuch*, pp. 85–91.

5. CIVIL LEADERSHIP IN DEUTERONOMY

Philip S. Johnston

Introduction

In every age and context, leadership is a crucial issue. Whether nation, business, college or church, the structure and exercise of leadership is fundamental to how a group functions. Who takes decisions, and on what authority? Is approval needed, and who gives it? Who resolves disputes, and who appoints them? What process ensures that it all works, and what happens if it does not?

This chapter will examine civil leadership in Deuteronomy. It will not look at religious leadership, except where civil and religious intertwine.[1] Further, it will not cover every aspect of civil leadership in the book, leaving to one side the pre-eminent roles of Moses and Joshua. And it will not engage with recent socio-anthropological study of the nexus of authority relationships within tribe, clan and family unit. Instead it will focus on the various groups of civil leaders portrayed in Deuteronomy, both those in the past and present of the narrative, and those in prospect in the settled society as envisaged by the law code. It will also briefly consider possible implications for the book's dating.

---

1. Here 'civil' is preferred to 'secular', since the latter term now carries anti-religious connotations inappropriate to ancient society. It excludes the explicitly religious leadership of priest and prophet.

Aspects of this have already been much studied: the royal pericope has been frequently and intensely examined, while recently scholarship has also focused on the role of elders and on the integrative themes of political conception and social justice.[2] Much of this study has focused on historical-critical and redactional issues, asking what era(s) a text reflects and what the implications are for dating different sections. Occasionally this discussion becomes rather circular, especially concerning the role of the king. This study will seek to build on previous scholarship, but will start with a focus on the text itself before moving to critical concerns and then theological reflections.

It will be helpful at the outset to define several terms. The Deuteronomic law code, or DL, is taken as chapters 12 – 26. Within DL, the central passage 16:18 – 18:22, sometimes labelled Israel's institutions or constitution, is a crucial section for this study; chapters 12 – 16 and 19 – 26 then form larger sections around this core. Most leadership terms in Hebrew are translated consistently into English, e.g. 'king', 'judge', 'elder', 'head' (of tribe). But a few are not, so to avoid confusion 'commander' will be used below for *śar* (a person of some seniority), and 'officer' for *šōṭēr* (an adjunct military or civilian official).[3] The terms 'leaders', 'leadership', 'officials' and 'officialdom' will be used collectively.

Civil leadership in narrative context

Initial appointment
The very first substantial section of the book deals with leadership. The opening paragraph presents the geographical and historical context in which Moses expounds 'this law' (1:5), beginning with a recollection of the summons forty years earlier to leave Horeb for the Promised Land, and adding a theological perspective (1:6–8). The account of the appointment of the tribal leaders

2. E.g. elders: Hanoch Reviv, *The Elders in Ancient Israel: A Study of a Biblical Institution* (Jerusalem: Magnes Press, 1989); Timothy M. Willis, *The Elders of the City: A Study of the Elders-Laws in Deuteronomy*, SBL Monograph Series (Atlanta: Society of Biblical Literature, 2001); political thought: Jean-Marie Carrière, *La théorie du politique dans le Deutéronome: analyse des unités, des structures et des concepts de Dt 16,18 – 18,22*, ÖBS 18 (Frankfurt: Peter Lang, 2001); social justice: Peter T. Vogt, *Deuteronomic Theology and the Significance of Torah: A Reappraisal* (Winona Lake: Eisenbrauns, 2006).

3. Outside Deuteronomy, *śar* is sometimes rendered as 'official', 'prince', and *šōṭēr* as 'recorder', 'scribe'. The different translations could reflect changes through time, but that must be a conclusion rather than a starting point.

(1:9–18) comes immediately after this, introduced by the vague phrase 'at that time'.[4]

Moses is aware that he cannot 'bear the heavy burden of [resolving] disputes' by himself, and instructs the people to choose 'wise, discerning and reputable' heads, which they agree to do. Moses takes these heads and appoints them as commanders of different rank and as officers. He then charges their judges to judge fairly, and to bring difficult cases to himself. The context clearly implies that those appointed are to act as judges in settling disputes. This would certainly be the heads/commanders, and might also be the officers, though the latter might play an adjunct, assistant role.

The similar account in Exodus 18:13–26 makes explicit that these appointments are for judicial purposes,[5] and also attributes the initial prompt to Jethro. However, there is another significant difference in the accounts. In Exodus (18:25) it is Moses who chose able men, but in Deuteronomy Moses asks the people to choose them. The two accounts could well be complementary: Moses instigated the process, but then sought tribal recommendations. Nonetheless, in a book whose backdrop is the succession of central leadership,[6] it is intriguing that the first reference to wider leadership records a process of appointment by recommendation from the people rather than centrally.

An interesting omission from both accounts of this episode is the category of elders. Other retrospective references (e.g. Deut. 5:23) imply that they already existed as leaders, but they are ignored here. While initially puzzling, this need not be problematic. It is quite possible that they had traditionally functioned for family and community disputes, and continued to do so in ways similar to those specified later in the legal section. But the new situation of unsettled, nomadic life was creating so many new issues that a different level of dispute resolution was needed. In any case, many of the heads and commanders appointed may already have been elders.

Early references
The next reference to earlier leadership occurs in the following episode, where the roles are reversed. Here the people suggest the course of action, namely prospecting the land, and Moses selects the scouting party of one man from

---

4. Unless identified otherwise, Scripture quotations in this chapter are from the NRSV.

5. Exod. 18:21–22, 25–26 also describes them as heads and commanders who judge.

6. Whether or not this is crystallized in Moses' death, as in the title of Dennis T. Olson, *Deuteronomy and the Death of Moses: A Theological Reading*, OBT (Minneapolis: Fortress Press, 1994).

each tribe (1:22–23). Again it is interesting to note divergence from the parallel account, this time Numbers 13, where Moses takes the initiative for both plan and selection.[7] While these two examples in Deuteronomy represent a small basis for generalization, they both depart from their parallel accounts in indicating some measure of shared responsibility between people and central leader.

The other significant feature in Deuteronomy's retrospective account is the scarcity of reference to popular leadership. The Exodus accounts repeatedly mention elders as intermediaries between Moses and the people;[8] but elders only feature once in Deuteronomy's historical purview, where along with tribal heads at Horeb they articulate the people's fear (5:23). Otherwise Moses directly addresses all Israelites. Collectively they were all involved in past events (Deut. 1 – 5), they instruct the following generations (Deut. 6), and they take responsibility for obedience and for fulfilment of the national mandate (Deut. 7 – 11). This direct address to Israel in general is by no means unique to Deuteronomy, but its pervasiveness here implies a vision of a society where responsibility is constantly decentralized.

Later references

As for the immediate narrative context, the only other references to civil leadership occur towards the end of the book in chapters 27 – 31, in two sets. First, two passages present joint civil–religious leadership. In chapter 27, first elders (v. 1) and then priests (v. 9) join Moses in charging the people, the former concerning the Mount Ebal memorial and altar, the latter concerning general obedience, though the literary inclusio implies that both groups were supportive of Moses in both respects. In chapter 31, there is a similar confluence of priests and elders, when 'this law' is entrusted to them for its septennial reading (31:9). Here the elders are the sole civil representatives, with no mention of tribal heads, commanders or officers, some of whom normally accompany elders in comprehensive lists.[9]

Second, two other passages indicate civil leadership on its own. In 29:10, those assembled before Yhwh are heads of tribes,[10] elders, officers, men, women,

---

7. Again there is an external prompt, this time Yhwh, Num. 13:1.

8. E.g. Exod. 3:16; 12:21; 17:5; 18:12; 19:7; 24:1.

9. E.g. Deut. 29:10; Josh. 23:2; 24:1.

10. MT reads 'your heads, your tribes', which looks erroneous. Many emend to 'the heads of your tribes'; others to 'your heads, your judges' (see *BHS* note), e.g. Moshe Weinfeld, *Deuteronomy and the Deuteronomic School* (Oxford: Clarendon Press, 1972),

children and foreigners, while in 31:28 it is simply 'the elders of your tribes and your officers' who assemble to hear Moses' song. Two surprising features are the omission of tribal heads in the second, and the inclusion of officers in both, since in other texts the latter play an adjunct role to commanders and judges. Diachronically this could reveal different redactional perspectives; synchronically it could represent elegant variation or indicate that officers actually had a wider civil role.

While not the focus of this study, the handover of individual leadership from Moses to Joshua also features in these later chapters. It was already noted back in 3:28, but is now more in view through Joshua's investiture in chapter 31 (vv. 7–8, 14–15, 23) and further mention in 32:44 and 34:9.

Civil leadership in Deuteronomic Law

General
References to civil leadership in the Deuteronomic Law (DL) occur as follows:

Text	Topic	Terms
16:18	appointment	judges and officers
17:9, 12	central court	judge ('who is in office in those days')
17:15	kingship	king
19:12	cities of refuge	elders (of the killer's city)
19:16–18	malicious witness	judges ('who are in office in those days')
20:5, 8, 9	warfare preparation	officers and commanders
21:2, 3–6	unsolved murder	elders and judges
21:19	rebellious son	elders
22:15, 18	alleged unchastity	elders
25:1–2	litigation	judges, judge
25:7	unwilling brother-in-law	elders

Nine of the eleven passages mention judges or elders or both, so these are clearly the most important agents for maintaining civil stability. A single passage

---

p. 101 n. 5. However, the latter is less likely, both textually, since 'heads' are nearly always mentioned in construct with 'your tribes', and contextually, since judges do not appear in other Pentateuchal portrayals of the Israelite assembly (unlike Josh. 23:2; 24:1).

refers to officers and commanders, and another to the king, so these leaders play a lesser role in Deuteronomy's perspective. These various terms and their settings will be examined below.

However, before proceeding, it is worth noting that references in Deuteronomy to officialdom are actually rare, indeed strikingly so. This is true not just of the retrospective narrative (see 'Civil leadership in narrative context' above), but also of DL itself. Here leadership terms occur in some laws, as listed above, but many more specify no leader responsible for enforcing the laws or mechanism for doing so.

In the first, large section of DL (12:1 – 16:17) there are no such references at all. To cite a key example, chapter 13 gives no indication of the investigative or judicial procedure to be followed: the apostate prophet 'shall be put to death', the apostate family member 'you shall surely kill', and for the apostate town 'you shall investigate and inquire and interrogate thoroughly' (13:5, 9, 14). The triple reference to inquiry in this last verse (cited here from NJPS) indicates the supreme seriousness of the apostasy, yet the actual procedure remains unstated. Similarly, in the middle 'institutional' section, the instructions regarding apostate worshippers in 17:2–7 and 18:9–13 make no mention of the assessment process,[11] even though the first passage almost immediately follows the appointment of judges. The third section (chs. 19 – 26) continues in similar vein. While there are several references to elders and judges as listed above, many important injunctions lack judicial procedure. For instance, displaced boundary stones (19:14) could be of great economic significance, and presumably any appeal procedure involved elders, possibly a central judge, perhaps also officers if they kept any records – but these are all unmentioned in the injunction.[12]

Of course, Deuteronomy is not a legal document with full and exact provision for each event (unlike, say, a university's Statutes and Ordinances). And it could well have been deemed appropriate to extrapolate procedures from the stated to the unstated. Nevertheless, the occasional nature of references to leadership gives the impression of devolved responsibility. Civil responsibility rests largely

---

11. Deut. 17:5 only states (lit.): 'you will bring out . . . to your gates . . . and you will stone them and they will die'.

12. Willis, *Elders*, p. 36 n. 6, adds: 'There are only scattered references elsewhere in the Hebrew Bible to legal proceedings and the appointment of certain groups of individuals to legal tasks . . . these examples do little more than demonstrate the variety possible in Israel's judicial affairs over several centuries, and their significance for elucidating judicial institutions and procedures in Deuteronomy is minimal.'

with individual Israelites, while officialdom exists as a light framework to enable all Israelites to exercise their responsibility.[13]

Elders

There are no references to elders in the first two sections of DL.[14] While the first section focuses more on religious matters, the actions against apostasy in chapter 13 would surely have involved elders, yet the text omits their role. The middle section also omits them, presumably because local eldership was a long-standing custom which did not need to be instituted or regulated. However, elders are mentioned in the third section, in five passages: they instigate the return of a refugee guilty of premeditated murder (19:12); they help measure the nearest town to an unsolved murder, then those from that town perform a ritual (21:2, 3–6); they witness and presumably endorse parental condemnation of a rebellious son (21:19); they punish the husband who falsely accuses his wife of premarital unchastity (22:15, 18); and they shame the man unwilling to marry his brother's widow (25:7). The last three of these clearly deal with family matters. But this is not necessarily a sign of limited, parochial authority, as sometimes suggested. The first two instances concern unlawful killing and involve dialogue between towns, while the third leads to capital punishment.

Judges

Like elders, judges are mentioned in five texts, though in contrast to elders there are two references to them in the middle section of DL. These provide a base for the three further texts, and indeed for much scholarly discussion.

The first text (16:18) instructs Israel to 'appoint judges and officers through-out your tribes, in all your towns'.[15] This is followed by the statement that 'they shall render just decisions', and the injunction to pursue 'justice, and only justice' (16:19–20). Most interpreters understand this injunction as addressed specifically

---

13. Also noted by Norbert Lohfink, 'Distribution of the Functions of Power: The Laws Concerning Public Offices in Deuteronomy 16:18 – 18:22', repr. in Duane L. Christensen (ed.), *A Song of Power and the Power of Song: Essays on the Book of Deuteronomy*, SBTS 3 (Winona Lake: Eisenbrauns, 1993), pp. 346–347.

14. See recent monographs of Reviv, *Elders*, and Willis, *Elders*, the latter focusing particularly on Deuteronomy.

15. Some think the king appointed judges, e.g. Gerhard von Rad, *Deuteronomy: A Commentary*, OTL (London: SCM, 1966), p. 118. However, Nelson demurs: 'Significantly, the king does not appoint these judges', Richard D. Nelson, *Deuteronomy: A Commentary*, OTL (Louisville: Westminster John Knox, 2002), p. 215.

to the judges, as occurs with appointments elsewhere, including in the account with which the book opens (1:16–17; cf. 2 Chr. 19:6–7, 9–10). However, Vogt rightly notes that the second person singular address of verse 18 ('you shall appoint') is maintained in the injunction of verse 19 ('you shall not distort'), and that this hardly fits the judges, given their plural number and the intervening third person reference ('they shall render', v. 18).[16] Vogt therefore argues that this injunction is addressed to the whole populace, stressing the collective responsibility for a just society. Again, these perspectives could well be complementary: the compiler took a standard pattern of judicial commission and instruction (as in 1:16–17), and purposely reworked it to widen the responsibility for justice to the whole community.

The second text (17:8–13) concerns a central court, which is simply assumed to exist (in contrast to the appointment process just discussed). This is clearly located at the central sanctuary, and the judge 'in office in those days' cooperates variously with 'the levitical priests' (v. 9)[17] and 'the priest' (v. 12). However, the passage states neither the method of appointment nor the manner of co-operation with the priesthood. This central judge's authoritative role is indicated by the appended phrase (lit. 'who will be in those days').[18] As Lohfink correctly emphasizes, this 'was not, as one often reads, a court of appeal, which could reverse the verdict of a court of first instance'.[19] Rather, it was for cases too difficult for the local court.

The third text (19:16–20) stipulates that a case involving a 'malicious witness' ('ēd ḥāmās) should go to the central court. This negative description of the witness could imply initial judgment in his local town, in which case this might be an appeal (contra the above). However, other explanations are possible: it could be proleptic, given the outcome sketched in the following verses; or it could imply a serious case where there is only one witness, which therefore does not meet the multiple-witness criterion but is still thought worthy of investigation.

---

16. Vogt, *Deuteronomic Theology*, pp. 210–211.

17. The Syriac misreads these as alternatives: 'to the priest or the Levite or the judge' (*BHS* note).

18. The same phrase only occurs elsewhere in 19:16 of the central judge, and in 26:3 of the priest receiving the firstfruits offering.

19. Lohfink, 'Distribution', p. 340. However, Lohfink immediately continues incorrectly: 'Rather, it was supposed to uphold – not overthrow – the judgments made by normal means in the local courts over particular cases.' The text does not say this.

In the two remaining texts, judges act locally. In one (21:2), they accompany elders in measuring town distances from an unsolved murder, presumably as neutral or at least trustworthy participants. The normal location of these judges is unstated, but they are probably those from the local towns. They could be joined by the central judge, since the officiating priests would also have to come from the central sanctuary.[20] And in the other (25:1–2), their sentence for flogging is limited to forty lashes. This latter text has first 'judges' then 'judge', implying some cooperation (unless the first is a generic/collective reference). Again, there are no further details, though it is easy enough to imagine how this might operate in practice.

Commanders and officers

Commanders (*śārîm*) appear only once in this section, in relation to warfare (21:9). After the priests and officials have variously addressed the troops, the commanders take charge. Clearly here they are senior military leaders. In chapter 1, they were appointed to general and judicial leadership in the early wilderness period, when the people faced periodic displacement and occasional battle. Commanders are then unmentioned in the narrative context of Deuteronomy, while the law code preserves only a military usage, with no regular, peacetime role for them.

Officers (*šōṭērîm*) are only mentioned twice in DL. In 16:18 they are to be appointed alongside judges, but with no role specified. And in 20:5, 8, they address troops before battle, to encourage non-participation by any soldier who is afraid, or is yet to benefit from recent developments (house, vineyard, wife). These texts align with the retrospective chapter 1, where officers accompanied judges and commanders (possibly the same group, see above). The reasons for non-participation in warfare imply that chapter 20 describes irregular militia in a conscript army, as was common in the ANE. So it is likely that these military officers had other roles, quite possibly as judicial adjuncts. Alternatively the term simply meant 'adjunct officers', and these could be different men in different contexts. Nonetheless, they are only mentioned very occasionally in DL, and clearly had supporting roles, so there is little need to delineate these roles further.

---

20. Many scholars assume this procedure is an unassimilated relic of pre-centralization involving priests from local sanctuaries. However, two other explanations are possible. One is that the 'levitical priests' were Levites who lived locally – after all, their only role is to 'pronounce blessings'. The other is that the central judge and priests were sent for, and the ceremony was then performed several days after discovery and burial of the body.

King

Because of the importance of the monarchy in Israelite historiography and ideology, and the importance of King Josiah's reform for the common dating of the text, the Deuteronomic pericope on the appointment of a king (17:14–20) has received detailed scholarly examination.[21] However, these issues often overshadow the civil leadership context of Deuteronomy itself. Alongside judges and elders with clear forensic responsibility, and commanders and officers with occasional leadership roles, the king is accorded no specific governance or judicial function. The indications of his authority come in the term itself (*melek*) with its connotations of power, the phrase 'like all the nations that are around me' with its obvious comparison, the preposition 'over' (*'al*, four times in vv. 14–15), and the reference to taking 'the throne of his kingdom' (v. 18). By contrast, his position is explicitly circumscribed in terms of nationality, military power (horses), sexual/social vanity (multiple wives) and wealth. Instead, he must focus on 'this law': having his own copy, reading it daily and adhering to it steadfastly. An integral part of this discipline is not 'exalting himself above other members of the community', a significant limitation of the power of kingship implied by the comparison with surrounding nations.

Many scholars read these restrictions as a late-monarchy reaction against rich and authoritarian kings, notably Solomon and his descendants like Manasseh. This is well illustrated by the term 'now' in Lohfink's otherwise admirable summary: 'The king is now no more than administrator and model Israelite.'[22] Similarly Nelson: 'The king is no longer the supreme arbiter of justice.'[23] However, this circumscription of power may not, or not only, be due to disillusionment with the monarchy as it was experienced. It fits with the book's pervasive vision of a decentralized society as already illustrated, and as such sits looser to historical moorings than is often envisaged.

Civil leadership elsewhere in the Hebrew Bible

Other indications of leadership in Israel form the backdrop to Deuteronomy and need to be sketched briefly. Elders seem to be the mainstay of civil society

---

21. See Jamie A. Grant, *The King as Exemplar: The Function of Deuteronomy's Kingship Law in the Shaping of the Book of Psalms*, SBLAB (Atlanta: Society of Biblical Literature, 2004), for detailed discussion and further references.

22. Lohfink 'Distribution', p. 349.

23. Nelson, *Deuteronomy*, p. 214.

in the pre-monarchy period. They head the lists of officials attending the convocation(s) with which the book of Joshua concludes (elders, heads, judges and officers, 23:2; 24:1), and they alone are mentioned as leaders who outlived Joshua (Josh. 24:31; Judg. 6:7). In the increasingly disjointed period of the hero-deliverer 'judges'[24] – who bear little resemblance to the later judiciary – it is the elders who provide local leadership, as in the stories of Jephthah (Judg. 11), the Benjaminites (Judg. 21), Boaz (Ruth 4) and the Philistine wars (1 Sam. 4). In the move to monarchy, the elders approach Samuel (1 Sam. 8), though notably it is Samuel who appoints the king, not the elders.[25] The elders lead the tribes at David's coronation (2 Sam. 5), are prominent in Absalom's short-lived court (2 Sam. 17) and head Solomon's dedicatory assembly (1 Kgs 8), though are surprisingly unmentioned in the schism account (1 Kgs 12). There are further sporadic references to elders right through to the post-exilic period,[26] where they play a prominent role in temple reconstruction (Ezra 5 – 6) and in Ezra's reform (Ezra 10:4). Despite occasional mention of 'the elders of Israel', their primary authority remained local. Thus they continued to exercise this role as wider civil leadership changed, from regional hero-judge to national king to imperial governor. The extent to which the authority of elders became eclipsed by that of judges remains to be seen (see below).

The role of judge is much less noted in Israel's literature after Joshua's convocation(s). The judges of the eponymous book are portrayed more as deliverer-leaders,[27] very different from the judgeship model of DL, though Deborah clearly settled disputes rather like the commanders of Deuteronomy 1, and the activities of several leaders are unspecified.[28] Samuel seems to have been a peripatetic central judge who then wanted to establish a judicial dynasty through his sons, but the elders rejected this in favour of 'a king to judge us'

---

24. The nominal participle 'judge(s)' only occurs in the book's introduction, of the group collectively (Judg. 2:16–19), not for any of the individual leaders. It does not occur for Samuel either, but is used of his sons (1 Sam. 8:1–2).

25. Jacob Milgrom, 'The ideological and historical importance of the office of judge in Deuteronomy', in Alexander Rofé (ed.), *Isac Leo Seeligmann Volume: Essays on the Bible and the Ancient World Volume 3* (Jerusalem: E. Rubinstein, 1983), p. 130, nevertheless describes the elders as 'king makers' with 'unbounded political power'.

26. E.g. 1 Kgs 21:8–11; Isa. 3:14; Ezek. 8:1.

27. Notably Othniel, Ehud, Shamgar, Gideon, Jephthah, Samson.

28. Tola, Jair, Ibzan, Elon, Abdon (Judg. 10:1–4; 12:8–15).

(1 Sam. 7:15 – 8:6).[29] From then on, apart from occasional historical reminiscences,[30] the Deuteronomistic History only associates giving judgment with
royalty, as in Absalom's revolt (2 Sam. 15:1–6) and Solomon's prayer (1 Kgs 3:9).
The king's responsibility to judge justly is similarly extolled in psalmody and
prophetic vision (e.g. Ps. 72; Isa. 11:1–5, 32:1–8; Jer. 22:1–5).

By contrast, the Chronicler notes six thousand 'officers and judges' in the early
monarchy (1 Chr. 23:4), and their presence at Solomon's assembly along with
commanders, leaders (*naśí'*) and family heads (2 Chr. 1:2). Further, it records that
Jehoshaphat 'appointed judges in all the land in all the fortified cities of Judah,
city by city', and 'certain Levites and priests and heads of families . . . to give
judgment for Yahweh and to decide disputed cases . . . at Jerusalem', with Levites
as their officers (2 Chr. 19:5, 8, 11). Judges are also involved in Ezra's reform
(Ezra 10:4).

Two particular judicial events during the monarchy period are worth noting.
First, in Ahab's Israel, Jezebel instructs the elders and nobles of Jezreel to seat
Naboth 'at the head of the people [*'am*]' and bring false charges. This duly
happens, and Naboth is then executed (1 Kgs 21:8–14). 'Nobles' (*ḥorîm*, lit.
'freemen') are clearly leading citizens,[31] and may have had some judicial authority
as such, but there is no explicit evidence of this.[32] Second, centuries later in
Judah, Jeremiah is seized by priests, prophets and 'all the people'. 'Commanders'
come up from the palace and Jeremiah presents his defence;[33] the commanders
and all the people, now won over, defend Jeremiah, supported by 'some of the
elders of the land', and Jeremiah is presumably freed (Jer. 26:7–19).[34]

---

29. For Moshe Weinfeld, 'Judge and Officer in Ancient Israel and in the Ancient Near
    East', *IOS* 7 (1977), p. 87, this and Judg. 11:9 show that 'in the premonarchic period
    "judges" were chosen by the elders'.

30. 2 Sam 7:11; 2 Kgs 23:22.

31. Cf. Isa. 34:11–12 (parallel with *śarîm*); Jer. 27:20; 39:6; Neh. 2:16, etc. The term may
    have had judicial connotations in certain regions and/or periods.

32. *Pace* Milgrom's assertion that the *ḥorîm* were state-appointed judges; 'The
    ideological', p. 129.

33. Here the *śarîm* are senior court officials, but the term 'commanders' has been
    retained for consistency.

34. Only the elders' contribution is cited, but this may indicate its importance to the
    prophetic redactor rather than its decisiveness to the outcome. A concluding
    comment (Jer. 26:24) notes Ahikam ben Shaphan's protection of Jeremiah, but
    this seems more general since it follows the account of Uriah's fate, and it implies
    a popular animosity towards Jeremiah different from the outcome here.

Civil leadership in historical-critical perspectives

In 1977 Weinfeld published an influential study comparing civil leadership in Israel and the ANE, focusing on judges but also discussing elders, commanders and officers, and citing numerous examples from Egypt, Anatolia and Mesopotamia. Weinfeld concluded that 'a common judicial pattern prevailed in the ancient Near East from at least the middle of the second millennium B.C. onward . . . [so] any attempt to draw a scheme of progression in this area is doomed to failure'.[35] But this has not prevented most scholars, including Weinfeld himself, from attempting to draw such a scheme regarding Israel. The typical scheme is that the traditional authority of elders was gradually superseded by that of royally appointed judges, and discussion centres on whether Deuteronomy builds on previous development in this direction, promotes it largely *de novo*, or reacts against it.[36]

Some scholars think Deuteronomy builds on previous royal reforms, possibly those of Jehoshaphat, and its laws reflects three stages of development.[37] (a) Initially elders alone had authority, as in some Deuteronomic laws. (b) Later, judges were appointed by the king to military settlements ('fortified cities') but without affecting procedures elsewhere, a process reflected to varying extents in 2 Chronicles 19 and the often associated passages of Exodus 18 and Deuteronomy 1.[38] (c) Finally, Deuteronomy seeks to extend state-appointed judges to all towns, and to reform the central court.

This view has been challenged on redactional and conceptual grounds. First, it credits at least some historical reliability to 2 Chronicles 19 (and Exod. 18; Deut. 1) as representing developments prior to the Deuteronomic reform, and many scholars question this. Second, it has difficulty accounting for the command that the people should appoint judges (Deut. 16:18), given the many other references to royal judicial responsibility. Willis speculates about when an author might have mistrusted royalty and proposed popular nomination

---

35. Weinfeld, 'Judge and Officer', p. 86.
36. Following the helpful outline of Willis, *Elders*, pp. 37–50.
37. Willis, *Elders*, pp. 37–38, cites W. F. Albright (1950), followed by A. Phillips (1970); and with revision G. C. Macholz (1972), followed largely by H. J. Boecker (ET 1980) and R. Wilson (1983).
38. Willis notes that Albright sees 2 Chr. 19 as historical, while Macholz places it alongside Deut. 1 simply as witness to some royal reform; nevertheless, both argue that it gives some indication of pre-Josianic central appointment of judges.

instead: perhaps in the dying northern monarchy, or later under Manasseh, or later still in the exile.[39]

The majority of scholars view Deuteronomy as promulgating widespread judicial reform alongside Josiah's centripetal cultic reform. In Weinfeld's summary, provincial sanctuaries had performed judicial functions, notably settling unsolved disputes by oath, lot or ordeal. But the abolition of these sanctuaries led to a vacuum which was then filled by the judges. 'Though the institution of appointed magistrates and clerical officers had undoubtedly existed before the Josianic reforms, it came into its full operational force only as a result of these reforms.'[40]

For Weinfeld, eldership still functioned for family litigation, but Levinson doubts even this.[41] For him, judges took over the very locus of judgment, the city gate, and inevitably displaced elders. However, as Willis notes, this does not account for further reference to elders both within Deuteronomy and beyond (e.g. Lam. 5:14),[42] or allow for different officials functioning in the gate area (cf. the king in Jer. 38:7).

Again, there are significant critiques of this perspective. A lesser one concerns the case of unsolved murder, where priests, judges and elders act concertedly with separate roles. A common defence is that the reference to priests is a later insertion,[43] but as it stands the text leaves a local role for priests. Another critique concerns the role of local judges before Josiah's time. Weinfeld allows their pre-Josianic existence, but without furnishing detail. However, if local priests did indeed resolve cases which were too hard for elders, as Weinfeld supposes, what was the need for judges?

Perhaps the most significant critique concerns the appointment of judges. It is often assumed that this was done centrally, i.e. by the king,[44] despite 16:18 being addressed to the people ('you'). It might be argued that this phrasing is

---

39. Willis, *Elders*, p. 41.

40. Weinfeld, *Deuteronomy*, p. 234. He immediately continues: 'It is by no means accidental then, that this institution is heard of so frequently' in Deuteronomy and the DH. But the cited and cross-referenced evidence he evinces hardly bears this weight.

41. Bernard M. Levinson, *Deuteronomy and the Hermeneutics of Legal Innovation* (New York: Oxford University Press, 1997), pp. 124–126.

42. Unless the elder laws are attributed to earlier strata; Willis, *Elders*, p. 43.

43. E.g. Weinfeld, *Deuteronomy*, p. 210 n. 6.

44. E.g. Weinfeld, 'Judge and Officer', p. 66: 'by a central authority (in contradistinction to the elders who were chosen by the local population)'.

simply parenetical, and/or that local proposal and central endorsement went together (as perhaps in the parallel texts Exod. 18 and Deut. 1). But this hardly fits with the account in 2 Kings 23 of a royally driven reform which went against popular support of local sanctuaries. Further, this perspective (like the previous) fails to account adequately for the limited powers attributed to the king in Deuteronomy itself.

A third scholarly perspective places significant elements of the DL in the exilic period and attributes to them a largely hypothetical or utopian outlook. For instance, the laws on elders, intended to give more responsibility to clan elders, are traced variously to the early exile, albeit with some memory of previous practice, or to the late exile with an entirely future orientation.[45]

However, the proposal that DL is composed largely in isolation from actual practice, hypothesizing the future rather than reflecting the present, is unlike all other extant ANE law codes. Just as there were similar legal officials across the ANE (see above), so there were similar law codes with a similar format, presenting typical examples rather than providing comprehensive coverage.[46] It is far more likely that Deuteronomy exemplifies this than that it offers a hypothetical utopia.

Finally, there is the seldom considered but still viable perspective that the DL contains genuinely ancient material, perhaps lightly modified in later eras. The arguments for this build on both the textual indices and the critiques of other perspectives. As noted from the start, Deuteronomy largely presents a non-hierarchical or flat model of civil leadership.[47] While it presents a single central authority in Moses, who hands over to Joshua, there is no provision for a continued central succession. And while the unsettled, nomadic period has commanders of thousands, hundreds, fifties and tens (1:15), there is no such hierarchical provision for the later settled occupation. As for civil leadership, elders continue to exert influence, even concerning homicide; the people themselves are to appoint judges; many laws stress the whole community's responsibility; a central court is envisaged, but only for hard cases; a king is

---

45. Willis, *Elders*, p. 45, cites for the former J. Bucholz (1988) and for the latter J. C. Gertz (1993). Bucholz posits further redactional layers to attenuate the influence of elders.

46. Cf. Raymond Westbrook, 'Adultery in Ancient Near Eastern Law', *RB* 7 (1990), p. 548: 'each code contains no more than a few aspects of a given ... problem'.

47. Lohfink, 'Distribution', describes the 'distribution of functions of power' as a reaction to kingship; also, '[i]n earlier times the king had also been supreme judge' (p. 348).

allowed but not mandated; the king has significant personal limitations and no specified judicial powers, but must simply obey 'this torah'.

This portrait of civil leadership certainly has many similarities with the pre- and early monarchy eras, notably the significance of elders, the lack of a significant hierarchy and the anxieties over kingship. The last of these is well demonstrated in the Gideon–Abimelech stories (Judg. 8 – 9) and in Samuel's institutional warnings (1 Sam. 8).[48] Of course, these texts as well as Deuteronomy 17:14–20 could reflect later disillusionment with Israel's kings, notably the arch-aggrandizer Solomon. But they could equally reflect a long-standing suspicion of monarchy as a regrettable option and one susceptible to corruption, a suspicion which also fuelled prophetic and historiographical critique of many royal incumbents.

By contrast, Deuteronomy's portrait of the judiciary is only partially reflected in this early period. Apparently Deborah 'used to sit under the palm of Deborah . . . and the Israelites came up to her for judgment' (Judg. 4:5). There is no explicit mention of such practice regarding other characters in the book, though several are recorded as having 'judged Israel'. However, this must be treated cautiously. The conclusions of accounts in roughly the first half of Judges, including that concerning Deborah, are that 'the land had peace for x years' (Judg. 3:11, 30; 5:31; 8:28), while the conclusions in the second half (including for the hero-deliverer Samson) are that the leader 'judged Israel for x years' (Judg. 10:2, 3; 12:7, 9, 11, 14; 16:31). Many scholars naturally surmise that two series of leaders have been combined in the book, with some conflation between the two. Nevertheless, alongside the explicit reference to Deborah, the several other references to leaders judging Israel (especially when no accounts of deliverance are attached to them) do suggest some recognized judicial role. This role is exercised explicitly by Samuel, with the added dimension of perambulation to Bethel, Gilgal, Mizpah and back to Ramah: 'he judged Israel in all these places . . . he administered justice' (1 Sam. 7:16–18). Samuel also 'made his sons judges in Israel' (1 Sam. 8:1), with disastrous consequences. Samuel stands apart from the leaders of the book of Judges, since he was clearly a national leader with prophetic and priestly functions. In this combination of roles and in his use of multiple cultic sites he clearly does not adhere fully to the Deuteronomic vision. Whether this means that such a vision had already been abandoned or had not yet been elaborated is of course part of the debate.

---

48. The story of Saul's rise (1 Sam. 9 – 12) has several echoes of the Abimelech narrative; see e.g. D. G. Firth, *1 & 2 Samuel*, AOTC (Nottingham: Apollos, 2009), pp. 125–126.

If Deuteronomy's vision was indeed ancient, then questions inevitably arise about its transmission in oral and/or written form. Who might have kept alive such a vision? And when was it committed to writing? Undoubtedly the laws are moulded by the book's general parenetic tenor which is quite different from other Pentateuchal strands. But we have no evidence of a suitable group preserving and moulding such a tradition. The few extant examples of proto-Canaanite script show that writing existed, but the surviving texts are brief and functional (e.g. the Gezer calendar), and very dissimilar to a lengthy theological treatise. Nonetheless, by the early monarchy there is an accumulation of traditions including the stories of the judges, Samuel, Saul and David. The different temper of these traditions, well known as the raw material of source criticism, also implies transmission in different contexts with different ideological perspectives. And one of these could possibly have been the circle which eventually gave us Deuteronomy.

Conclusion

In sum, Deuteronomy portrays a nation led by Moses and Joshua in its initial stages, but without a mechanism to perpetuate central leadership after entry into the Promised Land. The narrative mentions several types of local leadership in the pre-entry stage, and the law envisages some of these playing key roles in the adjudication of disputes. Judges and local elders are most commonly in view, with a limited military role for commanders and rather vague ancillary roles for officers. The single mention of a king, though important in some ways, gives little indication of his civil leadership or legal adjudication. There is a strong sense of the people themselves taking responsibility for justice, seen in the comparison of some narratives with their parallels elsewhere, the charging of the people in 16:19–20, and the scarcity of reference to official adjudication.

This portrayal of leadership reflects the pre- and early monarchy periods better than later eras, at least as these are presented elsewhere in the Hebrew Bible. However, if Deuteronomy's contents authentically reflect such early periods, the process of their distillation into the current book remains unknown. Later dates for the material contrast with this in both respects. Compilation and preservation in the late monarchy through to the post-exilic period is no more problematic than for most other Old Testament books. However, an origin in the late monarchy is problematic in that the book reflects neither the society nor its leadership as portrayed elsewhere, while an origin in the exile has similar problems compounded by the loss of kingship.

Whatever the dates of composition, redaction and finalization, Deuteronomy's vision of civil leadership can fairly be described as devolved, with most emphasis on the responsibility of all the people, helped by leadership and adjudication normally at local level, and an occasional 'light-touch' central authority. How this transposes to the many and varied contexts of today goes well beyond the current remit. But the contrast with some current leadership structures is significant.

6. PASSING ON THE FAITH IN DEUTERONOMY

David G. Firth

Introduction

That the book of Deuteronomy is interested in encouraging Israel to choose faith in Yahweh is, perhaps, to state the obvious. But this interest is not something it offers as simple observation. Rather, it is strongly hortatory. As Wright observes, 'Deuteronomy bends every rhetorical, literary, emotional, and moral skill to the task of equipping and motivating God's people to live for the purposes of God in each generation.'[1] Although larger-scale studies of Deuteronomy's rhetoric have been undertaken,[2] the purpose of this chapter is to focus more narrowly on the last part of this quote from Wright since detailed studies of this are lacking.[3] Deuteronomy is presented as a challenge to the generation about to enter the land not only to choose Yahweh, but also to pass on the faith

---

1. Christopher J. H. Wright, *Deuteronomy*, NIBCOT (Peabody: Hendrickson, 1996), p. 8.
2. See, for example, Gary Hall, 'Rhetorical Criticism, Chiasm, and Theme in Deuteronomy', *Stone-Campbell Journal* 1 (1998), pp. 85–100.
3. Patrick D. Miller, 'That the Children May Know: Children in Deuteronomy', in Marcia J. Bunge (gen. ed.), *The Child in the Bible* (Grand Rapids/Cambridge: Eerdmans, 2008), pp. 45–62, provides an excellent study that moves in this direction, but is more narrowly focused on the place of children.

it expounds to succeeding generations. The faith in Deuteronomy can be understood as acceptance of Yahweh as Israel's covenant God, and therefore the
need to live out the terms of that covenant. Because of this, each generation
can read Deuteronomy as its own challenge to faith in Yahweh and also to
passing on that faith.

But how does the book encourage each generation to pass on its faith in
Yahweh? It will be argued that passing on the faith is not simply an addendum
to the decision that is summoned from each generation. Rather, it is an integral
element of the whole of the book's rhetoric.[4] Indeed, for Deuteronomy it only
makes sense to summon a generation to faith if that generation also recognizes
the need to pass their faith on to subsequent generations. To explore this, we
will first look at references to passing on faith within the book's overall structure,
before considering in more detail those passages which explicitly exhort the
teaching of the faith or which show the problems caused when that faith is not
taken up by the next generation. *En route* we will consider Moses as the model
teacher who passes on the terms of the covenant he has received from Yahweh.
Beyond that, Deuteronomy also envisages Israel living out her faith in the
context of the nations, so the way that Israel shows her faithfulness to Yahweh
is itself instructive for the nations. For Deuteronomy, passing on the faith is
thus primarily focused on the need for subsequent generations to make covenant
faith in Yahweh their own, but it emphasizes this within a larger framework of
Israel's relationship to the nations. If this is correct, then the missiological
reading proposed by Wright[5] is not simply initiated by a reader with an interest
in mission but emerges fundamentally from the text itself.

In this light, Noll's recent claim that 'Deuteronomy's meager provisions for
public dissemination are predestined to failure'[6] misses the point. By focusing
only on the seven-year reading of the book (31:10–13) as an isolated element,
he fails to see that dissemination of the faith is integral to the whole book.
Indeed, Deuteronomy is aware of the fact that something only passed on at
long intervals would be subject to the extinction principle, in that on its own it

---

4. By 'rhetoric' I do not mean empty and sometimes specious arguments, but rather
   those techniques used to convince an audience of the position being argued. See
   Peter M. Phillips, 'Rhetoric', in David G. Firth and Jamie A. Grant (eds.), *Words and
   the Word: Explorations in Biblical Interpretation and Literary Theory* (Nottingham: Apollos,
   2008), pp. 226–265.

5. Wright, *Deuteronomy*, pp. 8–17.

6. K. L. Noll, 'Was There Doctrinal Dissemination in Early Yahweh Religion?', *Biblical
   Interpretation* 16 (2008), p. 425.

would not generate sufficient awareness of its content to sustain itself. But, as we shall see, Deuteronomy adopts a range of strategies to ensure that the faith it holds is regularly passed on.

The faith as the covenant

We have so far spoken of 'the faith' as something to be both believed and passed on in Deuteronomy. But as McConville has observed, something that is simply passed on does not have the same meaning for each generation.[7] This is because, in speech-act terms, Deuteronomy is presented as a speech from the past in which Moses addresses the generation about to enter the land, expounding the covenant and exhorting faithfulness to it, but also as a speech which is reheard by subsequent generations who then need to work out how the covenant and its structures continue to be relevant for them. Moses' illocutionary act within Deuteronomy thus has a different perlocution for subsequent generations. In spite of this, there remains a central core to Moses' message about faithfulness to the covenant that must shape the way each generation encounters this material.

The faith Deuteronomy seeks to pass on is rooted in the covenant, as it continues to be explored by subsequent generations. Although the form in which the covenant relationship is expressed varies, the dominant pattern in Deuteronomy emphasizes that Israel is Yahweh's people, at various points stressing this by describing them as Yahweh's *sĕgullâ* ('special possession') or *naḥălâ* ('heritage, property').[8] Israel is presented as a people who have known the grace of Yahweh in his choosing them through their ancestors and history, and who are now called to live out the terms of that relationship. The important point of this for Deuteronomy is that the covenant historically roots its message about the way ahead for Israel while also explaining why Israel needs to live out its calling to be Yahweh's people.

To take but one example, we can see this worked out in 7:1–11. Here Moses sets out the task of moving into the land, but does so by noting that it is Yahweh who will give the nations over to Israel (7:1–2). From this emerges a series of actions that will demonstrate Israel's commitment to Yahweh alone (7:3–5),

---

7. J. G. McConville, *Deuteronomy*, AOTC (Leicester: Apollos; Downers Grove: InterVarsity Press, 2002), pp. 41–42.

8. See Rolf Rendtorff, *The Covenant Formula: An Exegetical and Theological Investigation* (Edinburgh: T&T Clark, 1998), pp. 22–26.

actions that are rooted in Yahweh's faithfulness to his promises to the patriarchs (7:6–8). Yahweh's faithfulness shows that he keeps covenant, and therefore expects Israel to keep covenant (7:9–11). Israel's faith is thus an expression of the covenant, but already in this text we see the covenant presented in terms of what the current generation must do in the future (albeit, within the horizon of the book, an imminent future). Without mentioning the need to pass on this covenant faith, a text such as this already points in this direction because the covenant itself is here understood as something that will need to be worked out in a new context (life in the land), and it is this process of understanding and living out the covenant in the emerging setting of Israel's common life that drives the passing on of the faith.

Passing on the faith within the structure of Deuteronomy

There is reasonably broad agreement over the general structure of Deuter-onomy, though debate continues about the significance of elements within it.[9] In broad terms, we can speak of a prologue in 1:1 – 4:43, a central discourse in 4:44 – 28:68, and an appeal for covenant faithfulness in light of Moses' approach-ing death in chapters 29 – 34. The edges of these divisions continue to be debated, with some preferring to conclude the middle section at 26:19, while others make a good case for seeing 4:44 – 11:32 as a discrete section with chapters 12 – 28 then comprising a third major section.[10] For our purposes, it

---

9. Meredith G. Kline, *Treaty of the Great King: The Covenant Structure of Deuteronomy* (Grand Rapids: Eerdmans, 1963), has argued for the importance of covenant for understanding the whole of Deuteronomy. See also Dennis J. McCarthy SJ, *Treaty and Covenant* (Rome: Pontifical Biblical Institute, 1963), pp. 109–140, though he distinguishes between the central discourse and the frame of the book; and Ernest W. Nicholson, *Deuteronomy and Tradition* (Oxford: Basil Blackwell, 1967), pp. 43–45. However, there are problems with any attempt to align Deuteronomy's structure too closely with either Hittite or Assyrian treaties, and it is better to see these as part of the general background material which has been reshaped in the final presentation of Deuteronomy, so that covenant is a ruling metaphor rather than the formal guide to the structure of the book. Similarly, J. Gary Millar, *Now Choose Life: Theology and Ethics in Deuteronomy* (Leicester: Apollos, 1998), pp. 42–44.

10. See Millar, *Now Choose Life*, pp. 44–47. A more significant variation is offered by Duane L. Christensen, *Deuteronomy 1:1 – 21:9*, WBC (Nashville: Thomas Nelson, 2001), pp. lxx–lxxix. Christensen sees a major break at 3:22 with a major section

is sufficient to note that 4:44 – 11:32 is sufficiently distinct to be treated as a unit, whether we regard it as a complete section in its own right or as the general stipulations of the central discourse before the specific stipulations that follow from 12:1. Likewise, the question of whether we have a major break at 26:19 or 28:68 has little bearing on our discussion, because on either reading there is a significant section introduced at chapter 29. As such, we will work with a standard threefold division, but with the middle section itself divided into two parts.

Within each of the book's major divisions the passing on of the faith is stressed at key structural points. Thus at 1:5 we are told that Moses undertook to explain the *tôrâ* to Israel, though this was in accordance with all that Yahweh had commanded him (1:3). It is notable that the rare verb translated 'explain' (*b'r*) occurs elsewhere only in 27:8 in the concluding part of the central address, where the *tôrâ* is to be inscribed on the altar on Mount Ebal for subsequent generations. Thus an important link is formed between the book's opening and the conclusion to the central address on passing on the faith.[11] Later in the first section, in 4:9–10, the people are instructed to be sure to make the events at Horeb known to their children. Finally, 4:40 brings closure to the opening section by noting that it is the people's faithfulness to all that they have been commanded which is essential for continued enjoyment of life in the land by them and their children. Passing on of the faith is thus placed prominently at the beginning and the end of the opening section of the book, as well as being linked to the central address.

The theme of passing on the faith is also placed at prominent points in the central discourse. Since 4:44–49 is an introduction to the *tôrâ* and chapter 5 is Deuteronomy's record of the Decalogue and its reception, it is clear that the

---

running to 7:11. His subsequent divisions are more representative of the mainstream until 29:8, which he sees as a major break introducing several sections until the end of the book. But a major division at 3:22 seems unlikely because both 3:1–22 and 3:23–29 continue to recount events from Israel's past that led to them being on the borders of the land. Admittedly, 3:23–29 explain why Moses cannot go with the people into the land, but at most this is a shift within the first four chapters. Further, chapters 29 – 30 appear to have an internal unity of their own, making a major break at 29:8 also unlikely; see Takaaki Haraguchi, 'A Rhetorical Analysis of Deuteronomy 29 – 30', *Asia Journal of Theology* 15 (2001), pp. 24–37; and H. F. Van Rooy, 'Reconciliation in Deuteronomy', *Verbum et Ecclesia* 26 (2005), pp. 264–266.

11. See now also Edward J. Woods, *Deuteronomy: An Introduction and Commentary*, TOTC (Nottingham: Inter-Varsity Press; Downers Grove: IVP Academic, 2011), p. 79.

exhortation to faithfulness begins at 6:1. It is worth noting, though, that the Decalogue is presented as something to be learned (*lmd*) as well as done. The theme of passing on faith is particularly prominent in the whole of chapter 6. Thus in 6:1 we have Moses reporting that the commandments he is about to recount are those that Yahweh had commanded him to teach (*lmd*) the people, with the clear intention that this teaching should be passed on as the necessary precondition to their children's continued enjoyment of life in the land. The importance of this being passed on is made explicit in 6:5–9, with the expectation being that families will teach them (*šnn*) to their children, speaking of these things in the whole of life. In 6:20–25 we then have a teaching situation recounted within the setting of the Passover meal. We will look at each of these passages in more detail below, but the point to note at this stage is that passing on the faith is placed in a prominent position at the beginning of this section.

Similarly, the closure to each half of the central address places passing on the faith in a prominent position. This prominence is not matched by the intervening content, though these chapters largely provide the content of what is to be passed on. Hence in 11:18–25 we have a passage which largely repeats (though develops) 6:5–9 before mentioning the blessings and curses to be declared at Mount Gerizim and Mount Ebal (11:26–32), preparing for the prominence given to this at the end of the central discourse (27:1–26). The level of repetition between 11:18–25 and 6:5–9 indicates that these passages are to be read in light of one another, forming an inclusio within the first half of the central discourse. Likewise, the two references to Gerizim and Ebal form an inclusio for the second half of the central discourse, though as we have already noted 27:8 also provides an important link back to 1:6. Here Moses instructs the elders to write the words of the *tôrâ* on plaster over the stones of an altar at Mount Ebal, with the words of the *tôrâ* to be written 'clearly' (*b'r*). This is preparatory for the announcements of blessings and curses which form a model of public instruction, out of which chapter 28 provides a call to decision by outlining the alternative outcomes of life under blessing or curse.

The third major section is less cohesive than the first two, but finds its unity in the theme of the continuation of the covenant. It contains a recapitulation of covenant with an appeal for faithfulness in chapters 29 – 30,[12] and then a record of how the covenant continues beyond Moses in chapters 31 – 34. The slightly disparate nature of this material means that we no longer see the

---

12. Peter C. Craigie, *The Book of Deuteronomy*, NICOT (Grand Rapids: Eerdmans, 1976), pp. 354–366, describes these chapters as a concluding charge with an appeal for covenant faithfulness and then an appeal for decision.

technique of placing passages which discuss the passing on of the faith at the opening and closing point of the section. However, this emphasis is still included, though this time by placing it more centrally. An intriguing example occurs in 29:14–15 and 29:22. First, it is affirmed that the covenant is made not only with the current generation but also with those not present, while the punishment for failing to keep covenant will instruct both subsequent generations and foreigners of the importance of the covenant. In this instance the aspect of passing on faith is not carried out intentionally, but is regarded as something inherent in the covenant itself.

A more typical occurrence of passing on the faith occurs in 31:1–13. Here Moses indicates that he continues to have an instructional role. His teaching role is again placed in the foreground, though it is teaching shaped by his passing on of his role to Joshua. This public action is itself an act of passing on the faith, as Moses exhorts Joshua to faithfulness. Also, the task of passing on the faith is put into a formal setting as the *tôrâ* is placed with the ark so that it may be brought out every seven years as a continuing mode of instruction for all generations. But Moses' teaching role is not limited to the *tôrâ* delivered so far; it continues in his song which is equally to be taught to the people (31:19), acting as a continued warning against breaking covenant (31:19–22). As a result, Moses is said to have written both the words of the *tôrâ* and also the song which act as a continued witness against Israel (32:46). Although it is not quite as prominent, there is also a final reference to passing on the faith in 34:9. Here we read of Israel's acceptance of Joshua as Moses' successor, which is done 'as Yahweh had commanded Moses'.[13] Joshua's commissioning was an act of public instruction at the commencement of this section, and his acceptance at its conclusion shows that, for one generation at least, faith has been passed on.

Although we will need to look at these passages in more depth, this survey demonstrates that in each of the major sections of Deuteronomy the motif of passing on the faith is placed in a prominent position. It opens and closes the first two sections of the book, while the two halves of the second section also pivot around it. The theme occurs in the third section, not as prominently in chapters 29 – 30, but is again placed at the beginning and end in chapters 31 – 34. Given that virtually the whole of chapter 31 deals with this motif, it acts as the pivot for the whole section of chapters 29 – 34, with the brief closing reference to Joshua confirming that the practice has indeed begun. This indicates that Deuteronomy's rhetoric is not only a call to decision to covenant faithfulness,

---

13. Unless identified otherwise, Scripture quotations in this chapter are the author's own translations.

but in particular it is a call to faithfulness in which the covenant faith enshrined in the *tôrâ* is continually passed on.

Moses as the representative teacher

It would be easy to begin an examination of the detail of this topic by looking at those passages which exhort the teaching of the faith to others. But within the structure of Deuteronomy we have already noted that the initial presentation of this theme occurs with Moses passing the content of the covenant on to the generation who are about to enter the land, with the book closing as he hands over to Joshua before his death. That this is so structurally important to the book suggests that there is considerable value in Olson's suggestion that the *tôrâ* in Deuteronomy should be understood as a programme of catechesis, one in which Moses is the 'model teacher'.[14] Given the variety of ways in which *tôrâ* is used along with its various synonyms, 'catechesis' is perhaps too narrow a concept for it – but, when taken with the various terms for teaching we find across the book, it should be understood as a vital element of the *tôrâ*. As such, it is appropriate that we look at Moses as the teacher who passes on the faith to Israel before we look at those passages where Israel in turn passes on her faith.

The importance of Moses as the teacher is evident from the outset of the book. In 1:5 we are told that he 'began to explain this *tôrâ*'.[15] Von Rad regards this verse as a later addition on the basis of the fact that the *tôrâ* is not actually introduced until 4:44,[16] but this understands *tôrâ* in too restrictive a sense. Although *tôrâ* obviously includes the commands and stipulations presented from 4:44, it also incorporates the record of what has happened in the past and exhortation to faithfulness. Moreover, since 1:5 refers back to the command of Yahweh in 1:3, there is a clear context established for what Moses here undertakes.

But what is it that is described here? The verb used to describe Moses' activity (*b'r*) is a rare one, occurring in Deuteronomy only here and 27:6, and elsewhere

---

14. Dennis T. Olson, *Deuteronomy and the Death of Moses: A Theological Reading* (Minneapolis: Fortress Press, 1994), p. 11.

15. Although the verb following the hiphil of *y'l* needs to be translated as an infinitive in English, normal usage in Hebrew has it followed by a finite verb, here the piel perfect *bĕ'ēr*.

16. Gerhard von Rad, *Deuteronomy*, OTL (London: SCM Press, 1966), p. 37.

only in Habakkuk 2:2. In the other two passages, the word is clearly related to writing on a large surface. For this reason, it is not impossible that Deuteronomy understands from the outset that Moses is engaged in some form of writing. Indeed, some have insisted that only writing is meant here,[17] but the context requires that Moses' activity here includes some form of explanation.[18] If so, then this verb is chosen because it simultaneously points to Moses' exposition of the *tôrâ* in an oral context in which the *tôrâ* is 'writ large' before those portrayed as hearing him while also preparing for a final written form. Moses as the teacher would then continue to teach subsequent generations through what is written, which is itself a continuation from the oral setting. Such an interpretation is consistent with the fact that in 31:24 Moses is said to have 'written the words' of this *tôrâ*, while Moses' song in chapter 32 is intended to form teaching for the subsequent generations. Moses is the model teacher for his own generation, but through the written form of the text he continues to be the model teacher for all subsequent generations.

This interplay between Moses' role for his own generation and for those that follow continues through the book. Although the vocabulary of teaching is absent from 5:1–5, the brief report on how Yahweh delivered the Decalogue there insists that Moses is passing on something to be learned (*lmd*). Moses is thus not the originator of this covenant material.[19] This role is made more explicit in 6:1–2, where Moses reports that the commandments he is passing on represent what Yahweh commanded him to teach (*lmd*).[20] What is notable in this text, though, is that this teaching is not only so that the current generation may keep these statutes, but also subsequent generations, the idea being that Israel's days in the land would be multiplied to the extent that they continue to

---

17. A. D. H. Mayes, *Deuteronomy*, NCBC (Grand Rapids: Eerdmans, 1976), p. 116.

18. This is clearly the interpretation of LXX, which here uses *diasapheō*, 'to explain clearly', for *b'r*.

19. It is notable that this material is *not* called *tôrâ*, but it is still something to be learned, thus suggesting that (although the meaning of *tôrâ* is wider than 'catechesis') we cannot restrict the evidence for catechesis in the book to those places which mention *tôrâ*.

20. Craigie, *Deuteronomy*, p. 167, raises the possibility of this referring back to the mediatorial role assigned to Moses in 5:22–23. Although this is possible, it does not significantly affect the argument here. In any case, since such a teaching role for Moses has previously been raised in 4:5 and 4:14, it seems more probable that Deuteronomy does not look back to a particular moment where Moses took on this role, though the giving of the Decalogue is clearly a significant point.

pass on what they have received from Moses. If we are right in arguing that 1:5 presumes both oral and written instruction, then it is probable that Moses is the model teacher for subsequent generations through the written text, though he is initially the model teacher in his encouragement of oral instruction which conforms to what is written.

The combination of Moses' oral and written teaching being used to pass on the faith occurs again in 31:9–12. Here Moses' role in writing is made explicit, since he wrote (*ktb*) this *tôrâ* which was then given to both the levitical priests who carried the ark and to all the elders (*ziqnê yiśrā'ēl*). Although the immediate emphasis is on the levitical priests, since the *tôrâ* is to be read every seven years during the feast of Tabernacles, the reference to the elders indicates a concern with more than priestly activity alone. A consistent concern of the book is that the role of forming future generations in the knowledge of the covenant belongs to the whole people, and this concern is secured here by the reference to the elders. Since the elders would ordinarily be scattered across the nation, the implication is that the written text should be available more widely than the central sanctuary. This is made explicit in the directive to gather everyone in the towns at this time, so that those who did not go up to the central sanctuary would also learn the content of the *tôrâ*. Indeed, the community impacted by this is much wider than just those who would attend the feast at the sanctuary. The stipulation in 16:16 requires that all males attend the feast, but the readings in the towns were intended to cover the 'men, women, little ones [*tap*] and the sojourner [*gēr*]'.[21] This directive is notable therefore for the breadth of those covered by the teaching of the *tôrâ*, since it not only covers subsequent generations of Israelites, including male and female, it also covers those who were not ethnically included in the people but who had chosen to live within the community.

The association between Moses, the levitical priests and the elders continues in 31:24–29 and on into chapter 32. After the narrative of Joshua's commissioning (31:14–23), we return to the *tôrâ* being written (31:24) so that it could be placed with the ark where it would act as a witness against Israel.[22] The witness

---

21. On the significance of the *gēr*, see Jenny Corcoran's chapter in this book, 'The alien in Deuteronomy 29 and today', pp. 229–239.

22. Rather than seeing the narrative about Joshua as intrusive and thus evidence of various layers of redaction, Wright, *Deuteronomy*, p. 296, sees evidence of a chiastic structure in 31:14–29. If so, then it also indicates that the commissioning of Joshua continues the pattern of Moses as the model teacher, but a model now represented in the work of his assistant.

of the book of the *tôrâ* is that Israel has accepted the demands of the covenant, which in turn prepares for the claims made in Moses' song in chapter 32.[23] Because the book of the *tôrâ* is not only for the levitical priests but also for the elders and officers (31:28), it is again shown to be a work for all the people, enabling Moses to continue to teach the faith even as a negative witness against future unfaithfulness.

There is one other key point where Moses appears as the representative teacher in passing on the faith, though it occurs in a passage where he is not directly mentioned. In 17:14–20 we have the so-called law of the king, which requires that when a king comes to the throne he is to 'write a copy of this *tôrâ* from what is held by the levitical priests' (17:18). This is so that the king may not have his heart lifted up nor turn aside from the commandments because he fears Yahweh. Indeed, this practice is also to ensure a long reign, not only for a particular king, but also for his children. In this instance, we have only the study of the written text rather than oral exhortation. But since the written text is something which derives from Moses, then Moses is also the model teacher for the king, the one who therefore also ensures that faith is passed on within the royal family. As Vogt has stressed, the king is in this way the model Israelite,[24] following the pattern already established by Moses.

Instructions on teaching

That Moses is the nation's model means that, just as he had passed on the content and practice of covenant faith to them, so also they are to pass on their faith. As we shall note, this process of passing on the faith moves in two directions. The dominant direction is that Israel's faith is to be passed on to subsequent generations, in particular through parents passing on their faith to their children, thus creating a repeating cycle through successive generations.[25] But there is

---

23. Richard D. Nelson, *Deuteronomy: A Commentary*, OTL (Louisville: Westminster John Knox, 2002), p. 361.

24. Peter T. Vogt, *Deuteronomic Theology and the Significance of Torah: A Reappraisal* (Winona Lake: Eisenbrauns, 2006), pp. 218–219.

25. Nelson, *Deuteronomy*, p. 65, notes that passing on the content of a covenant to children is also an element of Assyrian vassal treaties. This parallel is important, though the parenetic nature of Deuteronomy means that even where it employs literary forms similar to those of the treaty texts, the parallels are not precise.

also an emphasis on the faith being passed on to those who are currently outside Israel, though this process is dependent upon the dominant one of parents passing on their faith to their children. However, where the processes for passing on the faith associated with Moses mixed oral and literary instruction, those considered here are based on oral practice and a resultant lifestyle which is then visible to others. Nevertheless, the oral instruction that is outlined here presumes the existence of a written point of reference.

That the issue of children is an important concern for Deuteronomy is made clear early in the book. In 1:34–40, Moses recounts the initial failure to enter the land, explaining that only Caleb and Joshua of the former generation would enter the land. It is particularly noted that Caleb would see the land and that it would be given to him and to his children (1:36). Likewise, it would be the children of those who did not enter the land at the first attempt who would possess the land (1:39). It is to those children that Moses is now presented as speaking. As such, they are at this point the recipients of Moses' instruction, though this is the precursor to them passing on their faith.

A more explicit concern with the role of parents in passing on the faith emerges in 4:9–14. In a typical hortatory turn, Moses warns the people to take diligent care of themselves because of the danger of forgetting what they have seen. Although the written text is important, a central element of Deuteronomy is its concern with remembering what has happened in the past because it is this that provides a framework with which to understand the *tôrâ*. Christensen thus observes that '[t]he essence of biblical faith is based on experience, not speculative reasoning'.[26] Although this point could be overstressed – wisdom texts like Ecclesiastes and Job surely engage in some speculative reasoning – it is certainly a valid observation for Deuteronomy. In particular, this warning reflects back on the experience of Horeb as outlined in Exodus 19. The emphasis here is that, although Israel did not see Yahweh, they heard him and ultimately received the Decalogue. For our purposes, it is particularly notable that Moses exhorts the people to make these events known (hiphil *yd'*) to their children and then subsequent generations because Yahweh had summoned them so they could learn (*lmd*, qal) to fear him and then teach (*lmd*, piel) their children (4:10). Although there is a shift in vocabulary from 'make known' to 'teach', the key principle is that a people who have heard Yahweh are to pass on what they have heard to subsequent generations, though they do so in a context of self-reflection that is aware of what happens

---

26. Christensen, *Deuteronomy 1:1 – 21:9*, p. 81.

to them if they forget these things. That is why Moses exhorts the people to remember while also teaching them. There is thus a crucial link between recalling events of the past and understanding them through the framework of the covenant, because both are necessary for subsequent generations to understand their faith.

A pivotal text on this theme is 6:4–9, a passage placed in the context of the *Shema*, the great summary of Israel's faith that is also a confession of faith.[27] More importantly perhaps, it follows on from the repetition of the Decalogue in 5:1–21 and then Moses' summary of the people's response at the time in the balance of chapter 5. This context is important, because it places the commitment of the *Shema* in a setting that makes sense of its confession of monotheistic faith.[28] The Decalogue has expounded the basic elements of Israel's faith so that the *Shema* can then be a great response to it, and also an essential element in the commandments given through Moses. Further, in 5:29 Moses recounts Yahweh as insisting that the reverence the Decalogue generates is also for subsequent generations. Indeed, we are told in 6:1–3 that Moses teaches these commandments in faithfulness to the command of Yahweh because these commandments are not only for the generation that Moses addresses, but also for

---

27. Although the *Shema* is often highlighted as a summary of Israel's faith, it does so by using phrasing which occurs elsewhere within Deuteronomy (4:1; 5:1; 9:1; 20:3; 27:9; cf. the similar phrase in 33:7). In each of 4:1; 5:1; 6:4 and 9:1, the imperative 'hear' introduces new material. As such, the suggestion of Bruce E. Willoughby, 'A Heartfelt Love: An Exegesis of Deuteronomy 6:4–19', *ResQ* 20 (1977), pp. 76–77, that it introduces the theme of 'heartfelt obedience to Yahweh' over-reads the text, and it should be considered rather as a rhetorical device to highlight the introduction of new material. Deuteronomy commands love, but it does so directly (e.g. 6:5).

28. Or at least monolatrous, depending on the interpretation of these terms. Wolfram Hermann, 'Jahwe und des Menschen liebe zu ihm zu Dtn. vi 4', *VT* 50 (2000), p. 52, makes the intriguing suggestion that the 'Hauptsache in v. 4 sei nicht die Aussage uber die Einheit Jahwes, sondern das Gebot, Gott von ganzem Herzen zu lieben' ('the principle concern in v. 4 is not the unity of God so much as the command to love God with the whole heart' [my trans.]). The complex issues of translation of Deut. 6:4 and their theological implications are neatly summarized by Timo Veijola, 'Höre Israel: Der Sinn und Hintergrund von Deuteronomium vi 4–9', *VT* 42 (1992), pp. 528–526; and Daniel I. Block, *How I Love your Torah, O Lord! Studies in the Book of Deuteronomy* (Eugene: Cascade, 2011), pp. 73–87.

subsequent generations of Israelites.[29] The emphasis on teaching here also picks up Yahweh's directive to Moses in 5:31, stressing the divine urgency that lies behind what is taught. The future blessing of the nation is said to be dependent upon their faithfulness to these commands.

As the nation lives out the commitments of covenant, its faithfulness is to be expressed in love for Yahweh. But this in turn raises the question of how future generations would know about Yahweh. It is this question that is answered by 6:6–9, a passage that stresses the oral setting of passing on the faith, but an oral setting that is also aware of a written text.[30] The picture it describes is one of a family that has its relationship with God at the centre of its life. The images it employs are those typically associated with the image of the life of faith as a journey, a journey during which an adult family member is expected to create opportunities to be accompanied by children who will be reminded of the things Yahweh requires. The immediate context presumes that the Decalogue will be central to this instruction. Although it cannot be limited to it, the Decalogue would provide the heart of the instruction described here. That is to say, the content of the instruction is based here not on what Yahweh has done so much as on what Yahweh requires. Nevertheless, since the Decalogue itself is predicated upon the saving acts of Yahweh (5:6), we should not see an absolute distinction at this point. Moreover, since Israel lived in a polytheistic context, the emphasis in the *Shema* on the uniqueness of Yahweh would naturally require some further explanation.

The actual processes of instruction are expected to be within the framework of daily life. Where Moses' instruction occurs as a set-piece address, the instruction within the family to subsequent generations is expected to occur within the routine experiences of life. What is described in 6:7 is therefore not simply a set of occasions during which the family was expected to speak of Yahweh. Rather, what we have here is an expression of the whole of life, so that Yahwistic faith permeated the whole of life, and in this setting the family could freely and openly discuss its faith. Indeed, this teaching was to be diligently

---

29. Nelson, *Deuteronomy*, p. 88, is open to the possibility that 6:2–3 have been added later to 6:1 because of the move to the second person singular. However, their place in a chiastic structure from 5:23 outlined by Christensen, *Deuteronomy 1:1 – 21:9*, p. 133, tends to confirm Christensen's thesis that the *Numeruswechsel* is a signal of structural boundaries (pp. xcix–ci), though not necessarily his larger argument about Deuteronomy as a form of poetry.

30. For our purposes I have assumed the unity of the text, though this is challenged by Veijola, 'Der Sinn', pp. 536–537, who finds several additions.

made, though it could only make sense in a context where faith was lived out in all areas.

The striking feature of this passage is the use of the verb *šnn*, most commonly translated as 'teach diligently',[31] the only time the verb is used with this sense. In all its other occurrences it means 'to sharpen' or some related sense.[32] On the basis of Ugaritic evidence it can be argued that there is an alternative version of the root that means 'to repeat, recite',[33] though one could achieve a similar result by arguing that the word is actually derived from *šnh*.[34] If we accept the more traditional derivation, then the diligence involved refers to sharpening children in their faith through instruction, whereas either of the alternatives would refer to regular repetition. It is difficult to make a firm adjudication either way on this – the traditional rendering recognizes an attested root and makes sense while avoiding the multiplication of roots in classical Hebrew. But the test of any proposed root is whether or not it provides a better meaning in context, and on this score the alternative proposal may be favoured.

However, it may also be that adjudicating in this way is unnecessary. Hebrew writers frequently play with roots with multiple senses, and we may have an instance of the intentional use of ambiguity here so that the root is effective in multiple ways.[35] The effect of this ambiguity, especially where a writer or speaker uses a relatively uncommon word as here, is that it destabilizes hearers and readers who may initially resolve the sense of the sentence in one way but are then forced to consider it in another way. In that the two meanings of the root can reasonably work in this passage, it is therefore probable that both 'sharpening' and 'repetition' are intended. Children are to be prepared for instruction and also to receive it continually. Thus the family was called to model faithfulness to Yahweh in its general life, and to instruct children through life so that they would know what Yahweh required and what it was to love him. Instruction is thus offered both through direct didactic discourse and

---

31. So ESV.

32. See Deut. 32:41; Pss 45:6 (etc.); 64:4 (ET 64:3); 73:21; 120:4; 140:4 (ET 140:3); Prov. 25:18; Isa. 5:28.

33. In that Ugaritic *tnn* = Hebrew *šnn*. See G. R. Driver, *Canaanite Myths and Legends* (Edinburgh: T&T Clark, 1956), p. 151.

34. Nelson, *Deuteronomy*, p. 87, notes this alternative.

35. On this model of ambiguity within the Old Testament, see David G. Firth, 'Ambiguity', in David G. Firth and Jamie A. Grant (eds.), *Words and the Word: Explorations in Biblical Interpretation and Literary Theory* (Nottingham: Apollos, 2008), pp. 159–162.

through a life that put this into practice, whether individually, within the family or in wider society.[36]

This process draws on both oral and written resources. That parents are to 'speak' of these things obviously points to an oral discourse that reflects on the exodus and Decalogue, as well as to the statutes that follow. But there also appears to be a written element. Although the statement that these words are to be 'on the heart' principally means that they are to be rehearsed orally, parents are also directed to 'bind them' on their hands and to have them between their eyes. Orthodox Jewish practice continues to follow this literally, though the preceding context would suggest that these directions are intended as a metaphor emphasizing the levels of commitment required. But the requirement that they be written on the doorpost is probably intended to be literal, meaning that there was some degree of writing involved. If so, then we see again the interplay between oral and written settings which characterizes the book. It is certainly true, however, that having at least some of the *torâ* written could be a useful trigger for generating the conversations imagined in 6:7.

A separate treatment of 11:18–21 may not seem to be required, since it largely repeats the wording of 6:6–9. In this instance, we return to one of the more typical verbs for teaching (*lmd*), a change that could be simply stylistic, though it also makes more explicit that parents here continue to follow the pattern of Moses. However, context is always crucial to interpretation, and 11:18–21 applies this similar language differently from 6:6–9. Rather than being a simple rep-etition of 6:6–9,[37] these verses extend their application in new ways. What is especially notable is that parents are here exhorted to the practice of faithful instruction of their children so as to ensure the abiding blessing of Yahweh, whereas 6:6–9 lays the foundation for subsequent generations not being tempted by other gods. These themes are not unrelated to one another within Deuter-onomy, and it is acknowledged throughout the book that it is necessary for Israel to remain faithful to Yahweh if they are to receive his blessings. Neverthe-less, chapters 6 – 11 are bookended by the theme of passing on the faith, with the implications complementing one another. The section begins by empha-sizing the importance of passing on the faith in order to avoid unfaithfulness. Now, as we come to the end of this section, a similar point is made for a more positive reason – because generational faithfulness was necessary for continued

---

36. Wright, *Deuteronomy*, p. 100.

37. So Cindy Erasmus, 'The Passing on the Faith Tradition within the Family', unpublished LTh (Hons) thesis, Baptist Theological College of Southern Africa (1996), p. 22.

enjoyment of the land. If it was then asked, 'How could they remain faithful?' a simple answer could be given – by ensuring that each new generation knew what Yahweh required. And it was seen as the primary responsibility of the parents to teach the faith to their children so that each succeeding generation would know the blessing of Yahweh. Instruction was crucial, and the family was a central place where it would happen.

A further text on this theme is found in 32:46 in the conclusion to the Song of Moses, where an overview of the coming life for each tribe is given. The language itself is fairly formulaic, but there are some significant developments generated simply by the context itself. While the reference to transmitting 'these words' possibly refers to the whole of the discourse of Deuteronomy, the immediate context suggests that it is the themes of Moses' song which should predominate. Nevertheless, as the passage moves from reciting the song to commanding the people to pass on what they know, the text now speaks of 'this *tôrâ*', indicating that the song was 'brought into conjunction with the law'.[38] It is important to note that here Moses' role as the representative teacher is established by the fact that he has recited (*dbr*) the song before the people, though the presence of Joshua[39] as Moses' designated successor is also noted. The song itself essentially provides a mechanism for Israel to see and understand Yahweh's role in their ongoing life. The instruction to be passed on is thus one whereby discernment as to Yahweh's involvement needs to be part of the instruction. However, the fusing of the song with the *tôrâ* means that the *tôrâ* provides the frame of reference for doing so. This means that passing on the faith goes beyond the mere understanding of facts, moving on to their interpretation. The Song of Moses, within the context of the *tôrâ*, provides a mechanism for doing this, and as this is also related to continued life in the land, it is apparent that Deuteronomy sees a developing understanding of what it means to live in covenant with Yahweh as essential to continued life in the land.

Not all processes of passing on faith depend upon parental initiative, because Deuteronomy also assumes that the regular patterns of worship will routinely provide opportunities to pass on faith, something that first appears in 6:20–25. The pattern of instruction expected here is somewhat different from what we have previously noted. Whereas 6:6–9 focused on the content of the laws, the intention here is to move beyond their content to their meaning. The setting is apparently the Passover, since the question posed by

---

38. J. A. Thompson, *Deuteronomy: An Introduction and Commentary*, TOTC (Leicester: Inter-Varsity Press, 1974), p. 304.

39. Here called 'Hoshea'.

the son is related to that indicated in Exodus 13:14, though the Passover itself is not specifically mentioned. The setting appears to be broadly liturgical, but the absence here of anything specifically tied to Passover means that the question takes on a wider frame of reference, being now about the whole of Yahweh's commands. Although this includes liturgical themes, it is now much wider. Where the teaching of 6:6–9 focused primarily on the requirements of Yahweh and only secondarily on his saving acts, that pattern is reversed here. That is to say, rather than outlining what Yahweh requires, the primary concern here is with Yahweh's saving acts, though these then become the motivation for faithfulness to the commands of Yahweh. The faith tradition that is passed on here is centred on the events of the exodus, while the story of the entry into the land is presumed.[40] These stories provide the living foundation of Israel's faith, a faith that the parents are expected to know, understand and explain to their children. Of course, it is also true that the stories themselves explain what it is that Yahweh has done, but they do not then proceed to explain what Israel is to do in response. Thus there is also a key application in the closing verses – the commandments have generated the question, and it is the account of the salvation achieved by Yahweh that is the central motivation for obedience to those commandments.

That chapter 6's model for passing on the faith includes both the content of what is required and the story of why this is required reflects the impact of the Decalogue. Chapter 5's recounting of the Decalogue began with the story of what Yahweh had done before outlining his requirements, whereas here the order is reversed. Nevertheless, it is not surprising that the theme of obedience to Yahweh's commands being necessary for continued enjoyment of the land again emerges here.

The possibility of liturgy providing a foundation for passing on the faith may also be implied in the requirement that those involved in celebrating the feasts of Weeks and Booths include male and female children and the resident alien, along with the Levite, widow, orphan and servants (16:11, 14). There is no explicit statement here about this task, but by insisting that all are to be involved in their celebration there is a clear implication that they too are to learn what these feasts mean in Israel's faith. Further, the faith is passed on and not only to subsequent generations, since inclusion of the *gēr* indicates that this concern moves beyond those with an ethnic claim to being the people of God.

---

40. The book of Deuteronomy is of course set on the borders of the land, but presumes that the conquest will be successful.

The possibility that Israel's faith might be passed on more broadly is indicated in 4:6–8. Here Moses has drawn on the events at Baal-peor (4:3–4) as a reason for Israel to keep the statutes. What is remarkable is that in encouraging Israel to keep the commandments, it is stated that doing so will demonstrate their wisdom and understanding in the sight of the nations. Israel is thus presented as if she were on a stage and the nations are those in the theatre watching her. At this point we are no longer interested in the relationship between written and oral instruction. Rather, instruction happens in the simple act of living out life within the covenant. Although Deuteronomy stresses the benefits to Israel of keeping the covenant, here we see the benefits for all the nations who, by seeing Israel live out Yahweh's requirements, are led to reflect on the greatness of both Yahweh and the *tôrâ*. The nations are not given the content of the covenant, but the nature of Israel's conduct as a reflection of the *tôrâ* is itself a means of passing on the faith and inviting them to share in what made Israel distinctive. The nations could also be shocked by Yahweh's judgment on Israel for their failing to keep covenant (29:22–28), which suggests that for Deuteronomy the faith could be passed on whether or not Israel was faithful to the covenant. The question, though, would be whether this happened because Israel stood under the blessing or under the curse. Either way, the nearness of the invisible God would be made visible in the concrete reality of Israel's life.[41]

Conclusion

It is apparent that Deuteronomy employs a variety of strategies to ensure that the faith is passed on, rather than this being a process destined to fail, as Noll has suggested. A passionate concern to pass on covenant faith is built into every level of the book. Its structure is designed to emphasize the importance of passing on faith, with Moses presented as the model teacher. From Moses, the dominant pattern assumes that the family is the central locus for this as his pattern is followed, through awareness of a written text and also a lifestyle of oral instruction. This instruction requires knowledge of the *tôrâ* and the underpinning story of salvation. But this is not only passing on facts, it is also passing on the ability to understand the covenant in Israel's emerging life. The faith is passed on not only through conscious instruction but also through common

---

41. For a missiological reflection on this passage, see Christopher J. H. Wright, *The Mission of God: Unlocking the Bible's Grand Narrative* (Nottingham: Inter-Varsity Press, 2006), pp. 378–380.

life, and not only to subsequent Israelite generations but also to the nations. In the handover to Joshua at the book's conclusion we see this process already beginning, anticipating its continuation through the generations and ultimately to the nations.

7. LIFE AND DEATH IN DEUTERONOMY

Heath A. Thomas

Introduction

When younger, the present author took a degree in literature in hopes of excavating that rich mine to unearth its gems. Literature has a special way of presenting the realities of what it means to be human, different from scientific explanation. This is one of the reasons why the humanities (literature, philosophy and the arts) remain a powerful resource for reflection and inspiration. 'Literature . . . offers us access to, and a way to share in, the entire range of human feeling over the ages. This is a gift like no other.'[1] And perhaps the most significant reality addressed in literature is one's mortality.

Life and death remain fundamental to the human condition in world literature in general, and all the more for Israel in the book of Deuteronomy. This is because the very concepts of 'life' and 'death' are not merely human realities in Deuteronomy, but are ever connected to the God of Israel and what he is doing in his world. For Deuteronomy, 'life' does not simply mean Israel's 'existence', but rather Israel's proper existence *before God in his divinely appointed place*. Conversely, 'death' does not simply equate to Israel's non-existence, but rather to

---

1. Arnold Weinstein, *A Scream Goes through the House: What Literature Teaches Us about Life* (New York: Random House, 2003), p. xx.

Israel's *rejection of God and banishment from his divinely appointed place*. These features locate Deuteronomy within its Ancient Near Eastern environment. As with its ANE neighbours, communal identity for Israel, as described in Deuteronomy, is rooted in the relationship between God, his land and his people. Deuteronomy presents life as Israel's embodied existence in Canaan and the threat of death as 'perishing' from the land that God has given them.

The purpose of this chapter is to explore the theological theme of life and death in Deuteronomy. It suggests that Deuteronomy presents a high theology of Yhwh as the giver of life for Israel; as they inhabit God's land, Israel are invited to choose Yhwh by choosing to obey his law; consequently the law portrays the 'good life' for Israel. Further, this chapter will demonstrate that Moses serves as a living exemplar of the importance of obedience to God through his law. In this way, law and life are complementary rather than conflicting theological concepts, because they both derive from God.

A narrative and rhetorical reading strategy serves as the methodological touchstone. Rather than a diachronic analysis of Deuteronomy or the Pentateuch, attention here is given to the narrative of the Pentateuch itself and its final book in particular, focusing on the theme of life and death. Helpful in this regard are recent narrative readings of Mann and McConville on the Pentateuch and the Primary History.[2] When read in this light, Deuteronomy is part of the story of God's purposes from creation onwards. This draws the particular story of Israel in Deuteronomy into the universal scope of redemption.[3] The rhetoric of Deuteronomy is vital to its message. Attending to its hortatory narrative reveals the book to be not only informative, but also transformative in its call to the reader.

He is your life: Yhwh

A central truth of Deuteronomy is that Yhwh is life for Israel. This most basic declaration appears in 32:39, where Yhwh says, 'I deal death and I give

---

2. Thomas W. Mann, *The Book of the Torah: The Narrative Integrity of the Pentateuch* (Louisville: John Knox, 1988); J. G. McConville, *God and Earthly Power: An Old Testament Political Theology* (London: T&T Clark, 2007). See also John Sailhamer, *The Meaning of the Pentateuch: Revelation, Composition, and Interpretation* (Downers Grove: IVP Academic, 2009).

3. See the especially rich work of Richard Bauckham, *The Bible and Mission* (Grand Rapids: Eerdmans, 2003).

life.'[4] This affirmation couples with a statement of his transcendent uniqueness: 'there is no god beside me.' The echoes of the great *Shema* of 6:4–5
reverberate here and proclaim that Yhwh, and he alone, remains the source of
all life for Israel. Moses admonishes God's people to choose Yhwh on the
rationale that '*He* will be your life and the length of your days' (30:20, emphasis
mine). Other versions obscure this theological point, for example JPS Tanakh
has: 'For thereby you shall have life and shall long endure.'[5] But the best
rendering of verse 20 treats Yhwh as the source of life and length of Israel's
days. As Barker rightly states, 'To choose life is to choose Yahweh.'[6]

Throughout the book, the transcendent uniqueness of Yhwh as the life-giver
to Israel distinguishes him from all other gods, those who would seduce Israel
into apostasy. Idolatry equates to 'forgetting' Yhwh as Israel's life. Idolatry in
any form will lead to death, a point elucidated in a number of texts (4:25–28;
8:19–20; 11:16–17). False gods lead Israel to their death precisely because *they
are not Israel's God*. Further, divine punishment accompanies idolatry and is a
form of discipline that, tellingly, culminates with Israel 'perishing' from the
good land that Yhwh has given them.

This teaching about life and death stands not as a theological abstraction.
Rather, it is a lesson borne out through the story of God and Israel narrated
within the book. As the holy victor over rival powers (Pharaoh and demi-gods
of Egypt), God reveals himself to be Israel's deliverer from that 'iron furnace'
(4:20) of Egypt, which is also described as a 'house of slavery' (5:6; 6:12; 8:14;
13:6, 11). Yhwh sustains and preserves this people in spite of their sin and
rebellion when he gives them life by miraculous provision of food and water
in the wilderness (8:15–16). Ultimately he prepares a place in which they will
live (6:10–11; 7:1–2). As they move into the land, he provides them the law, by
which they will live long in the days as they love the Lord their God with all

---

4. Unless identified otherwise, Scripture quotations in this chapter are the author's own
translations. For discussion of Deut. 32:29, see Fredrik Lindström, *God and the Origin
of Evil*, ConBOT 21 (Lund: CWK Gleerup, 1983), pp. 167–177.

5. See the discussion of Paul Barker, *The Triumph of Grace in Deuteronomy*, PBM (Milton
Keynes: Paternoster, 2004), p. 208. The masculine singular pronoun in v. 20 most
sensibly refers back to Yhwh rather than the instruction of God's *tôrâ* (*tôrâ* being a
feminine singular noun). So too J. G. McConville, *Deuteronomy*, AOTC 5 (Leicester:
Apollos; Downers Grove: InterVarsity Press, 2002), pp. 421, 430. Moses' final song
expounds this point in hymnic celebration, particularly in Deut. 33:26–29.

6. Barker, *Triumph*, p. 208. I do not share Barker's perspective on law in Deuteronomy,
however. See below.

their hearts (6:5; 12 – 26). Even if they rebel against him, the Lord himself will restore this rebellious, broken Israel and renew their days. He will punish his people through exile, but will remember his covenant love for them, bringing them out of that desolation (see 30:1–10). Although not explicitly connected to the teaching given in Deuteronomy 30, God's restoration of his people back *into* the land after their exile is akin to God bringing his dead people back to life, restoring them to their place of thriving before God.

On a holistic reading of the Pentateuch, God's vital work with Israel in Deuteronomy is part of the divine redemptive response to the problem of the sinful world elucidated in Genesis 1 – 11. The creation accounts (Gen. 1 – 2) and the story of Israel (Gen. 12 – Deut. 34) are drawn together in the Pentateuchal narrative. God causes Israel to thrive and 'multiply' whether in Egypt, the wilderness, or in the land of promise, echoing and fulfilling the command to humanity at creation, 'Be fruitful and multiply' (Gen. 1:28).[7] Further, this gift of 'multiplication' is such that their number might be compared to the number of the 'stars of heaven' (Deut. 1:9–10; 10:22), a phrase that resonates with Yhwh's promise to the patriarchs in Genesis 15:5; 22:17 and 26:4 and draws the Pentateuchal narrative closely together – from the primeval history, to the patriarchal stories, to the story of Israel. So Mann suggests that Abraham marks 'the promise of a new land, indeed, a new *world*' which also 'implies the creation of a new community' that is called by the name Israel; this community 'will be made by God and, at the same time, represent the continuing relation of all humankind to God'.[8] Deuteronomy presents this Israelite community at the borders of Canaan and foresees their life beyond.

To pursue this narratival trajectory in the Pentateuch, God gives Israel the land as a kind of Eden for them to inhabit. Eden/Canaan does not provide mundane life, but vibrant productivity for Israel. On the journey to God's land, Balaam's oracle hints at this point (Num. 24:5–9). His proclamation is at once retrospective and prospective – it remembers God's former garden and proposes that Eden might be rediscovered through God's people as they move into the land. Deuteronomy suggests this point as well, with a particular emphasis upon *the land* as Eden *redivivus*, particularly in 8:7–10. Both texts portray the land as one of abundance, water, foodstuffs, cultural resources and complete provision. The difference lies in their focus: while Balaam's oracle focuses on *God's people*

---

7. The language is precise – *Yhwh* has multiplied Israel. See Deut. 1:10; 7:13.

8. Mann, *The Book*, p. 28. See too the fine analysis of William P. Brown, *The Ethos of the Cosmos: The Genesis of Moral Imagination in the Bible* (Grand Rapids: Eerdmans, 1999), pp. 35–132.

in God's land, Deuteronomy's vision focuses on *God's land* as a gift for God's people. In the latter text, the adjective 'good' twice modifies the extensive description of the land, providing a frame in verses 7 and 10 that echoes the 'goodness' of creation in Genesis 1.[9] Deuteronomy then suggests that the good gift of God's land will draw God's people into praise and worship: 'You will eat your fill and you will bless Yhwh your God on account of the good land which he has given you' (8:10).

With its bounty of 'streams and pools of water', its 'wheat and barley, vines and fig trees, pomegranates, olive oil and honey', and its abundance of resources (8:7–9), the land itself is testimony to Israel that God provides to them resources for thriving in God's land. Canaan is the place where Eden will be modelled once again in God's world. McConville powerfully captures this thought:

> Through Israel, therefore, Deuteronomy shows the life of a nation as a microcosm of humanity (*'adam*) about to enjoy the blessings of the earth (*'erets*). All is set within the covenant, the means by which the basic problem of human existence exposed in Genesis 3 – 11 is to be overcome. The covenant with Abraham comes to maturity in Deuteronomy, the descendants of the patriarch having endured its (*sic*) lengthy servitude and seen God's judgement on its tyrannous overlords (Gen. 15.13–16). And the creative purpose is now embraced within the Mosaic covenant, which offers the means by which humanity/Israel may enjoy the paradisal blessings.[10]

God's divine favour and blessing on Israel derives neither from their power (7:7) nor from their righteousness (9:4–5), but rather from his faithful love to the patriarchs and his promise to them (7:6–8). The book's insistence upon divine initiative reinforces a theology of Yhwh's vitality; the gift of life has been given through divine grace. Israel is called upon to live well in the life/land that Yhwh has granted them by obeying his commands.

Yet, despite this real opportunity to embrace the gift of land and the God of life, Deuteronomy recurrently reveals Israel's wilful heart – they cannot but rebel against him. Deuteronomy 1 – 4 as well as the succeeding chapters 5 – 11 explicitly suppose rebellion, a supposition implicitly taken up within the law codes of chapters 12 – 26 since law and punishment presume the disobedience of God's commands, the very essence of rebellion. So the law provides not

---

9. R. Norman Whybray notes this as well. The curse of sin, then, is in a sense turned back as Israel lives well in God's land. See his *The Good Life in the Old Testament* (London: T&T Clark, 2002), pp. 43–44.
10. McConville, *God and Earthly Power*, p. 78.

only positive instructions for obedience but also negative instructions for disobedience. The blessings and curses in Deuteronomy 27 – 28 envisage Israel's disobedience as well.[11] Israel is forced to grapple with the fact that they may not embrace the God of life or the 'good life', but rather experience death, disease, wasting, famine and ultimately exile as a result of their sin (see Deut. 28).

But 30:1–10 powerfully reveals Yhwh as Israel's life, even through exile. After divine punishment, God will restore his people: 'Yhwh your God will circumcise your heart and the hearts of your offspring to love Yhwh your God with all your heart and soul, in order that you will live' (30:6). The image of 'circumcision of the heart' emphasizes that the very hope of Israel, its very life, lay 'not in its unaided capacity to respond [to God] but in God's unending commitment to remember mercy'.[12] This spiritual work within the heart of Israel remains unique. God would do a new thing in Israel so that they *would* love Yhwh, fulfilling the command for Israel to 'circumcise' their hearts in 10:16.[13] This point is echoed in the Song of Moses which notes that, whereas God's people may be 'wounded' in and through exile, nonetheless the blow will not be mortal: he 'will heal' his people (32:36–39). Divine healing comes in and through his initiative and divine act of restoration.

So Deuteronomy inculcates a theology of divine sovereignty and vitality, to which Israel is called to respond as shall be demonstrated below. Still, in the final analysis, Yhwh is in control of Israel's final destiny. He draws Israel out of Egypt. He alone sustains them in the desert. He alone provides for them as they prepare to enter into his Promised Land. He gives them law to provide a moral order for living well in that land. Yet, even if and when Israel rebels against him, Yhwh is sovereign to restore Israel their flagging faith and renew their life. In short, Deuteronomy presents Yhwh as the sovereign God of life.[14]

---

11. Note the difference between the portrayal of exile as punishment in Deut. 28 – 29 versus the portrayal in Lev. 26. For discussion, see Mark Boda, *A Severe Mercy: Sin and Its Remedy in the Old Testament*, Siphrut 1 (Winona Lake: Eisenbrauns, 2009), pp. 82–85, 111–112.

12. Christopher Wright, *Deuteronomy*, NIBC (Peabody: Hendrickson, 1996), pp. 289–290.

13. The language of God 'restoring the fortunes' of Israel that precedes this new life language in Deut. 30:3 intends a restoration of Israel to life as it should have been prior to exile – a veritable renewed humanity in a restored paradise. Indeed, in Deut. 30:5, God himself secures Israel's land and the people's productivity/multiplication, echoing covenantal promises.

14. Vogt argues along different lines but arrives at a similar theological conclusion: P. T. Vogt, *Deuteronomic Theology and the Significance of Torah: A Reappraisal* (Winona Lake: Eisenbrauns, 2006).

Life, Torah and choice

The God of life gives his law to Israel. It has been rightly suggested that the legal code in Deuteronomy 12 – 26 provides a 'moral order' in which Israel could live and thrive as they obey.[15] Law *mediates* life for Israel precisely because its source is in Yhwh. So the law is called Israel's 'wisdom' (4:6) as well as, tellingly, their very 'life' (32:47). It is Israel's 'wisdom', in the sense that the law shows Israel the way to follow God as well as the folly of disobeying him. Further, the law is Israel's 'life' because it is their means of continued habitation in God's land.

Remembering God's law equates to love and devotion to God, which then leads to well-being. McConville's translation of 32:47 captures this point: 'For these are no empty words for you; they are your very life, and by virtue of them you will have long life in the land you are crossing the Jordan to possess.'[16] These words exude fecundity and longevity for Israel. To obey law is to choose God and life, but the converse, of course, is true as well. Rejecting God's law is to embrace 'death' and 'curse' (30:15, 19).

But what is 'law'? The Hebrew word *tôrâ* certainly implies the legal code of Deuteronomy 12– 26 (often envisaged in terms of 'law/legal code'), but this term also covers the entire set of instruction given in the book.[17] To reduce *tôrâ* to a mere 'list of rules' is a thin understanding of a dense word. *Tôrâ* intends the instruction of God throughout the book.

Tôrâ is a challenging topic, especially in Christian quarters. Some view it in a negative manner, such as: (a) Israel's decline into religious legalism, a late development in the history of Israel's religion; or (b) a lofty standard too high for Israel and thus intentionally establishing Israel's failure; or (c) a form of works-based righteousness therefore opposed to the gospel. On these models, the law in one way or another proposes what *Israel does* in contradistinction to what *Yhwh does*.

But attempts to polarize human and divine action does not fit well within the theology of Deuteronomy. Its theology of law is not founded upon a dichotomy or polarization of legalism (human response) versus grace (divine initiative). Rather, it may be schematized: divine grace engenders human

---

15. J. G. McConville, *Law and Theology in Deuteronomy*, JSOTSup 33 (Sheffield: JSOT Press, 1984); Vogt, *Deuteronomic Theology*.

16. McConville, *Deuteronomy*, p. 447.

17. For further discussion on the meaning of *tôrâ* in Deuteronomy, see Mann, *The Book*, pp. 146–147; McConville, *Deuteronomy*, pp. 42–44.

obedience, human obedience to divine grace perpetuates divine blessing, which then leads to deeper human appreciation of divine grace.[18] Right human action comes in response to God's previous act of divine grace. In this way, the theology of divine faithfulness is emphasized without trivializing Israel's faithfulness to God in the book. As the God of life, Yhwh's purposes *will* be achieved through Israel despite their sin.

This implies a relational component working within the giving of law. The theology of election is important in this discussion. Israel did not *work* to become elected in the line of Abraham. Neither did they *work* to be chosen from the nations of the world or to be delivered from Egypt. Nor did they *work* to receive the law. Rather, all this is based upon the sovereign grace of Yhwh. Deuteronomy takes up this theme and suggests that God blesses Israel out of his grace (shown in his promise to the patriarchs) which then draws Israel to obedience to his word.[19]

The supremacy and uniqueness of Yhwh (the divine indicative) should lead Israel to love him in the whole of life (the divine imperative). Of course, Deuteronomy teaches the uniqueness of Yhwh in 4:39 and 32:39: there is none like him. But Israel's recognition of Yhwh's uniqueness ought then to lead them to proper action in the world. This point is at least intimated in the *Shema* and great command of 6:4–5: 'Hear O Israel, Yhwh is our God, Yhwh is One. You shall love Yhwh your God with all your heart and all your soul and with all your strength.' Yhwh's uniqueness (the divine indicative) then draws from Israel the proper response to him in love (the divine imperative). This very insight, however, rests within the context of a 'command' of law (6:2, 24). In this way divine initiative and human response are met in a delicate balance that prioritizes divine grace but necessitates (and envisions) human response on the basis of that divine grace.

The legal code in Deuteronomy 12 – 26, too, reflects this in its placement in the book.[20] Its setting between the first eleven chapters and the final seven chapters in the book is part of Deuteronomy's rhetoric. The code functions within the persuasive instruction of Moses (particularly his second sermon in the book),[21] and reminds Israel that after God has brought them to this place they are called to live in accordance with his moral order. The code *also* serves as a detailed set of stipulations that guide Israel's vassal relationship with their

18. McConville, *Law*, pp. 16–18.

19. Ibid., p. 17.

20. Patrick D. Miller, *Deuteronomy* (Louisville: John Knox, 1990), p. 10.

21. McConville, *Deuteronomy*, p. 212.

God, revealing a covenantal substructure. Yhwh has given his chosen people (divine election) the gift of law through his own divine initiative so that it might be observed within the land (human response). In so doing, the legal code presents a guide to covenant maintenance set within the story of Yhwh's purposes with Israel. Deuteronomy 1 – 11 rehearses God's faithfulness and grace to Israel as he has brought them to the plains of Moab. Deuteronomy 12 – 26 provides a vision for society as Israel moves into the land. The repeated description of the land as gift for Israel throughout Deuteronomy 12 – 26 reinforces the right way of human response: divine gift initiates human obedience, which perpetuates divine blessing as Israel embraces God's instruction.[22] And even if (and when) Israel disobeys, Yhwh's grace will preserve and restore them (Deut. 30). When understood in this way, law is not polarized against gospel. The law, then, is a gift that provides *the way to enter into the gift of God's land*.

But this raises the question of the nature of 'life' envisaged in Deuteronomy. Whybray describes it as not a random or dull existence but 'the good life'. It culminates in secure borders, food to eat, rest from enemies, communal well-being and justice amongst the society in accordance with Yhwh's law.[23] Weinfeld goes so far as to describe life in the book as a kind of 'happiness' at the level of the community as a whole.[24]

Moreover, *tôrâ* in Deuteronomy suggests that 'happy' life is infused by worship, as evidenced by the language of 'rejoicing' before Yhwh that frames the legal code of Deuteronomy 12 – 26.[25] In 12:7 and 26:11, Israel is called to 'rejoice' before Yhwh in worship. Deuteronomy's vision of life is shaped, then, by a liturgical frame. Within it, the legal code addresses different facets of communal living, and chapters 12 – 26 loosely follow the framework of the Ten

---

22. See Deut. 12:10; 13:12; 15:4, 7; 16:5, 18, 20; 17:2, 14; 18:9; 19:1–2, 10, 14; 20:16; 21:1, 23; 24:4; 25:15, 19; 26:1–2. One may note as well the strong emphasis upon protection of life in the law of the *talion* in Deut. 19:1–13, 21 (cf. Exod. 21:23–24). Just measure in retaliation is a means to protect life and reinforce the importance of vitality in God's law. For discussion, see Wright, *Deuteronomy*, pp. 224–226; Miller, *Deuteronomy*, pp. 146–147.

23. Whybray, *The Good Life*, pp. 42–45. Note as well the very helpful discussion of Hilary Marlow, 'Land of Hope and Glory', unpublished Tyndale Old Testament Lecture (2011).

24. Moshe Weinfeld, *Deuteronomy and the Deuteronomic School* (Oxford: Clarendon Press, 1972), pp. 307–313. This is explored further by Marlow, ibid.

25. For this distinctive language, see Deut. 12:7, 12, 18; 14:26; 16:11, 14; 26:11; cf. 27:7.

Commandments.[26] With this in view, Israel's obedience to law remains fundamentally an act of worship of Israel's God rather than an empty legalism.

The *tôrâ* in Deuteronomy teaches the supremacy of Yhwh in *all* aspects of Israel's life.[27] This includes regular communal celebrations (chs. 14 – 16), authority structures (chs. 16 – 18), human relationships and warfare (chs. 19 – 22), sexuality (ch. 22) and various other elements of community life (chs. 23 – 26). This rather expansive (but not exhaustive) vision of communal life reveals that Deuteronomy's 'good life' is not marked by a modern separation between secular and sacred spheres, but by a recognition that the transcendent uniqueness of Yhwh permeates the fabric of Israel's existence. Loving God *through his law*, in worship, throughout the whole of Israel's society, may be characterized as 'the good life'.[28]

If the good life comes to Israel through God's law, then the rhetorical force of the book draws Israel to decision. Israel is called to choose Yhwh by obeying his *tôrâ* within the subframe of Deuteronomy 11 and 30, where blessing and curse are laid before Israel. The hortatory declaration of 30:15–20 makes this explicit, especially in verse 19: 'Now choose [*bḥr*] life, so that you may live, you and your offspring.' The following verse clarifies the nature of the choice: 'to love Yhwh your God, to obey his voice, and to cling to him. For he is your life and the length of your days' (30:20).

Interestingly, the choice laid before Israel here is counterbalanced by Yhwh's 'choosing' throughout the book. But the balance is clearly asymmetrical. As O'Dowd notes, *Israel's God* does the choosing in twenty-nine of the thirty-one instances of the root *bḥr* – whether of Israel (7:6–7; 14:2) or the place of worship (12:5 – 17:10; 26:2).[29] But *Israel* does the 'choosing' when life and death are presented to them in 30:15–20. This reveals the general point on obedience drawn out in this section: in light of God's gracious 'choice' of his people in Deuteronomy 1 – 29, now God's people are called to 'choose' life in terms of Yhwh and his *tôrâ*. Deuteronomy's 'good and righteous world of life'[30] is set forth through divine law, but this ideal existence demands Israel's decision.

---

26. See John H. Walton's chapter in this volume, pp. 93–117; Wright, *Deuteronomy*, pp. 4–5; Vogt, *Deuteronomic Theology*, p. 29.

27. Vogt, *Deuteronomic Theology*; Joshua Moon, 'Preaching Deuteronomy as Christian Scripture', *Southeastern Theological Review* 2.1 (2011), p. 48.

28. See Vogt, *Deuteronomic Theology*, p. 228.

29. Ryan P. O'Dowd, *The Wisdom of Torah: Epistemology in Deuteronomy and the Wisdom Literature*, FRLANT 225 (Göttingen: Vandenhoeck & Ruprecht, 2009), p. 102 n. 108.

30. Ibid., p. 101.

Deuteronomy's rhetorical strategy on Israel's 'choice' matches the emphasis on the language of immediacy which occurs throughout the book. The term 'today' or a construction with similar meaning occurs in the book no less than seventy-four times, on the author's count. It comes in almost every chapter and functions as a rhetorical *Leitwort*, repeatedly drawing Israel to their present decision for Yhwh and his *tôrâ* 'today'. This is especially pertinent in the context of the covenant blessings and curses in Deuteronomy 27 – 28. Because of the emphasis upon 'today', it is reasonable to understand the force of chapters 27 – 28 as directed to readers on the plains of Moab. So the blessings and curses of chapters 27 – 28 give the audience a rhetorical decision point: will they embrace 'this law' or not? The blessings and curses reach their fulfilment in Deuteronomy 30, which then offers an urgent, genuine choice that Israel (and, to be sure, later readers) must make. In 30:15–16, God's story with Israel leads to a decision. Mann even suggests that listening to the story *demands* a response from the hearer, so that the 'significance of the narration in Deuteronomy is eviscerated if this demand for responsibility is ignored'.[31]

In 30:1–20, then, Israel is drawn to the point of choice. The rationale behind this is not to present a standard too high to keep, but rather to offer a genuine choice of life or death. Israel is called to 'choose life'. As they do, God will reside in their midst.

Because of the urgent call for decision, readings that would paint the hearers of Deuteronomy 30 as *purely* eschatological remain unconvincing. The language of 'today' (vv. 15, 16, 18, 19) is genuinely immediate.[32] Deuteronomy 30 does carry eschatological overtones, but these are properly set within the rhetorical strategy of the book. The future envisioned in Deuteronomy 30 is designed to spur Israel's appropriate response in the present. In this way, Deuteronomy 30 puts the accent on a theology of divine grace and sovereignty rather than on human achievement. The chapter describes both the potentiality of Israel's fidelity and (much more firmly) the certainty of God's sovereignty and commitment to Israel. God fulfils his purposes with Israel despite their sin.

Finally, when Deuteronomy is read within the larger story of the Pentateuch, the gift of *tôrâ* to Israel is divine grace with the redemption of the world in

---

31. Mann, *The Book*, p. 147.

32. Note the discussion of J. G. Millar, *Now Choose Life: Theology and Ethics in Deuteronomy*, NSBT 6 (Downers Grove: InterVarsity Press, 1998), who suggests the call for Israel 'today' is genuinely immediate, but impossible to heed. Rather Israel waits for God's eschatological renewal (cf. Deut. 30:1–14) and can only do their best to obey the law in the present.

mind. Israel's actualization of the 'good life' will draw the nations to wonder about this nation, this law and this God.[33] In light of God's gracious provision of the *tôrâ*, then, Israel's appropriate response is to choose the life that God sets forth within it.

On death's doorstep: Moses as exemplar

Deuteronomy's characterization of Moses stands out in the book. Other works have assessed Moses as a *speaker*, but here Moses is explored not only as a speaker but also as a character. Deuteronomy presents Moses as one who elucidates the book's teaching on Yhwh, law and life – in part by revealing the nature and meaning of his death. To grasp this point, the differences between Moses' speech, God's speech and the narrator's speech need to be clarified, along with the characterization of Moses within the Pentateuch.[34]

Moses is remembered positively as the prophet, mediator and intercessor for Israel. He speaks for God to the degree that his own voice carries the force of divine commands as is fitting to a true prophet of God. Moses is called a prophet in 18:14–22 and 34:10–12. Moses speaks the true words of God, in contrast with the false prophet (13:1–7), and is described as 'the man of God' (33:1). Although unique in the Pentateuch, elsewhere in the Old Testament (especially in Joshua–Kings) the title 'man of God' connotes a true prophet who faithfully delivers the word of God. So this title elevates Moses as the true prophet who faithfully declares God's word to the people.

---

33. Deuteronomy does not present a 'missional' teaching in the sense of the nations being the primary focus of Israel's fidelity to God. The nations *are* meant to observe Israel's devotion to God, but Deuteronomy's accent falls upon the uniqueness of Yhwh, Israel's election and God's call for obedience. On this point, Nathan MacDonald is correct in *Deuteronomy and the Meaning of 'Monotheism'*, FAT II/1 (Tübingen: Mohr Siebeck, 2003). Still, the teaching of God's uniqueness, Israel's election and her obedience to Yhwh are contextualized within the mission of God through his election of Abraham/Israel elucidated in the Pentateuch, as discussed above. See further O'Dowd, *The Wisdom*, pp. 107–108; Wright, *Deuteronomy*, pp. 8–14.

34. See the discussions of Robert Polzin, *Moses and the Deuteronomist* (New York: Seabury, 1980); Paul J. Kissling, *Reliable Characters in the Primary History: Profiles of Moses, Joshua, Elijah and Elisha*, JSOTSup 224 (Sheffield: Sheffield Academic Press, 1996), pp. 11–68.

Further, Moses stands as the mediator between Yhwh and his people, as texts like Exodus 20:18–21 and 24:2–8 vividly display, and Deuteronomy 5:1–4 rehearses. He serves God faithfully by declaring the words of the covenant. God's word is given to Moses, who then charges the people with it. He stands between God and his people as the law-giver, so that the instruction he promulgates is at once God's word and the 'instruction/law of Moses' (4:44). This is a point well remembered in the book of Joshua. Moses serves as the mouthpiece for God, the law-giver who offers parameters for Israel's life in the land.[35]

Moses is also the intercessor who pleads on behalf of God's people. So in Exodus 32 – 33 he bears the weight of Israel's election in prayer and calls upon God to be faithful to the descendants of Abraham on that basis. Seemingly at every point in Numbers, Israel blames Moses for their experience, and in response he mediates between God and the people in prayer. In this way, Moses is a kind of suffering 'servant' in the Pentateuch: the one who bears Israel's complaints against God and intercedes on behalf of a rebellious Israel. Through the repetition of this cycle, the Pentateuch portrays the virtue of Moses at prayer as an exemplar for faith in God amongst an obstinate, 'stiff-necked' generation.

Still, the Pentateuch does not paint Moses with the brush of naive idealism.[36] He remains an example of both *faithfulness* and *faithlessness*. The narrative from Exodus to Deuteronomy repeatedly highlights Moses' reluctance to respond to the command of Yhwh. One notes this early in the 'call narrative' in Exodus 3 – 4. At every turn Moses deflects God's plans for him. His reluctant responses to his call eventually lead to divine anger in Exodus 4:14. When similar terminology occurs elsewhere in the Pentateuch, some form of divine punishment normally follows.[37] The narrative implies that, while Moses' protestations against God may be understandable, they nonetheless remain unacceptable – let the reader be warned.

---

35. See Josh. 8:31–32; 23:6. Also 1 Kgs 2:3; 2 Kgs 14:6; 21:8; 23:25; 2 Chr. 25:4; 30:16; 33:8; Ezra 3:2; 7:6; Neh. 8:1, 14; 9:14; 10:29; Dan. 9:11, 13; Mal. 4:4.

36. A point at least acknowledged by Polzin, *Moses*, but he thinks that any negative portrayals serve to reinforce the authority of the Deuteronomist. Kissling's assessment, *Reliable Characters*, pp. 32–68, comes closer to the analysis offered here, as he sees Moses as a complex character with positive and negative aspects.

37. 'The LORD's anger burned against X', as in Exod. 4:14; Num. 11:1, 10; 12:9; 25:3; 32:13; Deut. 29:26. See also Josh. 7:1; Judg. 2:14; 20:3, 8; 10:7; 2 Sam. 6:7; 2 Kgs 13:3. Notice as well the alternative formulation 'the LORD became angry with X', in Deut. 1:34, 37; 3:26; 4:21; 9:8; 9:19–20; Josh. 22:18; 1 Kgs 11:9; 2 Kgs 17:18.

This portrayal of Moses' failings takes a mortal turn in Numbers 20:6–13. Here Moses and Aaron disobey Yhwh's command to 'order' (v. 8) the rock to produce water for the people. Moses strikes it with his rod twice here (v. 11), whereas at Meribah he struck it only once (Exod. 17:1–9). But regardless of how many times he struck the rock in Numbers 20:11, Yhwh's command was to 'order' water from the rock (v. 8). This disobedience against a clear divine command is equated with unbelief and a failure to 'consecrate' Yhwh before his people in verse 12, and then rebellion against his divine word in verse 24. This lack of faith and rebellion against Yhwh's word threatens the entire camp, since it infringes upon the very sanctity of God.[38]

Because Moses and Aaron did not trust Yhwh, the brothers are given a terrible sentence – they are stripped of their leadership roles as Israel enters the Promised Land. The narrative discloses what this means, when Aaron dies almost immediately after this act of faithlessness (vv. 23–29). The rationale given for his death comes in verse 24: 'because you [plural, indicating both Moses and Aaron] rebelled against my word concerning the waters of Meribah'.[39] Aaron's mortal punishment in the narrative foreshadows Moses' coming death, a reality explicitly declared in Deuteronomy (see below) and related directly to the incident at Meribah (32:50–51). This narrative of disobedience and its consequences serves as a powerful *negative* example, for the leaders of Israel, the populace at large and the reader.

In this way, the Pentateuch portrays Moses as a kind of paradox for God's people: an exemplar not only of *faithfulness* but also of *faithlessness*. The mixed nature of Moses' moral example must be taken seriously in order to interpret life and death in the Pentateuch in general and in Deuteronomy in particular. Deuteronomy's presentation of Moses underscores the theme of life and death presented in this essay.[40]

Deuteronomy characterizes Moses by extremes. He is described as the 'servant of Yhwh', both in his own words (3:24) and in those of the narrator's epitaph (34:5). In both cases, the title is honorific, indicating the unique place of Moses in Israel's story:

---

38. See the brilliant insights of Brown, *The Ethos*, pp. 95–99.

39. In the translation above, 'my word' is literally 'my mouth', indicating the close association between the command of God and the rebellion against his spoken command, which leads to death.

40. So the present interpretation of Moses' characterization differs from that of Polzin. Rather than it reinforcing the authority of the narrator (so Polzin, *Moses*), the character of Moses serves as an exemplar for *both* piety *and* waywardness for the reader.

His greatness lies in the fact that he has brought [Israel] to this point. In doing so, he has exhibited the great prophetic characteristics, not only of faithfully proclaiming the word of God, but of investing his own life totally in his servant role. This is why he is the servant *par excellence*. He lived his life on behalf of others; he himself is denied precisely that which is promised to them, into which he has led them.[41]

Yet Moses dies on the mountain at the threshold of, but *outside*, the Promised Land. In one sense, it is true that his work is done – he has transmitted Yhwh's instruction and has led Israel through the wilderness. Nonetheless, the terrible sadness of his exclusion from the land is almost palpable. He may gaze upon the land, signifying the surety of Yhwh's promise, but may not experience its bounty. Moses' vitality at the point of his death speaks to the great tragedy of this moment. Although strong and able to enter into Canaan, Moses is prevented from doing so. Why is he excluded from God's Eden for Israel?

To address this question, one needs to examine the presentations of Moses' death in the book. Three speakers describe Moses' impending death, and at different points: Moses at the start (1:37–38; 3:26; 4:21–24; 31:2, 27–29), the narrator (34:5) and Yhwh at the end (31:14, 16; 32:50–51; 34:4). In 1:37, 3:26 and 4:21, Moses explains to the people that Yhwh has denied his entry into the land and sentenced him to death because of *Israel's rebellion*. In the other texts mentioning his death, no explanation is given, save in 32:50–51. Here, as in Numbers 20:12, 24 and 27:12–14, Yhwh explicitly links Moses' exclusion to his sin of disobedience and dishonouring his name (see above).

But why is there a discrepancy between the former and latter presentations of his death? Some posit different literary sources for the presentations.[42] Others suggest that 1:37, 3:26 and 4:21 portray Moses as one who mediates for his people and suffers vicariously for their sin.[43] But the most attractive explanation comes from a close analysis of the voices within the narrative-dramatic presentation of Deuteronomy.

Moses is the first to speak of his death and its rationale. Deuteronomy portrays Moses as a preacher, exhorting the people to faith, today. Moses is

---

41. McConville, *Deuteronomy*, p. 478.

42. Miller questions the typical explanation of 32:50–51, that it stems from Priestly circles, in accord with Numbers, and so is not original to the Deuteronomist. Miller, *Deuteronomy*, pp. 243–245.

43. Dennis T. Olson, *Deuteronomy and the Death of Moses: A Theological Reading*, OBT (Minneapolis: Fortress, 1994). To my mind Olson's view is tenuous.

'the dying prophet' who is preaching 'to the people on the cusp of the land'.[44] As a good preacher, Moses' rhetoric instructs his audience but also draws them to the point of decision. In the first four chapters he does more than simply record the events of history. On the lips of Moses, this story is retold with a particular emphasis that recurs over and again: God has been gracious, but Israel has rebelled. Instead of rebellion, Moses' hearers should hear and respond with obedience. Moses compresses time and events in an extra-ordinary way, omitting material and shaping it to serve his rhetorical interests without betraying the general thrust of Israel's story in the wilderness.[45] By this homiletic device he draws God's people rhetorically towards *present* obedience.

The triple mention of his death in Deuteronomy 1 – 4 serves as a warning for Israel to obey God's word. In the first presentation (1:37), Israel's rebellion draws him into their punishment – death outside the land. So a successor to Moses becomes necessary as God's people journey with God (v. 38). In the second presentation (3:21–28), although Moses clearly draws on the events of Numbers 27:12–23, he omits the rationale for the death sentence recorded in Numbers 27:12–14. His death is only presented as an outcome of Yhwh's anger against him because of Israel (Deut. 3:26). And finally, as he charges Israel to obey Yhwh and avoid idolatry, he draws in his death notice once again (4:21–22): he will not go into the land, but they will. How then should they respond? 'Take care, lest you forget the covenant of Yhwh your God, which he made with you, and make a carved image, the form of anything that Yhwh your God has forbidden you. For Yhwh your God is a consuming fire, a jealous God' (4:23–24). Moses the preacher inculcates in his audience the consequences of sin and then illustrates the outcomes of sin: death.[46]

In the later presentation of 32:51, Moses' death notice serves as a warning to the reader in a different way. Yhwh speaks here, providing the 'final rationale' for Moses' death. God informs Moses (and clearly the reader) that the reason for his death outside the land is that he 'broke faith' against Yhwh by failing to 'consecrate' his name.[47] The first verb in verse 51 (*m'l*) often appears in legal

---

44. Moon, 'Preaching', p. 41.

45. Jean-Pierre Sonnet explains how Moses frames his discourse: *The Book within the Book: Writing in Deuteronomy*, BIS 14 (Leiden: Brill, 1997), esp. pp. 188–192.

46. My analysis differs from Sonnet, ibid., esp. pp. 188–190.

47. The verbs here are both plural, indicating that the sin applies not only to Moses but to Aaron as well. Deuteronomy's language here follows Num. 20 fairly closely and draws the texts together.

contexts and indicates a violation of legal obligations.[48] Here Moses failed to speak to the rock as Yhwh commanded him and instead struck it. This sin, however minor to Moses, nonetheless indicates to Yhwh a failure to consecrate him before Israel. Moses' rebellion against God's command implicates him in divine punishment – death outside the land.

For the audience on the plains of Moab, this serves as a severe warning – disobedience to Yhwh's 'word' ultimately leads to death. Moses dies outside the land not because he lives under the law but because he disobeyed the law.[49] The implied audience of the *book* of Deuteronomy gains this perspective all the more as the reader can hear the words of the narrator, Yhwh and Moses. Together these provide powerful testimony to hear and respond to Yhwh's word. Failing to obey his word leads to death outside the land – where Moses himself will die. In light of this, Moses as exemplar in Deuteronomy reinforces the importance of obedience to Yhwh's word. Rhetorically, the lesson of Moses in the book draws readers to the point of choice – will they obey God's word as proclaimed in Deuteronomy, or will they disobey? In particular, the example of Moses reveals that disobedience clearly leads to death.

Conclusion

This chapter demonstrates that life in Deuteronomy derives from Yhwh. Yhwh mediates life and 'the good life' for Israel through the *tôrâ*. Israel's proper response to the God of life is to choose to obey his gracious word and experience life. Moses serves as a powerful exemplar to reinforce the point. Death comes as a result of rebellion against Yhwh and his *tôrâ*. Such rebellion culminates with a disastrous experience, namely death outside the land of Israel, which is akin to being exiled outside the (albeit symbolic) Garden of Eden. This makes the point of drawing near to Yhwh and his *tôrâ* all the more pertinent for Israel and fits within Deuteronomy's rhetorical strategy for Israel to choose life, today.

© Heath A. Thomas, 2012

---

48. As in Lev. 5:15, 21; 26:40; Josh. 22:16, 31.

49. So my interpretation proceeds differently from the view of Sailhamer, *The Meaning*, pp. 559–562.

8. DEUTERONOMY IN THE INTERMARRIAGE CRISES IN EZRA–NEHEMIAH[1]

Csilla Saysell

Although most books of the Old Testament have been scrutinized for possible Deuteronomic influence at one time or another, this is generally understood in terms of editing rather than reception. Thus it is not surprising that Ezra–Nehemiah (EN) does not feature much in these explorations, as there is little if anything to be said about Deuteronomic editing in the book.[2] However, in a different sense EN is important because it is our earliest clear example of how Deuteronomy may have been received within the Old Testament, and thus it is a significant witness to reception history. The returned exiles draw on both Deuteronomy's theology and its legal regulations, and so demonstrate how a new

---

1. The material in this chapter is based largely on my PhD dissertation, published as *'According to the Law': Reading Ezra 9 – 10 as Christian Scripture*, JTISup (Warsaw: Eisenbrauns, 2012).

2. Among a collection of essays on Deuteronomistic influence, Crenshaw's paper on the Writings only mentions a few phrases (e.g. 'your servants the prophets', 'as at this day') and concepts (e.g. ban on intermarriage, importance of divine reputation) reminiscent of Deuteronomy in the liturgical prayers of Ezra 9 and Neh. 9, and that in a mere sentence each. J. L. Crenshaw, 'The Deuteronomists and the Writings', in L. S. Shearing and S. L. McKenzie (eds.), *Those Elusive Deuteronomists: The Phenomenon of Pan-Deuteronomism*, JSOTSup (Sheffield: Sheffield Academic Press, 1999), p. 155.

generation reworks the terms of the covenant within its own context. Moreover, EN is particularly interesting because it offers more than one interpretation of the same Deuteronomic laws in answer to a recurring crisis (intermarriage) and thus testifies to an engagement with the law which builds on Deuteronomy's theology.

In order to give some background to the post-exilic reading of Deuteronomic laws, this paper will first consider why Deuteronomy was so formative for EN and how the latter understood the function of the law in the former. This then will provide the context to the care that was taken to interpret Deuteronomic laws in the intermarriage crises of Ezra 9 – 10 and Nehemiah 13:23–31.

The understanding of the law

When Ezra sets out on his mission to bring back the law to Judah, the royal decree refers to 'the law/wisdom of your God which is in your hand' (7:14, 25),[3] suggesting a written document. Elsewhere in EN it is described as 'the book of the law of Moses/God' (Neh. 8:1, 18) or similar (Ezra 6:18; Neh. 9:3; 13:1). It is difficult to identify beyond reasonable doubt what this law book was, though it is likely to have been some form of the Pentateuch before its final editing. This may be derived from interpretations of the law in EN, which make reference to what we now know as Deuteronomic and Priestly regulations as well as to material from the Holiness Code.[4] Ezra 1 – 6 also adds its continuing witness to the importance of the written Torah in the life of the post-exilic community with its repeated 'as it is written' (Ezra 3:2, 4; 6:18).

It is noteworthy that out of the law collections in the Pentateuch only the Ten Commandments, 'the book of the covenant' and Deuteronomy are said to have been written down, and of these the last is the most emphatic. Overall, the significance of the written record is similar in all three: to testify to the stipulations of the covenant between God and his people.[5] In Deuteronomy this witness is somewhat negative, anticipating disobedience, which is evidenced

---

3. Author's translations throughout this chapter.

4. For a brief summary on the identification of the book of the law and further bibliography see H. G. M. Williamson, *Ezra, Nehemiah*, WBC (Waco: Word, 1985), pp. xxxvii–xxxix.

5. The two tablets are written (Exod. 24:12), then destroyed (32:19) when the covenant is broken, and rewritten (34:27–28) after the covenant is renewed (34:10). Likewise the 'book of the covenant' is mentioned in connection with a covenant ceremony (Exod. 24:7–8).

by the long list of curses following the covenant stipulations and which far outweigh the blessings promised for obedience. Indeed, the occurrences of the written law in Deuteronomy, which come primarily in the context of the covenant making, are largely connected to the curses rather than the blessings (curses: 27:3, 8; 28:58, 61; 29:20–21, 27; blessings: 30:10). Finally, this book of the law is placed in 31:26 'beside the ark' as 'a witness against you'.

The law also functions in a covenant context in EN, most obviously in Nehemiah 10 where the exiles commit themselves to keeping the law (Neh. 10:29). Although covenant (*běrît*) is replaced here by 'agreement' ('*ămānâ*, 9:38), the usual verb for making a covenant (*krt*, 'to cut') is retained. Moreover, the expression in 10:29, 'they are entering into a curse and an oath to walk in God's law', has some resonances with Deuteronomy 29:12, which states that Israel is 'to cross over into the covenant of YHWH and into his curse/oath'. Although the wording is not identical, the idea of entering into a sphere where curses for disobedience are operative is present in both. In fact, Israel's servitude and the land benefiting another people, which the exiles bemoan (Neh. 9:36–37; cf. Ezra 9:6–7, 9), are explicitly mentioned among the curses for disobedience in Deuteronomy (28:33, 47–48).

At the same time, beyond the written law's more negative function as a standard by which Israel is judged, it has a positive role unique to Deuteronomy of instilling in Israel the fear of YHWH.[6] This is exemplified in 31:9–13, where the law book is entrusted to Israel's leadership to be read every seven years at the feast of Booths, so that 'their children, who have not known, will hear and learn to fear the LORD your God' (v. 13). Similarly, the king is to copy and read the law book all his life, 'so that he may learn to fear the LORD' (17:19). Further, the law is Israel's wisdom and understanding in the sight of other nations (4:6), and provision to sustain as much as bread does (8:3). Indeed, keeping it means life and blessing in the land (30:15–16). Moreover, this is an authoritative text which Israel is to keep in its entirety without adding or taking anything away from it (4:2; 12:32), and which may be seen as an expansion on the principles established in the Ten Commandments, and accordingly placed alongside them. These notions of an authoritative law book (whatever its exact identity) and its influence seem to be reflected in 2 Kings 22:11 and in

---

6. Elsewhere in the Pentateuch there are some scattered reminders of God's gracious deliverance in Israel's feasts (Exod. 12:26–27; 13:8–9, 14–16; Lev. 23:39–43) and other visual *aides-mémoires* such as the tassels on garments to prompt Israel to obedience (Num. 15:37–41), but nothing so explicitly connecting the fear of YHWH with the written record of the law.

2 Chronicles 17:9, demonstrating a developing trend which finds its most explicit form within the Old Testament in EN.

As in Deuteronomy, the law is a positive force in EN, as when it is equated with wisdom in Artaxerxes' decree (Ezra 7:25, cf. v. 14). Moreover, the words are placed here on the lips of a Gentile monarch and the point is surely theological, echoing the nations' recognition of Israel's law as wisdom (Deut. 4:5–8). Nehemiah 9 further underlines the positive nature of Torah, describing it as 'just ordinances, true laws and good statutes and commandments' (v. 13). In the prayer's historic reflections the giving of Torah is sandwiched between God's guidance by the pillar of cloud and fire (v. 12; cf. Exod. 13:21–22) and the provision of manna and water from the rock (v. 15; cf. Exod. 16:4, 14–15; 17:6). This clearly reverses the chronological order of events as recorded in Exodus, where the law at Sinai (Exod. 19 – 20) follows the above. This non-sequential order may highlight the nature of Torah as a gift,[7] or it may simply indicate its centrality in the prayer.[8] It also associates law with guidance on the one hand and provision on the other, and this latter link is made explicitly in Deuteronomy itself (8:3). The pattern of guidance and provision is repeated as the prayer remembers God's continuing faithfulness despite the golden calf incident (Neh. 9:19–20), but significantly, instead of the law being mentioned again, it is replaced by God's Spirit giving instruction.[9] The parallel sequence of events in verses 19–20 and 12–15 creates a link between the law-giving and the instruction of the Spirit, and is perhaps an indicator of the dynamic nature of the law, the need to understand and interpret it rightly.

Recognizing that knowledge of the covenant needs to be reinforced, not only for those present but also for their descendants, is another typical theme of Deuteronomy (29:14). Whatever the book's *Sitz im Leben* might be, the narrative logic of this is clear. Moses is speaking to a generation already one removed from the exodus. It is imperative, then, that the children do not repeat the mistakes of their parents and that knowledge of the law is perpetuated to the following generation and beyond. Thus Deuteronomy endlessly exhorts

---

7. D. J. A. Clines, *Ezra, Nehemiah, Esther*, NCB (Grand Rapids: Eerdmans; London: Marshall, Morgan & Scott, 1984), p. 194.

8. L. C. Allen and T. S. Laniak, *Ezra, Nehemiah, Esther*, NIBCOT 9 (Peabody: Hendrickson, 2003), p. 136.

9. Clines suggests that this is because the law has already been given, so it cannot be repeated, Clines, *Ezra*, p. 195. However, it would have been possible to say that God did not take away his law or the verse could have mentioned the re-giving of the two tablets of stone (Exod. 34:1, 27–28).

Israel to remember, remember, remember.[10] It insists on actively teaching the commandments to the children (6:7; 11:19) and encouraging them to 'ask your father . . . your elders' (32:7). Likewise, all under the covenant should immerse themselves in the law day and night, and have written reminders of it on head, hand and doorpost (6:8–9; 11:18–21).

In EN this theme of teaching the law is reflected in the mission of Ezra, 'a scribe skilled in the law of Moses' (Ezra 7:6),[11] an expositor of the law who set his heart to study (lit. 'to seek out', *drš*), 'practise' and 'teach' it (7:10). EN takes this Deuteronomic emphasis one step further by implying the need for interpretation. Thus the community's decision to divorce the foreign wives in Ezra 10:3 is attributed to 'the counsel of my lord' (i.e. Ezra) and those trembling at God's commandment.[12] The verse also suggests that the crisis is to be dealt with 'according to [*k*] the law', which would indicate an interpretation arising out of the law. We see this perhaps less obviously when the book of the law is read publicly at the feast of Booths (Neh. 8:2–3) and the Levites help the people 'understand' (*byn*, v. 7), going round and either 'speaking distinctly or clearly' (*prš*, Neh. 8:8; cf. Ezra 4:18) or giving a translation into Aramaic,[13] or simply giving the sense paragraph by paragraph.[14] The leaders also gather separately to study under Ezra in order 'to gain insight' (*śkl*, Neh. 8:13), and their signed agreement to obey God's laws reflects early exegetical practices.[15]

---

10. The occurrence of *zkr* in Deuteronomy calling Israel to 'remember' her past or the commandments (fourteen times: 5:15; 7:18; 8:2, 18; 9:7, 27; 15:15; 16:3, 12; 24:9, 18, 22; 25:17; 32:7) far outnumbers similar usage in the rest of Exodus to Numbers (four times: Exod. 13:3; 20:8; Num. 15:39–40).

11. The original meaning of the root *mhr* is 'quick', but together with *sōpēr*, 'scribe', it becomes a stereotypical formula referring to an expert scribe who is skilled in exposition. Williamson, *Ezra*, p. 92.

12. The pointing of the Hebrew as *'ădōnāy*, 'the Lord', instead of *'ădōnî*, 'my lord', is unlikely to be correct. Williamson, *Ezra*, p. 143, summarizes the arguments thus: (1) God does not counsel but commands (Rudolph); (2) there is no such advice in the Bible; (3) God's involvement is mentioned at the end of the verse; (4) Shecaniah consistently refers to God as 'our God'. The mistaken pointing may be due to the increasing use of Adonai for 'the Lord'.

13. E.g. Fensham, following Schaeder. F. C. Fensham, *The Books of Ezra and Nehemiah*, NICOT (Grand Rapids: Eerdmans, 1982), p. 217.

14. Williamson, *Ezra*, p. 291.

15. D. J. A. Clines, 'Nehemiah 10 as an Example of Early Jewish Biblical Exegesis', *JSOT* 21 (1981), pp. 111–117.

EN's implicit emphasis on the need for interpretation indicates the gap between the circumstances when the law was originally formulated and those of the exiles, which can only be bridged by recontextualization (as we shall see in the intermarriage crises). It may also suggest something about the already established authority of the laws brought back by Ezra, which cannot simply be rewritten to adapt them to the post-exilic situation.

The use of Deuteronomic laws

Ezra 9 – 10

While EN clearly refers to many issues covered in the Priestly material, there is an overwhelming sense in which Deuteronomy seems especially significant for the exiles and we have already seen how this may be explained. Moreover, there is much in Deuteronomy's narrative context that has particular affinities with the returned exiles' situation. Both contexts look forward to issues arising from settlement in the land; both focus on Torah and on covenant commitment to YHWH; and both are faced with local inhabitants and neighbouring nations who are seen as potential threats to such obedience. For EN, however, the question comes into sharper focus via its struggle to define who belongs to Israel and thus where the boundary lies between herself and others. The issue is particularly exemplified by the intermarriage crises in Ezra 9 – 10 and Nehemiah 13:23–30. Both accounts engage with Deuteronomy in order to find a solution, but in the two cases the argument and the result are slightly different.

Ezra 9 – 10 combines two laws from Deuteronomy to reason against inter-marriages with 'foreign women' (*nāšîm nokrîyôt*, 10:2): Deuteronomy 7, which bans intermarriage with the seven Canaanite nations, and 23:3–6, which excludes Ammonites and Moabites from the assembly of YHWH for ten generations (i.e. 'for ever', cf. v. 6). That these Deuteronomic laws are indeed the background to the exiles' argument is clear from the list of nations mentioned in Ezra 9:1, and from Ezra 9:12, which quotes from both Deuteronomy 7:3 ('You shall not give your daughter to his son, nor shall you take his daughter for your son')[16] and 23:6 ('You shall never seek their peace or their prosperity all your days').[17] The identity of these women, variously referred to as 'the peoples of the lands'

---

16. Deuteronomy uses singular verbs and imperfects, while Ezra's are plurals and jussives. The latter also replaces *lqḥ* with *nś* for 'take'.

17. Again Deuteronomy uses a singular verb in contrast to the plural in Ezra, and the former's expression 'all your days forever' is replaced by 'forever' in the latter.

(Ezra 9:1, 11) and 'the peoples of the land' (Ezra 10:2), is unclear from the story, but the use of a prohibition against local inhabitants (on the analogy of the Canaanites) and another against other foreigners skilfully covers all eventualities. Since the historic Canaanite nations no longer existed by post-exilic times, the list seems to function not as a direct reference to these specific nations but as a comparison: any nation demonstrating the same abhorrent qualities would be unacceptable.[18]

Many commentators assume that the Ezran allusion to Deuteronomy 23 also includes verses 7–8, where the descendants of Edom and Egypt are excluded as well, but only for three generations. However, allusion to these verses is somewhat doubtful considering that the list in Ezra 9:1 does not mention Edom (though the parallel account of the events in 1 Esdras 8:68 does).[19]

The key term that sums up what is wrong with intermarriages is 'abominations' (*tôʿābōt*), which in Deuteronomy 7 refers to idolatry/apostasy (vv. 25–26) as frequently in the whole book (e.g. 13:15 [14]; 17:3–4). Abominations can also refer to the closely related sin of child sacrifice (e.g. 12:31; 18:9–10), as well as to issues such as the use of unjust weights (25:16) or eating unclean food (14:3). While 23:3–6 does not mention the worship of other gods or the term 'abominations', juxtaposition of this text with Deuteronomy 7 creates an interplay between the two. Thus the idea of abominations as idolatry/apostasy in Deuteronomy 7 carries over into the exilic understanding of why Ammon and Moab are unacceptable. Conversely, the hostility to Israel condemned in Deuteronomy 23 adds nuance to the meaning of abominations. A further aspect linked to the concept is the sin of sexual immorality, although in Deuteronomy 23 this may only be inferred. The hiring of Balaam (v. 5) evokes the later incident at Baal Peor of apostasy and sexual immorality (Num. 25; cf. Num. 31:16).[20] Further, the proximity of this law to several others dealing with sexual transgressions (adultery, rape, emasculation – probably for cultic reasons; 22:13 – 23:1) may also point to an implicit connection.[21] This is further reinforced by the stigma attached to Ammon's and Moab's origins as peoples descended from the incestuous relationship between Lot and his daughters (Gen. 19:30–38).

---

18. Williamson, *Ezra*, p. 130. C. E. Hayes, 'Intermarriage and Impurity in Ancient Jewish Sources', *HTR* 92/1 (1999), p. 12 n. 25.

19. For reasons why 1 Esdras mentions Edom, see my book, *'According to the Law'*, ch. 4.

20. The medieval Jewish exegete Rashi makes this connection in particular.

21. M. Fishbane, *Biblical Interpretation in Ancient Israel* (Oxford: Clarendon, 1985), p. 119.

The element most evident in EN from this cluster of associations with 'abominations' is the hostile attitude of 'the peoples of the land(s)' (e.g. Ezra 4:4–5; Neh. 2:19; 4:1–5). Apostasy/idolatry does not appear in the story, though it is easy to see how 'abominations' may be a stereotypical formula for describing the influence of other nations leading Israel to compromise its commitment to YHWH. It may also be a coded way of condemning idolatry, which in an explicit form would have elicited disapproval from the Persian authorities.[22] Further, the hint of sexual immorality may be the first step in the later Second Temple development of equating intermarriage with harlotry (*zĕnût*).[23]

As we have already seen regarding 'abominations', Ezra 9 juxtaposes Deuteronomic laws creating an interplay between texts. Further, such a combination of texts leads to an interpretation not quite intended by any of these laws on their own. We see this for instance in the way the exiles conclude that they must divorce their foreign wives, which is a wholly new development. Deuteronomy 7:2 prescribes the utter destruction (*ḥrm*) of the seven Canaanite nations and, presumably in anticipation that Israel will disobey, forbids any intermarriage (v. 3), but says nothing about what must happen once such marriages have been contracted. Deuteronomy 23:3–6 does not mention mixed marriages at all; rather, it simply commands the exclusion of the descendants. Neither text calls for the divorce of Canaanite or foreign wives, nor does any other law in Deuteronomy or the rest of the Pentateuch.[24] Yet the exiles clearly think that they handle the matter 'according to the law' (Ezra 10:3).

One way of explaining this is to see the divorces as a metaphorical reinterpretation of *ḥērem*: no longer as utter destruction but as a form of exclusion. Horbury argues for a shift in thinking during the Second Temple period that gradually substitutes the death penalty with exclusion from the community.[25] Due to the paucity of evidence it is difficult to prove or disprove his point, but

22. H. Maccoby, 'Holiness and Purity: The Holy People in Leviticus and Ezra-Nehemiah', in J. F. A. Sawyer (ed.), *Reading Leviticus: A Conversation with Mary Douglas* (Sheffield: Sheffield Academic Press, 1996), pp. 165–166.

23. C. Werman, '"Jubilees 30": Building a Paradigm for the Ban on Intermarriage', *HTR* 90/1 (1997), p. 14.

24. Williamson, *Ezra*, p. 151, tentatively suggests the divorce law in Deut. 24:1–4 as a possible background, but Ezra 9 – 10 makes no reference to any of the regulation's key words (*'erwat dābār*, 'naked matter, indecency'; *šlḥ*, 'to send'; *sēper kĕrîtut*, 'bill of divorce') and there is no explanation as to how the foreign women would fit the enigmatic 'indecency' as a criterion for divorce.

25. W. Horbury, 'Extirpation and Excommunication', *VT* 35/1 (1985), pp. 13–38.

if he is right then the events in Ezra 9 – 10 are not an isolated phenomenon but one of the earliest examples of a larger development. Another influence on the exiles' thinking may be the exclusion in Deuteronomy 23:3–6, which they apply to the wives as well.

A further influence of Deuteronomy is revealed in Ezra 10:2–3. When God's people took foreign wives they 'caused them to dwell' (*yšb*), while their divorce will 'cause them to go out' (*yṣ'*). Although these two verbs are fairly common in the Old Testament, in Deuteronomy it is YHWH who allocates lands to various people including Israel (2:5, 9, 19, 24, 31) and the latter's tenancy of the land is contingent on their obedience (4:40; 30:17–20; 32:47; cf. Ezra 9:12). Thus the marriages in Ezra may be seen as giving legitimacy to foreign people to live on the land and their sending away is an expression that they have no claim on it.

In the one instance where the verb *ḥrm* occurs (Ezra 10:8), it is used in the sense of confiscating the moveable property (*rĕkûš*) of Israelites who refuse to comply with the community's decision on divorce and who are also excluded. 1 Esdras 9:4 and Josephus (*Antiquities* 11.148) explain that such property is put in the temple treasury. While Deuteronomy 7 is the passage most commonly associated with *ḥērem*, 13:12–18 provides an Israelite parallel for the treatment of Canaanite nations. The Israelite city enticed into the worship of other gods is to be utterly destroyed (*ḥrm*), including people, livestock and other possessions. Verse 16 particularly warns against keeping any of the spoil; instead the city is treated as 'a whole burnt offering [*kālîl*] to YHWH', in contrast to Deuteronomy 7, where possessions are not mentioned apart from the destruction of idols (vv. 5, 25–26). Thus the twofold destruction of human life and of property as a whole burnt offering (Deut. 13) is transformed into the exclusion of the unrepentant and the confiscation of their property in the Ezran interpretation. The principle behind the treatment of Israelites worshipping foreign gods is also in line with 7:25–26, which sees the Israelite taking an idol into his house as one becoming *ḥērem* himself. Thus the refusal by some to deal with inter-marriages as the community sees fit leads to identifying the non-compliants with the purported abominations and treating them accordingly.

More than simply the fear of idolatry/apostasy, the exiles' reasoning includes the argument that 'the holy seed has intermingled with the peoples of the lands' (Ezra 9:2). The idea of all Israel as a 'holy people' is very likely derived from Deuteronomy 7:6, but the replacement of 'people' with 'seed' emphasizes physical descent. Although there is no obvious legal source for this develop-ment, arguably the *kil'ayîm* ('two kinds') laws in Deuteronomy 22:9–11 and Leviticus 19:19 provide the closest analogy. While these were originally agri-cultural regulations, one can see how they could be interpreted metaphorically to refer to intermarriages. These clusters of laws include sowing with mixed seeds in both, interbreeding of animals in Leviticus 19:19, and ploughing with two kinds of animals in Deuteronomy 22:10 (sometimes taken as a euphemism for sexual intercourse). Further, Deuteronomy's specification of seed among the vines, rather than simply two kinds of seed, may bring to mind the association of Israel as the vine or vineyard. Although Ezra 9 – 10 does not mention Israel as a vineyard, Ezra's prayer speaks of a protective 'fence' (*gādēr*, 9:9) around Judah and Jerusalem.[26] The word is most commonly used as a hedge or fence around a vineyard (Num. 22:24; Ps. 80:13 [12], cf. v. 9 [8]; Isa. 5:5) and thus 9:9 may be an allusion to this idea. There is a later example of using the *kil'ayîm* laws to ban intermarriage in the Qumran sectarian text 4QMMT (B75–82), and perhaps Ezra provides the first stepping stone in this development.

Thus Ezra 9 – 10 exploits the inherent possibilities in the Deuteronomic laws, though it goes beyond them to recontextualize the issues in its own post-exilic setting.

Nehemiah 13:23–31

In comparison, the intermarriage crisis in Nehemiah 13:23–31 uses Deuteronomic laws in a more straightforward way. The chapter quotes Deuteronomy 7:3 (v. 25) and lists intermarriages with Ammon and Moab (v. 23). Commentators generally agree that the inclusion of these two is probably a later interpolation whose purpose is to evoke the command in Deuteronomy 23:3–6.[27] Solomon's intermarriages are also mentioned as a deterrent (v. 26, alluding to 1 Kgs 11:1–8).

The main difference between the solutions of Ezra and Nehemiah is that the latter does not call specifically for the divorce of the wives; he merely extracts an oath from all the men. The content of the oath seems to be a recommitment not to intermarry (v. 25; cf. Neh. 10:31 [30]) rather than to send the wives and children away (cf. Ezra 10:3, 5). The laymen are also cursed (v. 25), one person from the high-priestly family is banished (v. 28) and a general imprecation is called down on the priests (v. 29), all of which suggest that these marriages could not be undone. Nehemiah's behaviour has often been interpreted as a temper tantrum, but it may have been a symbolic action to communicate the

26. Several English translations are misleading, using 'wall' here which evokes the Jerusalem city wall, but the usual word for the latter is *ḥômâ* (cf. Neh. 1:3; 3:33 [4:1], etc.).

27. E.g. Williamson, *Ezra*, p. 397; J. Blenkinsopp, *Ezra-Nehemiah: A Commentary* (London: SCM, 1988), p. 362; L. W. Batten, *A Critical and Exegetical Commentary on the Books of Ezra and Nehemiah*, ICC (Edinburgh: T&T Clark, 1913), p. 299.

Deuteronomic principle that God's judgment will come on those who have broken the terms of the covenant (Deut. 27:15–26; 28:15–68). As noted earlier, the commitment of the exiles in Nehemiah 10:29 to 'enter into' (*bw' b*) [the sphere of] a curse and an oath resonates with Deuteronomy 29:12, and it may give further support to the above interpretation.

Nehemiah 13:23–31 does not mention 'abominations' or the holiness of Israel either in a Deuteronomic sense (Deut. 7:6) or in the Ezran meaning of 'the holy seed'. Nehemiah 13:23 is primarily concerned about the descendants of mixed marriages losing their ability to speak Hebrew, which may be a cause for anxiety because it bars access to understanding Torah. Similarly, the quotation of Deuteronomy 7:3 and the example of Solomon may suggest a fear of idolatry/apostasy. It is possible that Solomon's sin is interpreted differently from the above in Nehemiah 13 (see e.g. Sirach 47:20, which sees Solomon's sin in terms of defilement of the family line). However, the overall tenor of Nehemiah 13 suggests a more straightforward Deuteronomic way of thinking despite the use of some non-Deuteronomic purity language.[28]

Conclusion

EN is clearly indebted to Deuteronomy for its understanding of the importance of the written law, not only as a witness to the covenant but as the source for instilling the fear of YHWH in his followers through teaching and remembering. EN, however, goes beyond Deuteronomy, recognizing the need to bridge the gap between the book's laws and the post-exilic context through interpretation. The interpretative moves especially in Ezra 9 – 10 seem to foreshadow later rabbinic techniques, particularly the way individual laws are used in conjunction with each other to provide answers to questions not envisaged by the original commandments. Both Ezra 9 – 10 and Nehemiah 13:23–31 show a more rigid thinking than Deuteronomy, clearly marking out the boundaries between 'us' and 'them'. It has no room for such categories as the *gēr* ('alien') and no explicit option for foreigners to be integrated into the community of Israel if they are willing to abandon 'abominable' ways. While Deuteronomy does not offer conversion either, its categories allow for this. Further, Ezra in particular defines Israel in ethnic terms and its understanding of the threat that foreigners pose goes beyond the apostasy/idolatry model suggested by

---

28. For issues of purity language in Neh. 13, see my book *'According to the Law'*, ch. 7.

Deuteronomy 7. Fusing 'abominations' with purity language, Ezra's solution is an object lesson of how the best intentions may in the end be counter-productive and fail to deliver the desired effect, as well as have adverse long-term consequences. In other words, by its very rigidity the Ezran interpretation can only reject but not protect the children of intermarriages from apostasy and its unequivocal identification of foreignness with abominations forecloses a more nuanced way of thinking regarding the connection between the two. Thus it keeps Israelites in a position of weakness by not allowing the process of healthy discernment to develop. Further, the truncated ending of Ezra 10:44 leaves open the question whether the proposed expulsion of the women took place at all (cf. 1 Esdras 9:36). Could this be an indication of a certain ambivalence or a hint of the practical difficulties in carrying out such a plan? While Nehemiah seems to be closer to Deuteronomic thought, it too can only lament the *fait accompli*, without providing a viable solution that could ensure long-term obedience.

Using Deuteronomic laws, EN incorporates into its story more than one answer to the question of how intermarriages are to be handled, without giving a final verdict. Thus its open-ended conclusion on the issue provides an implicit witness to the need for further reflection and interpretation that goes one step further than Deuteronomy's insistence to read, write and remember the law in order to fear the Lord, because of the continued need to recontextualize Deuteronomy's message.

9. THE PARATEXT OF DEUTERONOMY

Greg Goswell

There is a new interest in and respect for the insights of ancient readers of the Bible, whether Jewish (e.g. Rashi) or Christian (e.g. the Church Fathers). Part of the history of the interpretation of the biblical text that would otherwise be hidden from our view is preserved in its paratextual features. Like any other literary work, the book of Deuteronomy is made up of text and paratext. The term 'paratext' refers to elements that are adjoined to the text but are not part of it. The paratext of the Bible includes features such as the order of the biblical books, the names assigned to the books and the differing schemes of textual division within the books. This is what C. D. Ginsburg called 'The Outer Form of the Text', as opposed to 'The Text Itself', though he did not deal with the question of the titles assigned to the biblical books.[1] This study proceeds on the assumption that text and paratext, though conceptually differentiated, are for all practical purposes inseparable so that their interaction influences the reading of a text.[2]

---

1. C. D. Ginsburg, *Introduction to the Massoretico-Critical Edition of the Hebrew Bible* (London: Trinitarian Bible Society, 1897; New York: Ktav, 1966), pp. 1, 144.
2. For comments on the differentiation that I make, see Hendrik J. Koorevaar, 'The Torah Model as Original Macrostructure of the Hebrew Canon: A Critical Evaluation', *ZAW* 122.1 (2010), pp. 64–80 (64–66).

The modern readers I have in mind in this discussion are the biblical scholar (and scholar-in-training, the theological student), the well-read lay person who has access to non-technical commentaries and other aids, and 'the common reader'[3] who consults the Bible alone in private reading or whose knowledge of it comes from listening to it read and expounded in church services. It is only too easy for those who read (and even critically evaluate) texts to overlook the influence of the paratext on the reading process. Kevin Jackson bemoans the fact that paratextual elements are often unacknowledged and unexamined by scholars and non-scholarly readers alike, calling these elements 'invisible forms'.[4] My aim is to give the paratext of Deuteronomy greater visibility and to provide evaluative tools that can be used when interacting with the paratext of Scripture.

The placement of Deuteronomy

Where a particular book is placed relative to the other books that make up the Bible may influence a reader's view of the book, providing as it does hints of what the book may be about.[5] This paratextual feature is usually overlooked by the lay reader, and it is only quite recently that commentaries have begun to note the possible hermeneutical significance of canonical order.[6] There are a number of possible principles of order inferred by the reader, e.g. common genre, book size, similar theme, storyline thread.[7] It is storyline thread that determines the order of the books in the Pentateuch and the Former Prophets of the Hebrew canon (Joshua–Kings). The same principle is at work in the continuation of the narrative in the Histories section of the Greek canon (adding Chronicles, Ezra, Nehemiah, Esther). In the case of the Pentateuch,

---

3. Term derived from Dr Johnson's *Life of Gray* and used by Virginia Woolf, *The Common Reader* (London: Hogarth Press, 1925).

4. Kevin Jackson, *Invisible Forms: A Guide to Literary Curiosities* (New York: Thomas Dunne Books, 1999).

5. John H. Sailhamer calls this feature 'con-textuality', see *The Meaning of the Pentateuch: Revelation, Composition and Interpretation* (Downers Grove: InterVarsity Press, 2009), p. 216.

6. E.g. the brief discussion of the canonical placement of Song of Songs in Tremper Longman III, *Song of Songs*, NICOT (Grand Rapids: Eerdmans, 2001), p. 2.

7. For more detail, see G. R. Goswell, 'The Order of the Books in the Hebrew Bible', *JETS* 51.4 (2008), pp. 673–688.

the five books could hardly be put in any other order, despite the aberrant list of Melito, bishop of Sardis (died c. AD 190), who interchanged Numbers and Leviticus.[8] This sequence may be accidental: Leviticus is set at Mount Sinai (25:1; 26:46; 27:34), so its contents must *precede* the record of the Israelites' departure from Sinai in Numbers. Certainly, Deuteronomy is always placed in fifth and final position in listings of Pentateuchal books.

At this point my focus is on the placement of Deuteronomy within the library of scriptural books.[9] I will give consideration to its immediate location between neighbouring books (Numbers, Joshua) and its location at the juncture of two major canonical blocks, as the final book of the Pentateuch and abutting the Prophets (Hebrew canon) or Historical Books (Greek canon). Readers often presume that a book is more closely related to books next to it or nearby, and less closely related to books placed far from it.

Part of a 'Pentateuch'

Some scholars explain the division of the Pentateuch into five sections as due simply to the need to limit the length of scrolls in antiquity, for ease of handling. The Jewish name for the Pentateuch is *Chumash* (e.g. *Meg.* III, 74a), which recalls its five-book structure. The Hebrew word *Chomesh* ('a fifth') can refer to one of the five books of Moses (or one of the five books of Psalms). So, for example, the book of Exodus is called 'the second fifth' (*Sot.* 36b). Moshe Greenberg suggests that this is a largely arbitrary division, demonstrated by the fact that the whole is sometimes called 'the five fifths of the Torah',[10] which is equivalent to the Greek *hē pentateuchos* (*biblos*) ('five roll [book]'). Our designation 'Pentateuch' is derived through the Latinized form *pentateuchus* (*liber*). The average Bible reader is probably aware of this five-book grouping, but may not have thought in detail about how the five books might be connected or interact. It is claimed by some scholars that there are 'no natural divisions' between Exodus, Leviticus and Numbers, and that only Genesis and Deuteronomy 'have clearly distinct characters of their

---

8. Eusebius, *Historia ecclesiastica*, 4.26.13–14.

9. Pierre Bayard uses the term 'location', see *How to Talk About Books You Haven't Read*, trans. Jeffrey Mehlman (London: Granta Books, 2007), p. 11: 'what counts in a book is the books alongside it', namely how a book is situated relative to other books, and he makes use of the analogy of a library.

10. Moshe Greenberg, *Introduction to Hebrew* (Englewood Cliffs: Prentice-Hall, 1965), p. 175; see the Hebrew Bible edited by Norman H. Snaith (London: The British and Foreign Bible Society, 1958).

own'.[11] This view can be questioned, however, and Rolf Rendtorff is one who insists that each of the five individual books has a distinctive character, and that the division between them is by no means arbitrary.[12] Genesis is structured by means of a repeated genealogical formula (2:4; 6:9; 11:27, etc.), which ties the various parts into a unity. It is true that Leviticus continues the same historical setting (Sinai) as Exodus, but from Leviticus 1:1 onwards, the Lord speaks to Moses from the Tent of Meeting, and no longer from the top of the mountain.[13] Leviticus closes with a summary (27:34). Numbers describes the Israelites' departure from Sinai and the book begins with a precise date formula (1:1) and concludes with a summary (36:13). The hortatory or sermonic character of Deuteronomy (speeches by Moses to the people) differentiates it from what precedes. Placing the first five books under the title of *Chumash* or Pentateuch draws the reader's attention to the five-book structure of this canonical grouping and seems to assert their essential relationship one to the other. This suggests that neither the individuality of the books nor their inter-relationship is to be ignored or compromised in a reading of the Pentateuch.

Under the title 'Torah'

The word 'law' (the usual English rendering of *tôrâ*) has a legalistic ring that is not present in the Hebrew word, whose meaning is closer to 'instruction'.[14] In line with this, in the New Testament 'law' (Greek, *nomos*) can be used as a synecdoche to mean Scripture as a whole with no legalist nuance (see John 10:34; 12:34; 15:25; Rom. 3:19; 1 Cor. 14:21, where non-Pentateuchal texts are dubbed 'law'). Consequently, the name 'Torah' applied to the Pentateuch does not imply

---

11. R. Norman Whybray, *Introduction to the Pentateuch* (Grand Rapids: Eerdmans, 1995), p. 63; see R. Rendtorff, 'Is it Possible to Read Leviticus as a Separate Book?', in John F. A. Sawyer (ed.), *Reading Leviticus: A Conversation with Mary Douglas*, JSOTSup 227 (Sheffield: Sheffield Academic Press, 1996), pp. 22–35.

12. R. Rendtorff, *The Old Testament: An Introduction*, trans. John Bowden (London: SCM, 1985), p. 131.

13. As noted by Jean-Louis Ska, *Introduction to Reading the Pentateuch* (Winona Lake: Eisenbrauns, 2006), p. 18.

14. Barnabas Lindars, 'Torah in Deuteronomy', in P. R. Ackroyd and B. Lindars (eds.), *Words and Meanings: Essays Presented to David Winton Thomas on his Retirement from the Regius Professorship of Hebrew in the University of Cambridge, 1968* (Cambridge: Cambridge University Press, 1968), pp. 117–136. He emphasizes the didactic character of the word 'Torah'.

that Genesis–Deuteronomy contains nothing but legislation for the nation of Israel, though it does highlight the Sinaitic didactic portions that are given a central position in the corpus (e.g. Exod. 20 – 23; Leviticus; Num. 1 – 9).

The book of Deuteronomy introduces its contents as *tôrâ* (1:5, *hattôrâ hazzo't*, 'this instruction'), and the description is broad enough to encompass the hortatory character of the recorded speeches of Moses. In the next book, the word is used in expressions referring to Deuteronomy itself (Josh. 1:8, 'this book of instruction'; reminiscent of Deut. 28:61; 29:20; 30:10; 31:26), and Moses' successor Joshua is depicted as possessing this book (Josh. 8:31, 34; 23:6; 24:26).[15] The term 'Torah' used here in relation to Deuteronomy was later reapplied to the Pentateuch as a whole (e.g. Zech. 7:12; *Prologue to Sirach*; Josephus, *Against Apion* 1:38–41; Matt. 5:17; Luke 24:44; John 1:45; Acts 13:15). This suggests that all five books (not just the fifth) came to be viewed as instructional material for future generations as well.[16] So Deuteronomy is a good example of how earlier events in Israel's history are to be homiletically applied to later generations.

What precedes and follows

Deuteronomy is set off sharply from the preceding books by its style, being a series of speeches or sermons by Moses to Israel. Dennis T. Olson proposes that the previous book Numbers has a bipartite structure, with a shift of focus from the old generation who experienced the exodus and Sinai (chs. 1 – 25) to the new generation forty years later (chs. 26 – 36), with each section beginning with a census report.[17] Whether Olson's structure is accepted or not, his basic point about the contrast between the two generations holds good. There is an implied ethic based on the disobedience of the old generation and the obedience of the new: do not be like the first generation; follow the example of the second! Deuteronomy (following Numbers) picks this up and makes substantial homiletical use of the idea of successive generations in preparation for Israel's entry into the Promised Land. The failure of the first generation to enter the land

---

15. G. J. Venema, *Reading Scripture in the Old Testament: Deuteronomy 9 – 10; 31; 2 Kings 22 – 23; Jeremiah 36; Nehemiah 8*, OTS 48 (Leiden: Brill, 2004), pp. 193–195.

16. Cf. Brevard Childs, *Old Testament Theology in a Canonical Context* (Philadelphia: Fortress Press, 1985), p. 116.

17. D. T. Olson, *The Death of the Old and the Birth of the New: The Framework of the Book of Numbers and the Pentateuch*, BJS 71 (Chico: Scholars Press, 1985); see also Rolf P. Knierim, *The Task of Old Testament Theology: Substance, Method, and Cases* (Grand Rapids: Eerdmans, 1995), pp. 380–388.

(Num. 13 – 14) is referred to in the historical retrospective provided by Moses and in effect becomes a thinly veiled lesson about the need for the second generation to be obedient (Deut. 1:19–46). Likewise, the victories over Sihon and Og (Num. 21) are recalled by Moses (Deut. 2:31 – 3:21), as is the encouragement given at the time to the people and Joshua about what God is able to do against the Canaanite kingdoms they will face (Deut. 3:18–22).

In its position at the close of the Torah, Deuteronomy shows the continuing relevance of the experiences of the first Israelite generation at Sinai and in the wilderness to all future generations (e.g. 5:2–3: 'The LORD our God made a covenant . . . with us . . . all of us here alive this day').[18] Moses addresses the second generation of Israelites as if they were the first generation and had seen what their fathers saw at Horeb some forty years earlier. Similarly in 29:14–15, future generations are thought of as participants in the covenant on an equal footing with the generation addressed by Moses: 'Nor is it with you only that I make this sworn covenant, but with him who is not here with us this day.'

Looking in the other direction, the strategic positioning of Deuteronomy suggests that it is the link or bridge between the Pentateuch and the rest of the Old Testament.[19] Its pervasive influence is not due to its canonical positioning, but is largely the result of the theologically foundational nature of its contents. However, its placement does prompt the reader to look for its wider connections (without necessarily falling into the trap of Pan-Deuteronomism, of which R. R. Wilson is right to warn the unwary).[20] The connection is not simply with the book of Joshua,[21] nor even with the corpus Joshua–Kings (cf. the Deuteronomistic History),[22] but also, for example, with the prophecies of Jeremiah,

---

18. Unless identified otherwise, Scripture quotations in this chapter are from the RSV.

19. Duane L. Christensen, *Deuteronomy 1:1 – 21:9 Revised*, WBC 6A (Nashville: Thomas Nelson, 2001), pp. lxxxix–xcii, though Christensen's particular understanding of the role of Deuteronomy in the canonical process is highly speculative.

20. See the various essays contained in Linda S. Schearing and Steven L. McKenzie (eds.), *Those Elusive Deuteronomists: The Phenomenon of Pan-Deuteronomism*, JSOTSup 268 (Sheffield: Sheffield Academic Press, 1999), especially the essay by R. R. Wilson, 'Who Was the Deuteronomist? (Who Was Not the Deuteronomist?) Reflections on Pan-Deuteronomism', pp. 67–82.

21. Gordon J. Wenham, 'The Deuteronomic Theology of the Book of Joshua', *JBL* 90 (1971), pp. 140–148; J. Gordon McConville and Stephen N. Williams, *Joshua*, The Two Horizons Old Testament Commentary (Grand Rapids: Eerdmans, 2010), pp. 179–183.

22. M. Noth, *The Deuteronomistic History*, ET, JSOTSup 15 (Sheffield: JSOT Press, 1981).

Hosea and Malachi.[23] The depiction of the conquest in the book of Joshua picks up certain themes in Deuteronomy, such as the land, the religious danger posed by Canaanite culture, instructions on warfare, and tribal unity. The later history of the turbulent relationship between kings and prophets recounted in Samuel–Kings builds extensively on the brief passages in Deuteronomy that deal with the offices of king (17:14–20) and prophet (18:15–22), but other factors are also clearly at work, for there is no hint in Deuteronomy that the incumbents in these two offices will clash. It is no surprise that themes and modes of expression in the speeches of Moses are reused by later prophets, for Moses is the Deuteronomic paradigm of the prophetic office (18:15, 18). Many links can also be found between Deuteronomy and the wisdom thinking exemplified in Proverbs.[24] My fundamental point is that the final position of Deuteronomy within the Pentateuch suggests a way of reading the Pentateuch as a whole (as lessons for future generations) and also gives permission for the search for and discovery of various kinds of inner-biblical interconnections.

The name(s) of Deuteronomy

The titles assigned to the different books of Scripture are another element of the biblical paratext. Whether we realize it or not, a title influences our reading of a text and reflects the evaluation of earlier readers. The assigned title can exercise an influence on a book's reception and is also a window through which to glimpse an earlier stage of its reception history. Lack of close attention means that by default biblical titles are often treated as nothing more than identifying tags for referring to a given portion of Scripture.[25] This is certainly the case for the common reader. Most scholarly readers are aware of the alternative titles

---

23. Henri Cazelles, 'Jeremiah and Deuteronomy', in Leo G. Perdue and Brian W. Kovacs (eds.), *A Prophet to the Nations: Essays in Jeremiah Studies* (Winona Lake: Eisenbrauns, 1984), pp. 89–111; and in the same volume, J. Phillip Hyatt, 'Jeremiah and Deuteronomy', pp. 113–127; Hans W. Wolff, *Hosea: A Commentary on the Book of Hosea*, trans. Gary Stansell, Hermeneia (Philadelphia: Fortress, 1974), p. xxxi. Malachi's Deuteronomic theology provides the prophetic platform for the Ezra–Nehemiah reforms that were soon to occur, William J. Dumbrell, 'Malachi and the Ezra-Nehemiah Reforms', *RTR* 35 (1976), pp. 42–52.

24. Moshe Weinfeld, *Deuteronomy and the Deuteronomic School* (Winona Lake: Eisenbrauns, 1992).

25. Jackson, *Invisible Forms*, see ch. 1 on titles.

(Hebrew and Greek) assigned to the book of Deuteronomy, but this does not always impact interpretation (or not in the right way). The following discussion will give some appropriate tools for interpreting titles.

Gérard Genette provides a useful list of possible functions of any book title.[26] One function is to identify or differentiate a work, another to indicate its general contents, a third to highlight it to the public, and a fourth to indicate its form or genre. The first function of a title, unavoidable in practice, is to differentiate one literary work from others. An arbitrary title would fulfil this identifying function. But no biblical book was assigned an arbitrary title, even though some titles (e.g. Deuteronomy, Ecclesiastes) mean nothing to most modern readers, who use them as mere labels. A second function (as differentiated by Genette) is to indicate a book's contents or theme. Since no title can say everything about the subject of a text, titles inevitably simplify and are highly selective. The Greek title *Deuteronomion*, if understood to mean 'Second Law' or, better, 'Repetition/Copy of the Law', is a second function title. A third function is to recommend a literary work to a potential readership. The only biblical title to do this is 'Song of Songs' (i.e. 'The Greatest Song'). The fourth function (a specialization of the second) is to classify a book according to its form or genre. Generic titles were common in the ancient world, and titles like Chronicles, Proverbs and Lamentations fit this category.[27]

The title of a literary work is not necessarily applied by the author of the text, and in the case of the biblical books it is widely accepted that titles were not supplied by the authors. This is undoubtedly the case with regard to Deuteronomy. A biblical book title, therefore, is a post-authorial comment on the book to which it is affixed.

The Hebrew title

Following ANE custom,[28] the Hebrew titles of the first five books of the Bible are incipits (openings) consisting of the first significant words of the books

---

26. Gérard Genette, 'Structure and Functions of the Title in Literature', *Critical Inquiry* 14 (1988), pp. 692–720; idem, *Paratexts: Thresholds of Interpretation*, trans. Jane E. Lewin (Cambridge: Cambridge University Press, 1997), pp. 76–94.

27. For a fuller discussion of the application of these categories to biblical books, see G. R. Goswell, 'What's in a Name? Book Titles in the Torah and Former Prophets', *Pacifica* 20.3 (2007), pp. 262–277.

28. See W. G. Lambert and A. R. Millard, *Atra-hasis: The Babylonian Story of the Flood* (Oxford: Clarendon, 1969), pp. 32, 42, 43, in which colophons refer to tablets by their first line of text.

themselves. The use of opening words for a title does not necessarily mean that it is only a label, for an initial sentence might be aimed at orientating a reader and guiding the reading of a document. Evidence for this is the first Pentateuchal book, whose Hebrew name is *běrēšît* ('In the beginning'), the first word of the book (Gen. 1:1). As a book of 'beginnings' it is appropriately named, for it describes a series of origins: of the earth, of humanity, and of Israel (in the persons of its patriarchal forebears); so the title designates the general theme of the book. Exodus is named (*wě'ēllê*) *šěmôt* ('[Now these are] the names'), a reference to the names of the twelve sons of Jacob. These twelve names are not particularly used in the book, though it is here that the twelve-tribal nation of Israel is produced (Exod. 1:7) and the family of Jacob becomes 'the people of Israel' (1:9).[29] The rest of the Old Testament is the story of this nation. Likewise, Numbers is given the Hebrew title *běmidbar* ('in the wilderness'), the opening words being, 'The LORD spoke to Moses *in the wilderness* of Sinai' (Num. 1:1). This title serves to foreground the years of testing in the wilderness (even if not at Sinai) which occupy the central section of the book (chs. 11 – 21). It is these chapters that give the book its separate identity compared to the books on either side of it, for Numbers 1 – 10 share the same location as Exodus 19 – 40, and Numbers 22 – 36 are situated in the plains of Moab just as is Deuteronomy.

Deuteronomy is given the Hebrew title *děbārîm* ('words'), which is appropriate given the fact that the book consists almost entirely of speeches by Moses. Peter Craigie draws attention to the importance of the Hebrew title as a self-description of the book as 'a report of words which were spoken'.[30] So this title also serves to highlight the form in which divine revelation comes, namely as speeches by Moses to the people of Israel. In recent study of Deuteronomy, sometimes other models (e.g. the treaty analogy) have drawn attention away from the book's sermonic character.[31] Although Deuteronomy has affinities with ANE treaty texts, it is not the text of a covenantal treaty as such.[32]

---

29. This is the first application of the word 'people' (*'am*) to Israel in the Old Testament.

30. P. Craigie, *The Book of Deuteronomy*, NICOT (London: Hodder & Stoughton, 1976), pp. 17, 18.

31. E.g. Meredith G. Kline, *The Treaty of the Great King* (Grand Rapids: Eerdmans, 1963); Weinfeld, *Deuteronomy and the Deuteronomic School*, pp. 65–69.

32. The matter is more fully explored by Dennis J. McCarthy, *Treaty and Covenant: A Study in Form in the Ancient Oriental Documents and in the Old Testament*, Analecta Biblica 21 (Rome: Biblical Institute Press, 1963), who notes what he views as the rhetorical expansion of earlier covenantal elements. The treaty form has been nuanced in

The treaty model does not explain all the aspects of the book and indeed it may obscure some important features. The Hebrew title alerts us to the fact that in terms of actual content, Deuteronomy is mostly a series of four addresses (1:6 – 4:40; 5:1 – 26:19; 27:1 – 28:68; 29:1 – 30:20),[33] the first providing an historical review, the second expounding God's law, the third stressing the divine sanctions for disobedience, and the fourth peering into the future. The Hebrew title encourages such an understanding of the book, though reference to the Hebrew title is seldom if ever used to bolster arguments for it.

The Greek title

The title found in the Greek canonical tradition, *Deuteronomion* (so Vaticanus, Alexandrinus) is usually explained as referring to the 'Second Law', that is, the book is viewed as a repetition of the law in this second function title. The Hebrew expression *mišnēh hattôrâ hazzō't* in Deuteronomy 17:18 means 'a copy of this law', whereas the LXX rendering *to deuteronomion touto* is usually understood as meaning 'this second law'. There is no explicit or even implicit reference in the Hebrew text of Deuteronomy to an earlier body of instructional material (as preserved in Exodus and/or Leviticus). It is commonly stated that, for the LXX translation to be likely, the Hebrew demonstrative adjective *hazzeh* (masculine singular) would be needed instead of *hazzō't* (feminine singular). Therefore in both popular and scholarly commentaries on the book, the LXX title is often said to be a mistake and treated as irrelevant for interpretation. On the other hand, a comparison can be made with the expression in LXX Joshua 9:2c, *to deuteronomion, nomon Mōusē* (= Hebrew Josh. 8:32, *mišnēh tôrat mošeh*). This Greek text can be translated, '(Joshua wrote upon the stones) a copy of the law [or, a Deuteronomy], even the law of Moses.'[34] This text raises the possibility that the

---

personal ways, see J. G. Janzen, 'The Yoke That Gives Rest', *Int* 41 (1987), pp. 262–266; Kenneth A. Kitchen, 'The Fall and Rise of Covenant, Law and Treaty', *TynB* 40 (1989), pp. 118–135 (130).

33. Other scholars would divide the material on the basis of what they perceive as four major superscriptions at 1:1–5; 4:44–49; 29:1 (Heb. 28:69) and 33:1; e.g. Ska, *Introduction*, p. 39; Richard D. Nelson, *Deuteronomy: A Commentary*, OTL (Louisville: Westminster John Knox, 2002), p. 72.

34. The English translation provided by Sir Lancelot Charles Lee Brenton, *The Septuagint Version of the Old Testament with an English Translation* (London: Bagster and Sons, 1851), p. 290; cf. *NETS*, 'And Iesous wrote on the stones Deuteronomion [margin: i.e. *Deuteronomy*], a law of Moyses.'

LXX Deuteronomy 17:18 in fact refers to a duplicate copy, as does the Hebrew text, and further that the book was already called Deuteronomy when the Septuagint was produced.

The Latinized form of this Pentateuchal title has come into English through the Vulgate (*Deuteronomium*). Whether or not the Greek title is a mistranslation of Deuteronomy 17:18, the paratextual feature has affected how scholarly readers have approached the book. Its common interpretation, as a second body of laws different and distinct from those given at Sinai, reflects the hermeneutical problem of the relation between the laws as expounded in Deuteronomy and earlier forms promulgated at Sinai. This has been a preoccupation of both traditional Jewish exegesis and modern critical analysis. The former approach is harmonistic, while the latter tends to exploit differences.[35] In his comments on Leviticus 25:1 and Numbers 29:12, Rashi refers to Deuteronomy under the rabbinic name 'The Repetition of the Torah' (*mišnēh tôrâ*; *Meg.* 31b). The Hebrew equivalent of *Deuteronomion* is found in the Qumran Cave 4 Catena, where the work is called 'the Book of the Second Law'.[36] In correlation with this, *Jubilees* 6:22 speaks of 'the Book of the First Law' (presumably Exodus or Leviticus) as containing the law of Pentecost. The preoccupation of both rabbinic harmonization and critical analysis with comparing Deuteronomy and the Sinaitic legislation has sometimes failed to provide a positive theological exposition of Deuteronomy. More recent commentaries signal a new and more fruitful approach.[37]

The names of four of the first five books in the Greek Old Testament are allusions to specific passages from the respective books (the exception is Leviticus). For example, the LXX title of the second book (*Exodos*) refers to 'The Going Out [from Egypt]' and is a second function title. It summarizes the material up to and including chapter 18. It alludes to LXX 19:1, where the word appears (*tēs exodou*) when the Israelites arrive at Mount Sinai, the immediate goal of the deliverance (cf. Exod. 3:12). Exodus 19:4 could be read as a poetic summarizing of the events in the preceding eighteen chapters. This provides a credible division of the book into two halves (chs. 1 – 18, 19 – 40). Likewise,

---

35. See the discussion of S. R. Driver, *A Critical and Exegetical Commentary on Deuteronomy*, ICC (Edinburgh: T&T Clark, 1896), pp. iii–xix.

36. John M. Allegro, *Qumrân Cave 4.1 (4Q158 – 4Q186)*, DJD V (Oxford: Clarendon, 1968), p. 68.

37. E.g. Patrick D. Miller, *Deuteronomy* (Louisville: Westminster John Knox, 1990); and J. Gordon McConville, *Deuteronomy*, AOTC (Leicester: Apollos; Downers Grove: InterVarsity Press, 2002).

the LXX title of the fourth Pentateuchal book, *arithmoi*, or 'Numbers [of the census of Israel]', highlights the census lists of the two generations (chs. 1, 26) that are seen by Olson as the key to the book's organizational structure.[38] So the Septuagintal title of this book again provides an exegetical insight to assist the reader. The same applies to Deuteronomy.

In Deuteronomy 17, the first priority of the king is to write a duplicate of the standard copy of the law that is in the charge of the levitical priests. The LXX title of Deuteronomy highlights the instructions about the king as a key passage for the proper interpretation of this biblical book.[39] The king in Deuteronomy 17 is portrayed as a model Israelite,[40] so this is an appropriate passage for the Greek title to highlight as a guide to readers. In line with the Talmud (*Sanhedrin* 21b), Rashi in his commentary on Deuteronomy understands the Hebrew expression in 17:18 to mean there were 'two torah scrolls' (*šĕtê siprê tôrâ*), one to be placed in the king's treasure house and one to have with him. The king sets an example in writing and regularly reading the law, as all Israelites should do (see 6:7–9; 11:18–21; 31:9–13).[41] He habitually studies the law 'that he may learn to fear the LORD his God', a key Deuteronomic virtue applicable to all God's people (cf. 4:10; 5:26 [29]; 6:2; 14:23; 31:12). In this way the Deuteronomic ethic of obedience is to be modelled by the king. The king as the first citizen, the first among equals (*primus inter pares*), is to view his subjects as 'his brothers' (17:20; cf. 17:15),[42] so that the egalitarian teaching of the canonical book, rather than being undermined by the appointment of a king (a distinct danger, as shown by later Israelite history), is modelled by this key Israelite officer.

This text also anticipates the transformation of Moses' speeches into book form. By making the king the archetypal reader of the book in its future written

---

38. Olson, *The Death of the Old and the Birth of the New*.

39. The halfway point of the book in verses (according to the Masoretic notes) is not far away at Deut. 17:10.

40. Jamie A. Grant, *The King as Exemplar: The Function of Deuteronomy's Kingship Law in the Shaping of the Book of Psalms*, SBLAB 17 (Atlanta: Society of Biblical Literature, 2004), pp. 208–210; Ryan O'Dowd, *The Wisdom of Torah: Epistemology in Deuteronomy and the Wisdom Literature*, FRLANT 225 (Göttingen: Vandenhoeck & Ruprecht, 2009), pp. 77, 78.

41. See Dennis T. Olson, *Deuteronomy and the Death of Moses: A Theological Reading*, OBT (Minneapolis: Fortress, 1994), pp. 82, 83.

42. Gary N. Knoppers, 'The Deuteronomist and the Deuteronomic Law of the King: A Reexamination of a Relationship', *ZAW* 108 (1996), pp. 329–346 (330).

form (the completed Deuteronomy), 'Moses' speech projects its own reception – via the representativity of an exceptional reader'.[43] As noted by Sonnet, this royal portrait is in effect a flash-forward in time, picturing the future reception history of the completed book with a scene that carries an implied reception ethic for the people as a whole (cf. 31:9–13). By drawing the reader's attention to 17:18 as a key verse, the Greek title represents an exegetical insight for the guidance of future readers and fossilizes in time an ancient interpretative perspective on the use of the total canonical book.

The internal divisions of Deuteronomy

Whether Deuteronomy is read sequentially as a whole (*lectio continua*), as in the Reformed tradition, following Calvin's example, or read in excerpts, as by many modern readers and some lectionaries, the length of any reading portion inevitably influences the evaluation of its contents. The common reader is often guided (or misguided) by the traditional chapter divisions or by the sectioning provided by contemporary Bible versions. Those using a commentary will be influenced by the divisions suggested in it. In popular-level commentaries, divisions are often provided without comment or justification. In more scholarly commentaries, even when an explanation is provided, discussion of alternative subdivisions is seldom offered. Only scholars will be aware of and maybe influenced by the different divisions marked in the Hebrew text.

The division of the biblical text into chapters, sections, paragraphs and verses is not part of the text of Scripture if we limit text strictly to the words themselves, but is a paratextual feature. The different schemes of internal division within canonical books suggest alternate ways of understanding the biblical text. This newer area of biblical study is called Delimitation Criticism,[44] and has the potential of providing scholars with new tools to add sophistication to their analysis of texts. Breaks within the physical layout of a text serve a number of inter-related functions, which may be intentional or unintentional on the part

---

43. Jean-Pierre Sonnet, *The Book within the Book: Writing in Deuteronomy*, BIS 14 (Leiden: Brill, 1997), p. 79.

44. The term was coined by Marjo C. A. Korpel, 'Introduction to the Series Pericope', in Marjo C. A. Korpel and Josef M. Oesch (eds.), *Delimitation Criticism: A New Tool in Biblical Scholarship*, Pericope: Scripture as Written and Read in Antiquity 1 (Assen: Van Gorcum, 2000), pp. 1–50 (13).

of those responsible. The habits of readers in seeking meaning in texts suggest four possible functions of any such division (see below).[45]

The different schemes of division

As in the other Pentateuchal books, there are four types of major textual divisions in Deuteronomy. In this discussion I will largely ignore versification (the Masoretes counted 955 verses in Deuteronomy). The major divisions are the thirty-four chapters of our English Bible, the Hebrew open and closed paragraphs, the *seder* reading lessons (of later origin; thirty-two in L),[46] and the *parashah* reading lessons (ten in L).[47]

The chapter divisions of most English translations are those provided by Stephen Langton (1150–1228) to the Latin Vulgate.[48] They were then transferred to the margins of the Hebrew text by Rabbi Salomon ben Ishmael (c. 1330).[49] In the three cases where there is a difference between the Latin/English and Hebrew chapter divisions, the divergence is only one verse,[50] so this deviation may have been caused by the misplacement of a marginal note.[51] But this does

---

45. For more details, see G. R. Goswell, 'The Divisions of the Book of Daniel', in Raymond de Hoop, Marjo C. A. Korpel and Stanley E. Porter (eds.), *The Impact of Unit Delimitation on Exegesis*, Pericope: Scripture as Written and Read in Antiquity 7 (Leiden: Brill, 2009), pp. 89–114 (89–91); idem, 'Early Readers of the Gospels: The *kephalaia* and *titloi* of Codex Alexandrinus', *JGRChJ* 6 (2009), pp. 134–174 (139–142).

46. In L, upon which *BHS* is based, the *sedarim* are not numbered in the margin, though they are in the list that follows the Pentateuch; see David Noel Freedman et al. (eds.), *The Leningrad Codex: A Facsimile Edition* (Grand Rapids: Eerdmans, 1998), p. 252 (Folio 120 verso). In *BHS*, G. Weil numbers all the *sedarim* except the one at 20:1, in line with the Masoretic list of L (despite the fact that this *seder* is marked in the margin of L). According to Carmel McCarthy, *BHQ, Deuteronomy*, p. 5*, Weil's motivation may have been to bring the number of *sedarim* into conformity with the total of 167 for the Pentateuch provided in the Masoretic lists at the end of Deuteronomy.

47. In some Hebrew Bibles, e.g. the edition of Snaith, there are eleven *parashiyyot*, with one placed at 31:1 (no. 52), giving a total of fifty-four for the Pentateuch as a whole.

48. Beryl Smalley, *The Study of the Bible in the Middle Ages* (Oxford: Basil Blackwell, 1952), pp. 221–224.

49. Ginsburg, *Introduction*, p. 25.

50. Eng. 12:32 = Heb. 13:1; Eng. 22:30 = Heb. 23:1; Eng. 29:1 = Heb. 28:69.

51. David Marcus, 'Alternate Chapter Divisions in the Pentateuch in the Light of the Masoretic Sections', *Hebrew Studies* 44 (2003), pp. 119–128, esp. p. 121.

not explain the wider variation that sometimes occurs (e.g. 1 Kgs 4:21–34 in English = 5:1–14 in Hebrew, a variation of fourteen verses).[52]

The Hebrew paragraphs are marked by spaces in the text and are a feature of the oldest texts we possess. There are two types: the 'open' paragraph, which starts on a new line, and the 'closed' paragraph, which continues on the same line after a short space. In later printed Hebrew Bibles (but not in L), an 'open' paragraph is marked by the Hebrew letter *peh* (the first letter of *pĕtûḥā'*), and a 'closed' paragraph is marked by the Hebrew letter *sāmek* (the first letter of *sĕtûmā'*). According to Josef Oesch, the segmentation of the biblical text (seen already in the biblical texts among the Dead Sea Scrolls) is part of a long reading tradition that included such divisions.[53] Oesch saw the likely origins of the divisions in the desire of the author (or redactor) to protect the correct understanding of the text by dividing it into sense units.[54] Certainly, as stated by Emanuel Tov, '[t]he subdivision itself into open and closed sections reflects exegesis on the extent of the content units'.[55] There is significant variation in the placing of paragraphs in Hebrew manuscripts. The practice of putting *peh* or *sāmek* in the vacant space is of a later date than the paragraphing itself, and there is also variation as to whether a paragraph is marked as 'open' or 'closed'.[56]

As well as this, the Hebrew Bible has been divided into 452 *seder* lessons (pl. *sedarim*), indicated by a large *sāmek* in the margin. These specify thirty-two (or thirty-one) weekly liturgical readings in Deuteronomy as part of a three-year cycle associated with the Palestinian tradition. The *sedarim* at times divide the text at what seem unlikely places (e.g. 12:20; 15:7; 18:14). Whether or not

---

52. See the attempted explanation of Jordan S. Penkower, 'The Chapter Divisions in the 1525 Rabbinic Bible', *VT* 48 (1998), pp. 350–374. For a listing of the differences, see Patrick H. Alexander et al. (eds.), *The SBL Handbook of Style for Ancient Near Eastern, Biblical, and Early Christian Studies* (Peabody: Hendrickson, 1999), Appendix E.

53. Josef Oesch, 'Textgliederung im Alten Testament und in den Qumranhandschriften', *Henoch* 5 (1983), pp. 289–321, esp. p. 318. For a collation of open and closed paragraphs in texts of Deuteronomy among the Dead Sea Scrolls, see *BHQ*, Appendix B, pp. 14*–15*.

54. Josef Oesch, *Petucha und Setuma: Untersuchungen zu einer überlieferten Gliederung im hebräischen Text des Alten Testaments*, OBO 27 (Freiburg: Universitätsverlag, 1979), p. 339.

55. Emanuel Tov, *Textual Criticism of the Hebrew Bible* (Minneapolis: Fortress, 1992), p. 51.

56. For a table of differences in the Masoretic manuscripts of the Tiberian type for Deuteronomy, see *BHQ*, Appendix A, pp. 10*–14*.

the Christian reader views them as helpful for exegesis, these partitions continue
to influence those who read the Hebrew text liturgically.

There are also longer sections, marked in the margin by an abbreviation of
the word *parashah* (pl. *parashiyyot*). They are associated with the Babylonian
tradition and appear only in the Pentateuch, providing fifty-three lessons (ten
in Deuteronomy) for a one-year lectionary cycle.[57] They are a feature of modern
Jewish Bibles in English (e.g. Soncino, jpsv). The revised edition of Duane
Christensen's commentary on Deuteronomy takes cognizance of this lectionary
cycle of ten weekly readings in his outline of the book,[58] but this is rare among
Christian commentators.

These four schemes of division have separate origins but will be considered
together, since they reflect alternate ways of reading the same text. These diverse
ways of dividing Deuteronomy influence its interpretation and suggest
competing perspectives on the book. Nevertheless, the substantial overlap of
schemes of totally different origins suggests that the divisions are neither
arbitrary nor without sense.

The functions of divisions

A division separates one section of a text from another. This is its first and
most obvious function. In the case of Deuteronomy, this serves to demarcate
different speeches, or to differentiate different topics, arguments or sections
in a speech. For example, a major break is indicated at 16:18 by the *parashah*
and *seder* reading schemes, signalling a change of topic from cultic matters
(tithes, festivals) to Israelite office bearers, and the start of *seder* 17 coincides
with a change of topic to that of the king (17:14). A new paragraph begins at
this point in most English versions. Likewise, the chapter division and closed
paragraph at 18:1 alerts the reader to the start of a discussion about the priests
(18:1–8).

A second function of a division, the inverse of the first, is to join material.
It demarcates a unit, suggesting that the material enclosed within its boundaries
is closely related in meaning. A literary portion is assumed by many readers to
be a unit of meaning. For instance, Deuteronomy's *seder* 13 concerns three

---

57. For further discussion of the Babylonian and Palestinian reading cycles, see
    Charles Perrot, 'The Reading of the Bible in the Ancient Synagogue', in Martin
    Jan Mulder (ed.), *Mikra: Text, Translation, Reading and Interpretation of the Hebrew
    Bible in Ancient Judaism and Early Christianity* (Assen/Maastricht: Van Gorcum,
    1990), pp. 137–159.

58. Christensen, *Deuteronomy 1:1 – 21:9 Revised*, pp. xciii–xciv.

scenarios of incitement to covenant breach, by a prophet, a fellow Israelite or worthless men who lead astray a whole city, linked by the refrain: 'Let us go after/serve other gods' (13:2, 6, 13).

A third function of a division is to highlight certain material in a text, making it more prominent to the reader. Material is accentuated by placing it at the beginning or end of a demarcated section. Readers tend to see the beginning as indicating what a section is about,[59] and tend to look to the end for a summary statement of theme. For example, *seder* 15 begins with the instruction to act generously towards a poor brother (15:7), and the ethical principle is then applied in the *seder* to the seventh-year release of debt, the release of a Hebrew slave, and the three main annual festivals (15:7 – 16:17). The placement of 4:24 ('For the LORD your God is a devouring fire, a jealous God') and 18:13 ('You shall be blameless before the LORD your God') at the close of their respective *sedarim* (nos. 4 and 17) turns these verses into punchlines. In some Hebrew Bibles, the initial letter of 18:13 (the final verse of its *seder*) is a large letter (*Tav*).[60] Some English Bibles follow this division, for example NIV, but others do not. The NRSV starts a new paragraph at 18:15, a division followed by the Revised Common Lectionary.[61]

The mirror image of the third function is the fourth, to downplay or ignore certain textual features. This often goes unnoticed simply because of the character of the function itself – for example, the traditional textual divisions (whether Jewish or Christian) fail to suggest that the contents of Deuteronomy 12 – 26 are organized according to the order of the Ten Commandments as posited by Stephen Kaufman and others.[62]

When analysed in this fashion, the status of text divisions as commentary on a text is revealed. But the traditional divisions reflect the interpretative decisions of preceding generations, so may mislead the contemporary reader.

---

59. Similarly James Muilenburg: 'the delimitation of the passage is essential if we are to learn how its major motif, usually stated at the beginning, is resolved', 'Form Criticism and Beyond', *JBL* 88 (1969), pp. 1–18 (9).

60. E.g. R. Kittel, *Biblica Hebraica* (Stuttgart: Privileg. Württ. Bibelanstalt, 1925), and the Hebrew Bible edited by Snaith.

61. First Lesson for Fourth Sunday after the Epiphany, Year B. (This lesson also ends at v. 20, before the final two verses on prophetic discernment.)

62. S. Kaufman, 'The Structure of the Deuteronomic Law', *Maarav* 1/2 (1978–9), pp. 105–158; see the chapter by John Walton in this volume, pp. 93–117.

The alternate sense units of Deuteronomy

A few further illustrations. The second *seder* division in L at 2:2 (coinciding with the second paragraph division) marks an important turning point in Moses' account of their journey from Egypt, with the divine command to 'turn northward' (towards the Promised Land). Perhaps due to the constraint of the traditional chapters, commentaries routinely start a new section at 2:1 (Christensen is an exception), even when there is a recognition that 2:1 is the sequel to the command to the Israelites in 1:40 to turn back the way they have come (McConville), and the section starting at 2:1 is given the heading 'Turn north' (Nelson).

The third *seder* lesson (2:31 – 3:22; coincides with a closed paragraph in L) encompasses the story of the victories over Sihon and Og, together with the lesson that God is also able to give the Israelites victory over the Canaanite nations across the Jordan (3:21–22). Not without reason, some commentaries start the section at 2:24, when the Israelites enter the territory of Sihon (McConville), or at 2:26, when messengers are sent to Sihon (Nelson). The fourth *seder* lesson (3:23 – 4:24) is bounded by an inclusio of Moses' exclusion from the land as a salutary lesson for Israel (3:23–29; 4:21–22). Alternatively, within the boundaries of Deuteronomy 4 there is a focus on the danger of idolatry (with an open paragraph break at 4:1 in L, and a space in 4QDeut[d]). What sets off 4:25–40 (= *seder* 5) from the preceding part of the chapter is the new concern over the danger of *future* idolatry ('When you beget children . . .'). There is a new paragraph at 4:25 in various English versions (ESV, NIV, NEB). The final verse of the *seder* returns to the theme of children (4:40, 'with you, and with your children after you').

The chapter break at 13:1 (Heb. 13:2), which is also the start of the thirteenth *seder* lesson and an open paragraph break, supports a division at this point. The alternate divisions of the text make 12:32 either the last verse of the English chapter or the first verse of the Hebrew chapter.[63] Both ways of dividing the text highlight this instruction as a general statement ('Everything that I command you you shall be careful to do; you shall not add to it or take from it'), either as a conclusion to the section about false worship or as an introduction to laws about the false prophet. The similarity of this verse to 4:2, which introduces the reference to events at Baal Peor, confirms for Kaufman a connection of

---

63. According to Jack R. Lundbom, either is possible because of similarities of the verse with 12:1 (framing ch. 12) and 13:18 (framing ch. 13): 'The Inclusio and Other Framing Devices in Deuteronomy I – XXVIII', *VT* 46 (1996), pp. 296–315 (306–308).

12:32 with the subsequent laws of apostasy in chapter 13.[64] On the other hand, a chapter division at 13:1 is favoured by the fact that a number of nearby textual sections are also introduced by the casuistic introductory particle *kî* ('when/if') (12:20, 29; 13:1, 6, 12).[65]

In the Hebrew Bible, the regulations concerning the three great annual festivals (16:1–17) form the closing part of *seder* 15 that starts at 15:7 (coinciding with a closed paragraph). The *seder* opens with the theme of generosity towards the poor (15:7, 'you shall not harden your heart or shut your hand against your poor brother'), which is thereby turned into a topic sentence for this textual division. An important aspect of the explanation and application of the instructions about the annual feasts is the need to include vulnerable social groups in the festal celebrations (16:11, 14). The reader might not have noticed this feature if the section was understood to start at 16:1.

Conclusions

This study of the paratext of Deuteronomy has shown that the positioning of this book relative to other biblical books – as the final book in the Pentateuch; following Numbers and preceding Joshua; and at the strategic joint between the Pentateuch and the rest of the Old Testament – has hermeneutical significance. Consciously or unconsciously, the reader's evaluation of Deuteronomy is affected by the company it keeps in the library of scriptural books.

The material marshalled in this chapter shows that the title given to a literary work fulfils certain functions and that titles may influence interpretation. In the case of Deuteronomy, the Hebrew title is a generic classification of the book as speeches, while the alternate Greek title, by highlighting 17:18 as a key verse, indicates something about the book's content and its ongoing use by the people of God. It is best to view the placing of titles on biblical books as commentary on the text. Like all commentary, the titles are to be neither lightly discarded nor readily accepted, but weighed and tested by a reader's own consideration of the book's contents.

There is the danger of allowing the chapter divisions in the English Bible with which Christian readers are familiar to control their reading of the text. This does not, however, give them permission to exclude from consideration other traditional textual divisions (whether ancient paragraphs, *sedarim* or

---

64. Kaufman, 'Deuteronomic Law', p. 127.
65. See the discussion provided by Marcus, 'Alternate Chapter Divisions', pp. 127, 128.

parashiyyot). More often than not, a division represents a considered and insightful reading of the text. However, the fact that there are different schemes that do not entirely coincide shows that they are interpretations of the text, with competing views of the meaning of the text. It would be helpful if commentators more often discussed alternative ways in which the text may be divided into meaningful sections, and provided an explanation for why a particular way of dividing the text has been chosen.

10. THE ALIEN IN DEUTERONOMY 29 AND TODAY

Jenny Corcoran

Introduction

This chapter explores ways in which the covenant renewal in Deuteronomy 29:10–15 provides a helpful paradigm of distinctive inclusivity for contemporary ecclesiology. To show the relevance of this passage, I first explore the detail of these verses and how they relate to the wider understanding of non-Israelites in Deuteronomy. I then briefly outline Wright's paradigmatic approach, noting how Blenkinsopp adds a helpful dimension and why this becomes so appropriate for this study. Finally I look at some points of application of Deuteronomy 29 to contemporary ecclesiology.

Deuteronomy is an obvious text to explore in terms of understanding the social and ethical constructs of the people of God, and of exploring how these themes relate to Christianity. The book draws together many of the key themes of Israelite religion, including covenant theology,[1] and has a significant influence on the rest of the canon of Scripture.[2]

---

1. W. Brueggemann, *Deuteronomy*, Abingdon OTC (Nashville: Abingdon Press, 2001), p. 17.
2. C. J. H. Wright, *Deuteronomy* (Carlisle: Paternoster Press, 1996), p. 1.

The resident alien within the covenant of Deuteronomy 29:10–15

Deuteronomy 29:10–15 presents the covenant renewal at Moab and shows a remarkable inclusivity[3] of vision for the covenant people of God as, for the first time, the *gēr* ('resident alien') is formally included.[4] The identity of God's people is to be strikingly different from that of the surrounding nations. All, regardless of age, gender, status and ethnicity, stand equally before the Lord: leaders, men, women and children – and the word for children here describes particularly young children. The covenant is intended to be inclusive from its very inception,[5] and no group is to be excluded from participation and blessing.[6]

The narrative context of these verses sees Israel standing on the edge of the Promised Land, looking across to what they will be fighting to claim. Before they begin this task of conquest, God calls them to stand and renew the covenant in order to be established as his people.[7] At this high point of reaffirming their unique identity as God's chosen people, it would be understandable if what was presented was a summons to maintain their unique religious identity and ethnic purity. Instead, the surprise is that the *gēr* is included alongside the native-born Israelites.

In these verses the resident alien, by becoming a covenant partner, assumes responsibility to keep the law alongside the Israelites. The law then provides identity, dignity and protection to a group who are predominantly poor, vulnerable and marginalized.

As well as sharing in the rights and responsibilities of the community, the resident alien is drawn into the salvation story of the people of God, finding a place within the historical and eschatological story of hope between God and his people. In 29:13 Moses announces to the gathered people that God has called them to be his people 'as he swore to [their] fathers, to Abraham, to Isaac and to Jacob'.[8] The resident aliens standing alongside the Israelites as covenant

---

3. Brueggemann, *Deuteronomy*, p. 261.

4. J. G. McConville, *Deuteronomy*, AOTC (Leicester: Apollos; Downers Grove: InterVarsity Press, 2002), p. 416.

5. D. Christensen, *Deuteronomy 21:10 – 34:12*, WBC (Nashville: Thomas Nelson, 2002), p. 718.

6. Wright, *Deuteronomy*, pp. 286–287.

7. G. von Rad, *Deuteronomy*, OTL (London: SCM Press, 1966), p. 180.

8. Unless otherwise identified, Scripture quotations in this chapter are the author's own translation.

partners are included within the scope of these words, implying that they too are children of Abraham, Isaac and Jacob. In Brueggemann's description they are drawn into the 'rootage of the past'.[9]

The future dimension of the covenant is represented through the repetition of the word 'today', which occurs five times in these five verses (29:10, 12, 13, 15 [x2]).[10] Future generations are called to 'choose today' for themselves and enter into the inclusive, multi-generational identity of the people of God.

'Your' resident alien

Resident aliens are not only to be included within the covenant community, the Israelites are to show a particular responsibility for them. This is implied by the description of them as 'your resident alien', living 'within your camp'. The resident alien is identified with Israel five times in Deuteronomy, as 'yours' four times (5:14; 24:14; 29:11; 31:12) and 'his' once (1:16). The phrase 'within your gates' occurs of them (sometimes alongside other groups) six times (5:14; 14:21, 29; 16:14; 24:14; 31:12) and 'in your midst' twice (16:11; 26:11), as well as 'in your camp' here. The resident alien is included in those who are to benefit from the triennial tithe, in order that they may eat 'within your gates' (14:28). All this reinforces the Israelites' duty of care towards the non-Israelites who were settling amongst them.

The 'alien' in the wider context of Deuteronomy

Deuteronomy uses two different terms when writing about foreigners, *gēr* and *nokrî*. (The word *tôšāb* is often used as a synonym of *gēr* elsewhere in the Old Testament, but does not appear in Deuteronomy.) The terms are used to demarcate sharply between two groups: foreigners who are open to faith in God, the *gērîm*, and those who are not, the *nokrîm*.[11] This difference is crucial for understanding how Deuteronomy views and treats those who are not ethnically Israel, and so for understanding 29:10–15 and how it fits into the theology and ethics of the book.

---

9. Brueggemann, *Deuteronomy*, p. 22.

10. Following MT versification, so NIV. The NRSV splits vv. 14–15 differently, with one 'today' in each verse.

11. H. Ringgren, '*Nokrî*', in G. J. Botterweck, H. Ringgren and H.-J. Fabry (eds.), *Theological Dictionary of the Old Testament* (Grand Rapids: Eerdmans, 1998), vol. 9, p. 426.

Nokrî

The term *nokrî* is used to describe someone or something that is 'alien' or 'other'. People described as this are normally thought of as dangerous or hostile towards Israel.[12] There are five occurrences of *nokrî* in Deuteronomy for people, and a further two for gods (31:16; 32:12). Three of the uses of *nokrî* for people inform the Israelites that it is permissible to treat the *nokrî* differently from themselves, and, interestingly, differently from the *gēr* as well (14:21; 15:3; 23:20). There is also a prohibition against making a *nokrî* king in the future (17:15).

The other use of *nokrî* (29:22) is interesting in terms of this study, but it is helpful to understand two further words first, *gôyîm* and *'ammîm*. Millar argues that, where a distinction is made between these two terms for 'peoples' in Deuteronomy, the *gôyîm* are seen more negatively and as a potential threat, while the *'ammîm* are described more neutrally and at times positively.[13] He goes on to describe how the *'ammîm* become the 'audience' who observe God's love for Israel, witnessing the story of redemption and thus finding themselves in a position of potential blessing.[14] The significance of this for the *nokrî* can be seen in 29:22, where they are among those who will see the curses that God will pour out on Israel. There is a sense that they are not simply onlookers but also understand what they are seeing. As the *nokrî* are then receptive onlookers, in Millar's terms they become like the *'ammîm* and are in a place of potential blessing. This is not the overall impression that Deuteronomy gives about the *nokrî*, but it does allow for the possibility that at the end of the book, as it looks to the future, there might even be hope for them.

Gēr

The word *gēr* is used in Deuteronomy to describe a foreigner who has a 'special status'.[15] Unlike the *nokrî*, the *gēr* is loved by God (10:18). Deuteronomy frequently mentions the *gēr* in the same phrase as the orphan and widow (10:18; 14:29; 16:11, 14; 24:17, 19, 20, 21; 26:12, 13; 27:19). All three groups were generally considered 'economically weak'[16] and therefore vulnerable, in need of

---

12. A. Konkel, '*Nokrî*', *NIDOTTE*, vol. 3, p. 109.

13. J. G. Millar, *Now Choose Life: Theology and Ethics in Deuteronomy* (Leicester: Apollos, 1998), p. 149.

14. Ibid., p. 149.

15. A. Konkel, '*Gēr*', *NIDOTTE*, vol. 1, p. 837.

16. L. Epzstein, *Social Justice in the Ancient Near East and the People of the Bible* (London: SCM Press, 1986), p. 116.

care and protection. Various instructions encourage proper justice or provision of food for these vulnerable groups.

In several contexts where the word *gēr* occurs, the Israelites are reminded that they were themselves *gērîm* (10:19) or slaves (16:12; 24:18, 22) in Egypt. God expects that Israel will remember his concern for them in their vulnerability and that this will encourage them to protect the *gēr* from exploitation and starvation.[17] This reminder becomes a key theological point in Deuteronomy, and will be explored more fully below.

The *gēr* is overtly included within those expected to obey the laws of the nation, and Moucarry argues that the range of laws the *gēr* is expected to observe demonstrates how they were integrated into the national life of Israel.[18] They were to observe the law, and not engage in behaviour prohibited to ethnic Israelites.[19] As well as 'civil' rules and regulations, the *gēr* should observe the Sabbath, and could offer sacrifices and participate in religious festivals.[20] Deuteronomy does not directly mention the involvement of *gēr* at Passover, although it does not prohibit this, while Exodus and Numbers expressly permit them to celebrate the Passover provided they are circumcised. The resident alien is also mentioned in the instructions regarding the septennial public reading of the law to Israel in 31:12. Here the alien is included, standing alongside the men, women and children of Israel, as they gather to hear the law. As with the Israelites, the *gēr* is expected here to listen, to learn, to fear and to follow all the words of the law.

Deuteronomy 24:19–21 instructs Israelites to leave a portion of the harvest in the fields, on the olive trees and on the vines for the alien, the orphan and the widow, i.e. for the economically vulnerable. Woods comments that the identical structure of the three instructions, 'When you ... do not ... it shall be for ...', suggests ownership of this portion by the vulnerable.[21] This part

---

17. J. Goldingay, *Theological Diversity and the Authority of the Old Testament* (Grand Rapids: Eerdmans, 1987), p. 135.

18. G. Moucarry, 'The Alien According to the Torah', trans. J. Smith, *Themelios* 14.1 (1988), p. 18.

19. B. Blatchley, 'The Resident Alien: Principles of Pentateuchal Provision and their Relevance to the Treatment of Asylum Seekers in the UK Today', unpublished essay, Wycliffe Hall (2004), p. 13.

20. R. De Vaux, *Ancient Israel: Its Life and Institutions*, 2nd ed. (London: Darton, Longman and Todd, 1965), p. 75.

21. E. J. Woods, *Deuteronomy: An Introduction and Commentary*, TOTC (Nottingham: Inter-Varsity Press; Downers Grove: InterVarsity Press, 2011), p. 254.

of the harvest is no longer the possession of the farmers to do with what they want, even if it would be to show generosity towards those in need. Instead, God instructs them that this is now the possession of the widow, orphan and *gēr* by right, a significant claim given the importance of the land in the covenant between God and Israel.

Is a gēr a foreigner?

Cairns claims that the word *gēr* in 29:11 most probably refers to the Gibeonites of Joshua 9,[22] and that gathering wood and drawing water is about assisting in sacrificial and purificatory rites at the temple.[23] However, the wider use of the two words for alien in Deuteronomy gives little evidence to support Cairns's view, and it is much more likely that *gēr* has the same meaning here as elsewhere in the book. Gathering wood and drawing water illustrate the type of activities of those doing menial work in Israel. This in turn supports the view that resident aliens would most likely be poor and would need to hire themselves to more wealthy members of the community in order to survive.

Following Bultmann, Na'aman argues that the *gērîm* are not foreigners at all, but refugees from within Judah displaced by Sennacherib's campaign.[24] He supports his argument by highlighting the distinction between the *gērîm* and the *nokrî*, connecting the needs of the *gērîm* with those of the Levite and arguing that there are no other laws providing for the needy of Judahite origin.

While this is an interesting perspective, it is not consistent with the overall presentation of the *gērîm* in the text. For example, the explicit inclusion of the *gērîm* in religious festivals would not require clarification had they already been recognized as followers of Yahweh. Van Houten also argues that the *gērîm* were not ethnically Israelite and that throughout the Old Testament they never lose their own ethnic identity.[25]

'The assembly of the LORD'

While demonstrating that there is an inclusivity in Israel in Deuteronomy, it is important to address those occasions that appear especially nationalistic. One example of this is chapter 23, which describes particular groups of

---

22. I. Cairns, *Deuteronomy: Word and Presence* (Grand Rapids: Eerdmans 1992), p. 257.

23. Ibid., p. 257.

24. Nadav Na'aman, 'Sojourners and Levites in the Kingdom of Judah in the Seventh Century BCE', *ZABR* 14 (2008), pp. 237–279.

25. C. van Houten, *The Alien in Israelite Law* (Sheffield: JSOT Sheffield Academic Press, 1991), p. 160.

people who are to be excluded from the *qahal*, the assembly, some on the basis of ethnicity.

For each of the prohibitions in Deuteronomy 23 the phrase *biqĕhal yhwh* ('in the assembly of the LORD') is used. The word *qahal* occurs another five times throughout the book (5:22; 9:10; 10:4; 18:16; 31:30), but not in the exact phrase seen in this chapter, suggesting that what is intended here is something quite specific. In support, there may well have been ethnic Israelites unfortunate enough to fulfil the description of 23:1, and therefore be excluded from this 'assembly of the LORD' but still part of the Israelite community. Rather, it appears that this phrase describes a specific cultic activity or activities from which some Israelites and some foreigners were excluded. However, this does not prevent them from participating in other religious festivals, as demonstrated by the specific mention of the resident alien as part of the community that celebrates both the feast of Weeks and the feast of Tabernacles in Deuteronomy 16.

Paradigm as a hermeneutical approach

Having explored the detail of the text, it is now important to outline the hermeneutical approach adopted so that insights can be gained for contemporary ecclesiology.

Wright's paradigmatic hermeneutic provides a helpful way of viewing the people of God in the Old Testament as a pattern for the people of God in the New Testament and beyond. Wright compares his approach with the way in which learning a set pattern in grammar can help one when presented with a new language.[26] There are limitations to his approach,[27] but the concept of establishing a pattern that enables processing of new situations is attractive and appropriate for this particular task. While Wright primarily utilizes his paradigmatic approach to draw out a missiological hermeneutic of the Old Testament,[28] it is entirely appropriate to adopt his approach for a more ecclesiological focus.

---

26. C. J. H. Wright, *Old Testament Ethics for the People of God* (Leicester: Inter-Varsity Press, 2004), pp. 65–66.

27. For further discussion see W. Janzen, *Old Testament Ethics* (Louisville: Westminster John Knox, 1994); and C. Rodd, *Glimpses of a Strange Land: Studies in Old Testament Ethics*, OTS (Edinburgh: T&T Clark, 2001).

28. This is apparent in his commentary on Deuteronomy, e.g. Wright, *Deuteronomy*, p. 12, but for a fuller understanding of his approach see also C. J. H. Wright, *The Mission of God: Unlocking the Bible's Grand Narrative* (Leicester: Inter-Varsity Press, 2006).

A further reason why Wright's paradigmatic approach is particularly appropriate is that it echoes the way Deuteronomy presents the past action of God's
dealings with his people as a paradigm for their dealings with the resident alien.
God's rescue of his people from slavery in Egypt is a recurrent refrain throughout Deuteronomy, reminding them of their own story in order to influence
their behaviour towards others. God's treatment, protection, love and deliverance of the Israelites becomes the paradigm for their treatment of the vulnerable
within their own community, including the resident alien. This supports Wright's
argument that his hermeneutical approach is not something that he reads back
into the Old Testament, but was part of God's theological plan in creating and
structuring Israel in a specific way.[29] This paradigm is not limited to Deuteronomy (the focus of the present study), but can be seen elsewhere in the Old
Testament as well, and there are links between what is seen here and the theology
of Genesis 12 and Isaiah 40 – 55.

In his exploration of 'conflict and accommodation' in Israelite religion,
Blenkinsopp makes important observations about the behaviour of Israel
towards the resident alien. He argues that the treatment of this group of out-
siders is significant in the struggle to maintain a balance between the distinctive
practices of the Israelites and their openness towards those of other nations.
Deuteronomy inhabits the narrowest of edges between exclusivity and inclusivity, and many passages emphasize one perspective over the other. Blenkinsopp
writes that the collective memory of Israel was intended to prevent ultimate
exclusivism and to shape a more positive response towards the resident alien.[30]
This could be summarized as a paradigm of hospitality that originates in a story
of rescue.

Theological significance of the *gēr* in the covenant renewal at Moab

The experience of slavery was fundamental to the identity of Israel,[31] as can be
seen in the frequency of references to the exodus in Deuteronomy. The forty-
nine separate references to Egypt, spread evenly through the book, show its
continued importance to the book's theology. Six verses (5:15; 6:21; 15:15; 16:12;

---

29. Wright, *Old Testament Ethics for the People of God*, p. 321.

30. J. Blenkinsopp, 'Yahweh and Other Deities: Conflict and Accommodation in the
    Religion of Israel', *Int* 40.4 October (Richmond: Union Theological Seminary,
    1986), p. 366.

31. Millar, *Choose Life*, p. 153.

24:18, 22) make a specific connection between Israel's own experience of slavery in Egypt and the need to keep the law that God is giving to them. Towards the end of the book a warning of possible future slavery in Egypt (28:68) concludes the curses that will occur if Israel breaks the covenant they have just affirmed. These verses highlight what McConville describes as Deuteronomy's vision of Israel as 'a delivered people, on the verge of a land, a people consisting of "resident aliens" (15:15), who go back into exile, and can come from it again'.[32]

The people God called before him at Moab were to create, through the covenant, an ethnic identity that would be visibly and dramatically different from that of the surrounding nations. They were to become a paradigm of an hospitable community, embodying a distinctive inclusivity for the surrounding nations to witness. This was to be a community in which there was no room for a 'pyramid of social stratification'.[33] Even though in 29:10–15 the people are listed in separate groups, they are called to stand together as equals before God. The only differentiation these verses permit is between God and the gathered people, not among the people themselves. As a nation they are to live a life of justice, love, righteousness and compassion, because these are the qualities of their God.[34]

As they live this out, the presence of the resident alien is a visual reminder of their status as redeemed slaves, always holding before them their own story and encouraging them to adopt the behaviour that God modelled for them. This story of redemption was not just to be seen within the cult but also in their day-to-day life, from the way they practised justice to the way they harvested their produce. Supporting Blenkinsopp, Hanson writes that the structures and institutions of Israel were not just accidental or convenient, but were inherent within their social and communal ethic, in order to remind them of the nature of the God they worshipped, the God who revealed himself through the exodus.[35]

The law becomes particularly significant for land use and ownership, as agricultural generosity is encouraged with the reminder that Israel are themselves strangers in the land and are not the ultimate owners.[36] At the end of

---

32. McConville, *Deuteronomy*, p. 44.

33. P. Hanson, *The People Called: The Growth of Community in the Bible* (Louisville: Westminster John Knox, 2001), pp. 22–23.

34. Ibid., p. 172.

35. Ibid., p. 23.

36. V. Matthews and D. C. Benjamin, *Social World of Ancient Israel 1250–587 BCE* (Peabody: Hendrickson, 1993), p. 83.

Deuteronomy, Israel are still standing outside the Promised Land. It is here that the covenant renewal occurs, in a place where they own no land and have nothing except their freedom from captivity. 'This freedom is the foundation of God's covenant with a liberated people, since the very "space" in which Israel's legislation is given is freedom.'[37]

Ecclesiological implications

Having looked at the theology of the passage, I will now briefly draw out some of the ecclesiological implications of seeing it as a paradigm for the people of God today. This will involve the paradigm of hospitality and the way in which the people of God were called to be distinctive but not exclusive, influenced by their 'collective memory'.

Wright argues that Deuteronomy must be allowed to challenge the church today in terms of whether it embodies justice, compassion and love in its witness to wider society.[38] Throughout Deuteronomy God displays a deep concern for justice and for the vulnerable, illustrated in Israel's redemption, and his people are expected to reflect this concern.[39] This particular passage also suggests that the church should live out its paradigm of hospitality as a community that is inclusive, regardless of ethnicity, age, gender and social status.

The resident aliens reminded the people of God that they themselves were merely stewards of the land that was generously given to them. This too has implications for the church as it engages in conversations regarding care for the environment.

An aspect of this paradigm is that the modern resident alien reminds the church community of their own redeemed status before God. This would be problematic if the resident alien is reduced to a representative function within the people of God, devaluing their own intrinsic worth in God's sight. An important counter is the recognition that, as argued throughout this chapter, the resident alien was drawn into full covenant membership. They were not only given the protection the law afforded to them but also, and significantly, they had to keep the law and not behave in ways that would dishonour God in the

---

37. J. Ska, 'Biblical Law and the Origins of Democracy', in W. Brown (ed.), *The 10 Commandments: The Reciprocity of Faithfulness* (Louisville: Westminster John Knox, 2004), pp. 155–156.

38. Wright, *Deuteronomy*, p. 14.

39. Goldingay, *Theological Diversity*, p. 135.

sight of other nations. Far from being simply an *aide-mémoire* for the Israelites of their redeemed state, or a recipient of hospitality, the resident alien was a fully participating member of the religious community.

This draws the discussion into an important question for contemporary ecclesiology, namely at what point new church members should be expected to adopt Christian norms, values and ethics. This is not a simple question and will surely elicit a complex response, reflecting the variety of perspectives on the right order for new Christians of 'believing', 'belonging' and 'behaving'.

If the collective memory of the Israelites provided the theological impetus for their behaviour, then what is the collective memory for the church? Is it a story of rescue from slavery, that will encourage an attitude of love and hospitality towards the marginalized? Further questions need to be asked about how the church goes about appropriating this paradigm in practice. This is beyond the remit of this chapter, but there can be no doubt that concerns for real hospitality and justice for the oppressed will lie at the core of an answer. This will be made more possible through churches and individuals engaging with the individual and corporate story of rescue at the heart of this paradigm and reimagining it today.

Conclusion

As I have shown, the use of the word *gēr* in 29:10–15 reveals in microcosm an attitude of distinctive inclusivity among the people of God. It is a crucial passage for understanding how the book as a whole relates to the alien, and how the people of God were to tread the fine line between maintaining their distinctive identity and welcoming foreigners within their community. With Wright's paradigm and other insights, it has been possible to begin exploring some of the implications of this passage and its theology for contemporary ecclesiology. This involves church communities being very aware of the story that creates their corporate identities, and of how it shapes their attitude towards those who are 'resident aliens' in their own society.

11. GENOCIDE IN DEUTERONOMY AND CHRISTIAN INTERPRETATION

Christian Hofreiter

Divinely commanded genocide?

When the crusaders reached Jerusalem in July 1099, they fasted, prayed and circumambulated the city, as the Israelites had done around Jericho. Once the city had fallen into their hands, a massacre ensued:

> Girls, women, matrons, tormented by fear of imminent death and horror-struck by the violent murder wrapped themselves around the Christians' bodies in the hope to save their lives, even as the Christians were raving and venting their rage in murder of both sexes. Some threw themselves at their feet, begging them with pitiable weeping and wailing for their lives and safety. When children five or three years old saw the cruel fate of their mothers and fathers, of one accord they stepped up the weeping and pitiable clamour. But they were making these signals for pity and mercy in vain. For the Christians gave over their whole hearts to murder, so that not a suckling little male-child or female, not even an infant of one year would escape the hand of the murderer.[1]

---

1. Albert of Aachen, as quoted in B. Z. Kedar, 'The Jerusalem Massacre of July 1099 in the Western Historiography of the Crusades', *Crusades* 3 (2004), pp. 15–75 (22f.).

It is hard to imagine anyone reading this report without feeling deep moral revulsion. And yet there are texts in Deuteronomy that appear to say that once God commanded his people Israel to engage in an extermination campaign that might well have included scenes like the one described above. Is it possible that God at one stage actually commanded genocide?

In fact, at least one rationale given for the Jerusalem massacre was that 'the crusaders remembered how King Saul, who had spared Agag, had aroused God's anger and perished'.[2] What God had commanded Saul, and what Deuteronomy enjoins in various places, is the practice of *ḥērem*. Used as a verb in the hiphil it means 'consecrate a city and its inhabitants to destruction; carry out this destruction; totally annihilate a population in war'.[3] While 'genocide' is a twentieth-century term, it is defined along similar lines, i.e. as 'acts committed with intent to destroy, in whole or in part, a national, ethnic, racial or religious group', including 'killing members of the group'.[4]

This chapter addresses moral and hermeneutical challenges posed by the concept of *ḥērem*.[5] The term itself is especially prominent in Deuteronomy and the so-called Deuteronomistic History: of the seventy-nine times the verb and corresponding noun occur in the OT,[6] more than half are within the corpus of Deuteronomy to 2 Kings.[7] While Deuteronomy is not the first book in canonical order to mention the term,[8] the *ḥērem* texts in it are particularly important because as part of the law they have enjoyed enhanced prestige and authority, and they set the scene for the Deuteronomistic History.

As Israel approaches the Promised Land, it engages in *ḥērem* warfare, which is either directly commanded or retrospectively endorsed by YHWH (2:33–34;

---

2. Bartolf of Nangis, as quoted in ibid., p. 20.

3. N. Lohfink, '*ḥrm*', in G. J. Botterweck et al. (eds.), *Theological Dictionary of the Old Testament* (Grand Rapids: Eerdmans, 1974), pp. 180–198 (188).

4. Article 2, United Nations Convention on the Prevention and Punishment of the Crime of Genocide (1948).

5. For a historical-critical introduction, see Lohfink, '*ḥrm*'; P. D. Stern, *The Biblical Herem: A Window on Israel's Religious Experience* (Atlanta: Scholars Press, 1991).

6. I will generally use OT (Old Testament) to indicate a specifically Christian approach to this collection of texts, and HB (Hebrew Bible) for approaches that differ from the classical Christian position.

7. Lohfink, '*ḥrm*', p. 181.

8. It is used in the context of war in Num. 21:1–3, but also – with a different meaning – as part of a penal code (Exod. 22:19) and in Priestly writings (Lev. 27:28, 29; Num. 18:14).

3:2–6). This total destruction is also at various points described as the direct action of YHWH (3:21; 31:4). From the narrative perspective of Deuteronomy, these accounts are located in the past. Other *ḥērem* commands, by contrast, point to the future. *Ḥērem* is commanded in three contexts: against the seven nations of Canaan (7:1–2), against idolatrous Israelite cities (13:12–17) and against Canaanite cities in the land (20:16–18). The reason given is the danger that Canaanites or apostate Israelites might otherwise seduce Israel to follow other gods (e.g. 7:4–16; 13:13; 20:18).

Other passages indicate that Israel is not displacing the Canaanites because of any supposed moral excellence, but rather because of Canaanite depravity (9:4–5; 12:31; 18:10–12). In addition, the idea of a divine gift of land combined with divine assistance in the destruction of previous inhabitants is not limited to Israel, but extends to other peoples in the region as well (2:20–22; cf. also 2:10 – 12:23). This does not obviate the moral challenge involved, but should be borne in mind as one evaluates claims that Deuteronomy is irredeemably ethnocentric.

Jews and Christians have not formed their views on *ḥērem* on the basis of Deuteronomy alone. Numbers contains the first canonical description of *ḥērem* warfare (Num. 21:1–3). Joshua describes how the Israelites carried out the Deuteronomic *ḥērem* commands: while they did not annihilate all the Canaanites (Josh. 13:1–7; cf. Judg. 1:28–33; 2:1–3) they utterly destroyed a good number of cities (e.g. Josh. 6:21; 8:25; 10:28–42; 11:8–18) and repeatedly left no survivors (e.g. Josh. 10:18–30; 11:8–14). After the conquest account in Joshua, *ḥērem* is mentioned much less frequently. The only other major narrative involves the failure of Saul to obey the divine command and totally devote the Amalekites to destruction, and the ensuing judgment upon him and his descendants (1 Sam. 15; cf. Exod. 17:14–16; Deut. 25:17–19).

Devout readers of the Bible have found these passages to be morally unpalatable and theologically challenging ever since antiquity. The cognitive dissonance caused by these texts can be summarized as a severe tension between three tenets, claims or deep-seated intuitions:

1. God is good, loving and just.
2. The Scriptures bear faithful witness to God.
3. Both the concept and the practice of *ḥērem* are morally revolting.

The tension arises from the fact that the Scriptures are understood to say that God has commanded and commended *ḥērem*, and that *ḥērem* appears deeply unjust, unloving and even evil. This in turn calls into question the goodness of God, or the veracity of the Scriptures, or our moral intuitions about the atrocious nature of genocide. For Christians, the complication of a perceived tension between the OT and the NT is added.

This chapter will show that faithful readers have been aware of these challenges for millennia and have developed a number of markedly different ways for addressing them.[9] The various approaches will be presented and their respective strengths and weaknesses evaluated in order to stimulate current readers to think through the 'costs and benefits' of adopting one or another reading strategy.

Most strategies amount to a more or less radical reappraisal of at least one of the three claims above. Some have questioned the goodness of God (e.g. Marcion), others have called for a re-evaluation of our moral intuitions (e.g. Augustine), yet others insisted that the killing of humans is not God's intended message to Christian readers of these texts (e.g. Origen). In addition, each approach is based on explicit or implicit views on how God has revealed himself over time, how the Scriptures contain that self-revelation, and how the OT relates to the NT.

Questioning the goodness of God

After a period of 'uncritical' reception of the ḥērem of Deuteronomy and Joshua (e.g. Wisdom 12:2–11; Acts 7:45; 13:19; Heb. 11:30–31; Jas 2:25; *1 Clement* 12:6–8; *Barnabas* 12:8–10), warfare texts were at the centre of a second-century debate about the continuing significance of the Hebrew Scriptures for Christians. The controversy was occasioned by Marcion of Sinope, who famously posited an irreconcilable antithesis between the Jewish Bible and the Christian Scriptures (for him a truncated version of Luke and ten Pauline epistles). The only work composed by Marcion himself is usually referred to tellingly as *Antitheses*; in it he contrasted the God of Jesus Christ with the Demiurge, the God of creation (what some today would call 'the God of the OT').

According to Adolf von Harnack, the most influential Marcion scholar of the twentieth century, in the *Antitheses* 'the opposition of the acts of war of the Jewish God to the gentleness of Jesus played a major part'.[10] Among the *Antitheses*, as reconstructed by Harnack, are the following: 'Joshua conquered the land with violence and cruelty; but Christ forbids all violence and preaches

---

9. While the Jewish reception history of these texts is deeply fascinating, space only permits a consideration of Christian interpretations.

10. A. von Harnack, *Militia Christi: The Christian Religion and the Military in the First Three Centuries* (Philadelphia: Fortress Press, 1981; German ed., 1905), p. 47.

mercy and peace.'[11] 'The prophet of the God of creation, when war came upon the people, went up to the top of the mountain and stretched out his hands to God so that he might destroy many in the battle. Yet our Lord, because he is good, stretched out His hands, not to destroy, but to save men.' 'The prophet of the God of Creation, so that he might destroy more of the enemy, stopped the sun from setting until he should finish slaying those who were fighting against the people. But the Lord, because He is good, says, "Let not the sun go down upon your anger."'

Marcion does not actually deny any of the three tenets set out above. However, his solution is radical: there is not one God, but two. The Hebrew Bible (HB) bears truthful witness to one of them, the Gospel and epistles to the other. The first is cruel and to be rejected; the other, previously unknown but now revealed in Jesus Christ, is good and to be worshipped. On the upside, this approach allows Marcion to uphold his moral convictions, for example about war, and to maintain a 'high view' of Jesus and Paul. However, the cost is of course enormous: Jesus and his apostles are totally cut off from their historical setting in devout Judaism, and the God whom they loved and worshipped is turned into a demon. Also, for the theory to work, the Gospels and epistles must be heavily redacted to remove any positive references to the HB.

Unsurprisingly, this most radical of solutions was unacceptable to the emerging Great Church, and Marcion himself was excommunicated in AD 144. While Marcion's solution was beyond the pale, it is worth noting that this first sustained ethical critique of OT warfare texts did not emerge from some 'enlightened' paganism, but rather from a close reading of the Gospels and epistles. In fact, Marcion and his followers claimed to be nothing other than faithful Christians. In an important sense, therefore, the controversy about the ethical status of these OT texts emerged as an in-house debate among those who saw themselves as followers of Jesus.

Over the centuries, few have been attracted to Marcion's stark ontological dualism positing two gods. However, it is by no means uncommon to contrast the 'OT God' with the 'NT God', even at times in evangelical publications.[12]

---

11. The first antithesis is reconstructed from a homily by Origen, the following two from the anti-heretical *Adamantius Dialogue* (written c. 300); cf. A. von Harnack, *Marcion: das Evangelium vom fremden Gott. Zweite, verbesserte und vermehrte Auflage* (Leipzig: J. C. Hinrich'sche Buchhandlung, 1924), pp. 89, 272*–273*; and ibid., pp. 90, 281*.

12. Cf. e.g. C. S. Cowles, 'The Case for Radical Discontinuity', in C. S. Cowles et al. (eds.), *Show Them No Mercy: Four Views on God and Canaanite Genocide* (Grand Rapids: Zondervan, 2003), pp. 13–44.

Attempts have also been made to question the goodness of God within a monotheistic framework, for example by post-Holocaust Jewish theologians such as David Blumenthal, who argues that God sometimes is plainly abusive.[13]

Radical approaches of this nature, however, have never won over a majority of Jews or Christians, and it is hard to see how they could be integrated into anything resembling classical theism. In fact, God's goodness and justice is so fundamental an axiom in Jewish and Christian faith that it is usually held to be indubitable. It is something Christians and Jews reason *from*, rather than reason *for*.

Questioning our moral intuitions

Once Marcion's criticism had been raised, Christians who accepted the OT as Holy Scripture found it necessary to explain how it coheres with Christian doctrine and practice, especially as recorded in the documents eventually recognized as the Scriptures of the NT. The most influential approach in this field goes back to Augustine of Hippo (354–430). In terms of the three propositions set out above, Augustine emphasizes the need to readjust our moral intuitions. But he also points out ways in which the OT and NT are significantly different, while not being mutually exclusive.

The most directly relevant remarks are found in his *Questions on the Heptateuch*.[14] Deuteronomy is fundamental to Augustine's approach to *ḥērem* texts. For example, commenting on Joshua 21:41–43, he quotes Deuteronomy 7:1–3 and 20:10–17 in their entirety and interprets the narratives of Joshua–Kings as partial fulfilment of these and other promises and commands. In his view, the fulfilment is partial because of Israel's failure to completely carry out the annihilation command.[15]

Augustine comments on the crucial passage: 'Joshua left nothing that breathes alive. As the Lord had commanded his servant Moses, and as Moses had similarly commanded to Joshua, so did Joshua. He did not fail to do anything that the Lord had commanded Moses' (cf. Josh. 11:14f.). He continues:

---

13. Cited in E. A. Seibert, *Disturbing Divine Behavior. Troubling Old Testament Images of God* (Minneapolis: Fortress Press, 2009), p. 70.

14. Written c. 419; cf. A. D. Fitzgerald, 'Quaestiones in Heptateuchum', in A. D. Fitzgerald (ed.), *Augustine through the Ages: An Encyclopedia* (Grand Rapids: Eerdmans, 2000), pp. 692–693. There is at present no translation of the entire work in English.

15. Augustine, *Questions*, VI, 21.

No one should think it cruel that Joshua left not a single survivor in the cities handed over to him, for this was what God had commanded. But those who think that God himself is cruel, and who for that reason do not want to believe that the true God was the author of the Old Testament, are as mistaken about the works of God as they are about the sins of men. They are ignorant of the punishment each person deserves to suffer and, therefore, think it a great evil if what is about to collapse is overthrown, and if mortal men die.[16]

While Augustine's comments refer to a passage in Joshua, the importance of Deuteronomy is again clear: the text in question refers back to what YHWH had commanded Moses, presumably the Deuteronomic *ḥērem* commands. Augustine's approach has three prongs, in his order:

1. *Divine command.* The human actors (here Joshua and, by implication, the Israelites) are absolved from the charge of cruelty because they acted under divine orders. This reasoning is an example of what ethicists call divine-command theory, according to which certain actions are good by virtue of their being commanded by God (rather than God commanding certain actions by virtue of their being inherently good). The underlying dilemma was famously raised by Socrates in Plato's dialogue *Euthyphro*: 'Is the pious loved by the gods because it is pious, or is it pious because it is loved by the gods?'[17] Augustine opts decidedly for the latter.

2. *Divine justice.* If that same charge of cruelty is levelled against God himself, or used as an argument against the OT (here the Manicheans and other opponents of the HB are clearly in view), this is due to a lack of understanding both of God and of human sinfulness. Unlike these critics, God surely knows what each person deserves to suffer. Augustine here appeals to the goodness and justice of God as an indubitable premise, an axiom *from* which he argues. The same deep-seated conviction underpins Abraham's intercession on Sodom's behalf (Gen. 18:25) and Paul's argument in Romans (Rom. 3:6; 9:14), and has been taken as axiomatic by the vast majority of Jews and Christians throughout the ages.

---

16. *Questions*, VI, 16, my translation; cf. John R. Franke (ed.), *Joshua, Judges, Ruth, 1 – 2 Samuel* (Downers Grove: InterVarsity Press, 2005), p. 67.

17. Plato, *Euthrypho*, 10a.

3. *Relative severity.* Finally, Augustine points out that death is not so terrible a punishment for beings who are already death-bound. In other words, the Canaanites would have died in any event. While their life span was shortened, their destiny was not fundamentally altered. Here Augustine attempts to put into perspective the relative severity of the punishment.[18]

While these arguments may deal with the moral nature of the commands, they do not yet address the antithesis Marcion and others pitted between the OT and the NT. Augustine addresses these further concerns most directly in *Answer to Faustus.* The Manichean bishop Faustus seems to have focused his criticism of the OT on Moses' actions: slaying the Egyptian, ordering the Israelites to despoil the Egyptians, waging war (especially against Amalek) and commanding death for those worshipping the golden calf. Similar criticisms could of course be levelled at the *ḥērem* texts.

Once more, Augustine's fundamental premise is that God is just and that therefore anything he commands is also just and must be obeyed.[19] The reasons Augustine envisages for the divine command (here, to despoil the Egyptians) vary widely: it may be that the Egyptians 'were sacrilegious and wicked'.[20] Then again, 'perhaps the Hebrews were *permitted* to do these things in accord with their desires and thoughts rather than *ordered* to do them'.[21] Or there may in fact have been 'totally hidden' reasons. Whatever the case, the bottom line for Augustine is that 'one must yield to God's commands in obedience, not resist them with an argument'. To object to God's commands is the sign of an 'ignorant and false goodness of the human heart' which 'contradicts even Christ and does not want the wicked to suffer any evil'.

Turning directly to the alleged contradiction between Jesus' command not to retaliate (Matt. 5:39) and divine commands to wage wars, Augustine attributes the difference to the 'order of the times',[22] and the fact that 'the Old Testament, with its earthly promises, veiled and, in a certain sense, wrapped in deep shadows the secret of the kingdom of heaven, which was to be revealed at the proper

---

18. It is possible that the psychological force of his argument was considerably stronger in antiquity than in our day, at a time when the average life span was much shorter and when many died in infancy.

19. Augustine, *Answer to Faustus, a Manichean* = *Contra Faustum Manichaeum* (Hyde Park: New City Press, 2007), XXII.71, p. 349.

20. Ibid., XXII.71, p. 348.

21. Ibid., p. 349, my italics. The three following quotations are found ibid.

22. Ibid., XXII.76, p. 352, 'rerum dispensationem ac distributionem temporum ordo'.

time'.[23] In the Old Testament, 'it was first seen that these earthly goods which include human kingdoms and victories over enemies, for which the city of the impious that is spread throughout the world is especially accustomed to pray to idols and demons, belong only to the power and judgment of the one true God'. However, 'when the fullness of time came, so that the New Testament, which was veiled by symbols of the Old, might be revealed, it had now been shown by clear testimony that there was another life, for whose sake this life ought to be held in contempt, and another kingdom, for whose sake it was necessary to endure most patiently the opposition of all earthly kingdoms'. And so, 'The patriarchs and prophets waged wars for their kingdoms in order to show that the will of God also gives such victories; the apostles and martyrs were slain without resistance in order to teach that it is a better victory to suffer death for faith in the truth.'[24]

There is thus a sense in Augustine that God's self-revelation progressed and even changed markedly over time. However, there is no total discontinuity: even '[i]n the Old Testament the prophets knew how to die for the truth', while at the same time Christian emperors, too, 'put their complete confidence in the Christian faith and received a most glorious victory over their godless enemies, who had placed their hope in the worship of idols and demons'.[25] This link of OT warfare with wars waged by 'Christian emperors' against their 'godless enemies' adumbrated one of the darkest aspects of biblical interpretation by Christians.

However, it should also be noted that Augustine's interpretation is by no means restricted to a literal reading of these texts. He is convinced that wonderful treasures are hidden in even the most obscure passages of Scripture.[26] For him, all scriptures 'speak of Christ'. In fact, when Augustine preaches to his flock, he usually dwells much more on the allegorical reading.

In sum, Augustine's approach upholds two of the three premises: the goodness and justice of God and the faithfulness of the scriptural witness. The cost, however, is not insignificant: to set aside our moral intuitions regarding 'acts committed with intent to destroy, in whole or in part, a national, ethnical, racial or religious group' – including the indiscriminate slaughter of infants – is no small thing. In addition, despite Augustine's comments on the difference between OT and NT dispensations, he is willing to see a certain continuity between divinely mandated warfare in the OT and wars conducted

---

23. Ibid.; also the two following quotations.
24. Ibid., p. 353.
25. Ibid.
26. Ibid., XXII.94, p. 369; also the following quotation.

by Christian emperors. This left the door ajar for a literal application of these texts; the example above from the crusades is a terrible reminder that this application did not remain theoretical.

Among those who followed broadly Augustinian lines with respect to warfare and ḥērem texts are Thomas Aquinas, John Calvin, Hugo Grotius, and – to give but one of several contemporary thinkers – Richard Swinburne.[27] The explanations suggested by Augustine are still found among commentators today: some stress Canaanite sinfulness and judgment, others emphasize the importance of pure worship, others speculate that the command may have been a concession to Israel's hardness of heart, yet others emphasize that God's reasons remain deeply mysterious.

One of the reasons why Augustine's approach continues to appeal to many evangelicals in particular is that it avoids the accusation which he put to Faustus, of approaching the Bible

> in such a way as to remove all authority from the heart of the scriptures and to make each person his own authority for what he approves or disapproves of in any scripture. That is, each person is not subject to the authority of the scriptures for his faith but subjects the scriptures to himself, with the result not that something is pleasing to him because he finds it written in their lofty authority but that it seems correctly written because it has pleased him.[28]

Questioning the Scriptures

Some ancient interpreters, however, held that precisely this kind of critical evaluation was needed. According to Ptolemy, a second-century Gnostic teacher, different parts of the HB were inspired and authoritative to varying degrees: parts were pure but imperfect, others interwoven with injustice, and yet others purely symbolic and allegorical. In addition, some parts were concessions to the hardness of human hearts, or even the teachings of those who honour God with their lips but whose hearts are far from him.[29] The discriminating reader

---

27. R. Swinburne, 'What does the Old Testament Mean?', in M. Bergman et al. (eds.), *Divine Evil? The Moral Character of the God of Abraham* (Oxford: Oxford University Press, 2010), pp. 209–225.

28. Augustine, *Answer to Faustus*, XXXII.19, p. 421.

29. B. Layton, 'Ptolemy's Epistle to Flora', in B. Layton (ed.), *The Gnostic Scriptures: A New Translation with Annotations and Introductions* (New York: Doubleday, 1995), pp. 306–315.

had to sift the wheat from the chaff, using the teaching of Jesus as criterion: 'the Savior's words enable us to determine what is valuable in the law and what is not.'[30]

This Gnostic approach to the HB was rejected by the Great Church, but it may well represent the way many Christians today actually read the OT. While for much of the nineteenth and twentieth centuries questions of historical accuracy were the major issue concerning the trustworthiness of the OT, recent debates have more often focused on what has been called its ethical veracity. Wes Morriston, for instance, has recently argued that divine commands to wipe out entire nations constitute 'a strong *prima facie* case against inerrancy', i.e. the view 'that there are no serious mistakes in any book of the bible'.[31]

Randal Rauser, who describes himself as 'a systematic and analytic theologian of evangelical persuasion',[32] seems to reach a similar conclusion. In his view, the sense that 'genocide is always a moral atrocity' is such a morally powerful intuition for 'properly functioning, moral adults' that it forces a choice between concluding that either there is no perfect being or that 'Yahweh did not order people to commit genocide', the position which he himself advocates.[33]

As the previous section shows, however, the claim that 'genocide is always a moral atrocity' has repeatedly been denied in the Christian tradition. Rauser puts forward four arguments to establish it. First, 'it is always wrong to bludgeon babies', an assertion which he believes 'every rational, properly functioning person cannot help but know'.[34] Second, 'war creates, rather than merely uncovers, moral monsters'.[35] *Ḥērem* warfare thus would have had an inescapably corrupting influence on the Israelites. Third, the biblical rationale for 'the Canaanite genocide' evinces 'the typical elements . . . that are always invoked to justify genocide', i.e. 'division between an in-group and out-group, demonization of the out-group and an injunction to destroy the out-group'.[36] Given the

---

30. Ptolemy's argument in *Ad Floram* 4,3ff., as summarized by A. Pasquier, 'The Valentinian Exegesis', in C. Kannengiesser (ed.), *Handbook of Patristic Exegesis: The Bible in Ancient Christianity* (Leiden/Boston: Brill, 2004), pp. 454–470 (460).

31. W. Morriston, 'Did God Command Genocide? A Challenge to the Biblical Inerrantist', *Philosophia Christi* 11.1 (2009), pp. 7–26 (7–8).

32. R. Rauser, 'Randal Rauser', http://randalrauser.com/about/, accessed 21 June 2011.

33. R. Rauser, '"Let Nothing that Breathes Remain Alive": On the Problem of Divinely Commanded Genocide', *Philosophia Christi* 11.1 (2009), pp. 27–41 (33).

34. Ibid.

35. Ibid., p. 35.

36. Ibid., p. 37.

widespread parallels between Israelite and non-Israelite justifications for genocide, it 'is implausible to believe that the Israelites' genocide is the single divinely mandated exception in a long history of horrifying atrocities'.[37] Fourth, 'reason and experience establish that belief in the Canaanite genocide has contributed to a long history of moral atrocities'.[38]

If one accepts Rauser's arguments and wishes to uphold the traditional Christian belief that YHWH is God, the perfect being, one should consequently reject the claim that YHWH ordered the Israelites to commit genocide. If the Scriptures are understood to claim the contrary, they are wrong. Rauser's forceful arguments show why self-identifying evangelicals increasingly accept this possibility.

Questioning a static view of revelation

Historically, Christians have rarely considered outright rejection of parts of Scripture a viable option. By contrast the idea that God reveals himself progressively over time, clarifying and at times correcting earlier perceptions of his self-revelation, is ancient. This view is usually called progressive revelation. It is related to the concept of accommodation, i.e. the understanding that God accommodates his self-revelation to the capacities of its recipients. For an analogy, think of a Nobel prize laureate using rather different language to explain her research to, say, other specialists in her field, undergraduate students and her own pre-school children. Examples of this can be found in both the OT and NT, for example the Chronicler's 'clarification' that it was Satan rather than YHWH who incited David to hold a census (cf. 1 Chr. 21:1 and 2 Sam. 24:1). The classic presentation of God accommodating himself not only to the *cognitive* but also to the *moral* capacities of the recipients of revelation is Jesus' teaching on divorce. Here Jesus points out that certain Mosaic laws were given because of the people's hardness of heart, rather than because the commands reflected God's perfect and immutable will (Mark 10:5 and par.).

As we have seen above, Augustine, for instance, is prepared to entertain the thought that the Israelites were not in fact *commanded* but rather *permitted* to despoil the Egyptians – to satisfy their covetous, sinful desire. *Mutatis mutandis*, the same line of argument could be pursued in describing the *ḥērem* commands as a divine concession to the barbaric customs of warfare in the ANE and to the hardness of hearts of God's people.

---

37. Ibid., p. 39.
38. Ibid.

Hubert Junker, for instance, argues that hardness of heart and brutal times account for the human element in these parts of scriptural revelation. However, he adds, Christians are also bound to affirm the 'thus says the LORD' aspect of revelation. When pressed as to why God would, even for a brief moment in time, condescend to the point of using such barbaric customs for his providential purposes, Junker suggests that the answer is unfathomable, a deep mystery. He does affirm, however, that judgment and the protection of the true faith from paganism were among God's aims, and that in the end God will be seen to have acted justly *vis-à-vis* any and every one of his creatures.[39]

In an article on Amalek, Eleonore Stump also invokes the idea of progressive revelation, but in a rather unusual way. On her reading, the attempt to combat idolatry by devoting idolaters to destruction failed, and was bound to fail – as God had surely foreknown. However, the people of God needed to *experience* the failure of this strategy for overcoming idolatry. The command and the failure are all part of the divine educational strategy: 'In the miserable process of formation through experience, one of the things a people can learn is what will not work to enable a people to become just, good, and loving.'[40]

The way Junker and Stump apply progressive revelation to *ḥērem* texts allows for a firm commitment to the goodness and justice of God and to the faithfulness of Scripture. However, since God did indeed command his people to exterminate others, the moral intuition regarding the atrocity of genocide has to be re-evaluated, possibly along the lines of a Kierkegaardian 'teleological suspension of the ethical'. Such an approach, however, remains vulnerable to the challenge that the end cannot justify the means, especially if the means are as ghastly as genocide.

Questioning our interpretations

The final group of approaches seeks to uphold all three convictions, i.e. the goodness and justice of God, the faithful testimony of the Scriptures and our moral intuitions about genocide. Despite great variation in detail, these approaches have in common the view that the prima-facie or literal reading of

---

39. Hubert Junker, 'Der alttestamentliche Bann gegen heidnische Völker als moraltheologisches und offenbarungsgeschichtliches Problem', in *TThZ* 56 (1947), pp. 74–89.

40. E. Stump, 'The Problem of Evil and the History of Peoples: Think Amalek', in M. Bergman et al. (eds.), *Divine Evil?*, pp. 179–197 (197).

these OT texts is not the one we should adopt. This may be because God intends Christians to understand the passages as allegory, myth, metaphor or hyperbole.

Allegory

The historical origin of allegory in Greece, centuries before the Christian era, is likely connected with the interpretation of authoritative texts whose literal meaning had become problematic.[41] Similarly, '[w]hen the Christian Church took over the Old Testament, it did so on the understanding that some of it should be understood in non-literal ways'.[42] However, it should also be noted that by the second century AD allegorical interpretation was not primarily a defensive hermeneutical move; rather, by that time 'an aptitude to be interpreted allegorically was part and parcel of sacredness in texts'.[43]

Allegorical readings of OT texts are found in the NT itself (e.g. Gal. 4:25–26; 1 Cor. 9:9–10; 10:4). With respect to the destruction of the Canaanites and the Amalekites, some of the earliest Christian sources (i.e. of the late first and early second centuries) interpret these texts allegorically – *before* Marcion's trenchant critique! The author of *1 Clement*, for instance, interprets the scarlet sign hung from Rahab's house as signifying the blood of Christ, and reads the entire Jericho episode as signs of things now fulfilled in Christ. The author of *Barnabas* makes much of the homonymy between Joshua and Jesus (the names are identical in Hebrew and Greek), interpreting YHWH's prediction to blot out Amalek (Exod. 17:14) to mean that 'in the last days the Son of God will cut off by its roots all the house of Amalek' (*Barnabas* 12:8–10). It is not entirely clear to whom Barnabas thinks Amalek refers. However, a similar interpretation is found in Justin Martyr, whose comments on the same passage are unambiguous in identifying the referent of Amalek: 'He makes it manifest that through Jesus . . . the demons would be destroyed.'[44]

The fullest example for the allegorical interpretation of *ḥērem* is found in the twenty-six surviving sermons that Origen of Alexandria (c. 185–254) preached

---

41. Cf. F. Siegert, 'Early Jewish Interpretation in a Hellenistic Style', in M. Saebo, *Hebrew Bible/Old Testament: The History of Its Interpretation, Vol. 1, From the Beginnings to the Middle Ages* (Gottingen: Vandenhoeck & Ruprecht, 1996), pp. 130–198.

42. Swinburne, 'What Does the Old Testament Mean?', p. 24.

43. J. Barton, *The Spirit and the Letter: Studies in the Biblical Canon* (London: SPCK, 1997), p. 54.

44. Alexander Roberts et al. (eds.), *The Apostolic Fathers. Justin Martyr. Irenaeus* (Grand Rapids: Eerdmans, 1885 [1867]), Dialogue with Trypho, p. 131. Interestingly, the Greek word Justin uses here is the same by which the Septuagint routinely translates *ḥērem* (*exolethreuein*).

on the book of Joshua.[45] While his comments are thus not explicitly concerned with the *ḥērem* texts in Deuteronomy, his hermeneutical approach could be readily applied to them as well.

Two things are worth noting at the outset. First, in Origen's time, allegory was by no means primarily a defensive reading strategy; rather, it was the way learned and pious Alexandrians had been interpreting their sacred Scriptures for centuries. Second, while certain 'Origenist' opinions (that Origen may or may not have held himself) were condemned as heretical almost 300 years after his death, he certainly understood himself as a traditional 'man of the Church' and spent his life defending what he had received as traditional Christianity against heretics and pagans.

To understand Origen's interpretation, it is important to consider a series of commitments with which he approaches the Bible. First, Origen fundamentally believes that 'all Scripture is divinely inspired and useful' (2 Tim. 3:16).[46] Second, he admits that the presence of warfare texts in Scripture is puzzling for a Christian, but he trusts the decision of the apostles with respect to the canon and reconciles the tension by affirming a figurative meaning:

> Unless those physical wars bore the figure of spiritual wars, I do not think the books of Jewish history would ever have been handed down by the apostles to the disciples of Christ, who came to teach peace, so that they could be read in the churches. For what good was the description of wars to those to whom Jesus says, 'My peace I give you . . . ' 'not avenging your own self . . . suffer offence'?[47]

Third, Origen claims, 'We who are of the catholic Church do not reject the Law of Moses, but we accept it if Jesus reads it to us, so that when he reads we may grasp his mind and understanding.'[48] Finally, Origen reasons that if all Scripture is inspired by God, its true meaning must be worthy of him: 'For you ought to know that those things that are read are indeed worthy of the utterance of the Holy Spirit.'[49] Where Marcion's understanding of what is worthy of God (*theoprepes*) led him to reject the Hebrew Scriptures, Origen apparently works with a comparable concept to decide the true, Christian

---

45. Origen, *Homilies on Joshua* (Washington: Catholic University of America Press, 2002).
46. Ibid., XX.2.
47. Ibid., XV.1.
48. Ibid., IX.8
49. Ibid., VIII.1.

meaning of the OT. In fact, Origen opines that a literal reading of certain texts not only led the heretics astray but might even lead immature believers to 'believe such things about [God] as would not be believed of the most savage and unjust of men'.[50]

Like the author of *Barnabas* and Justin Martyr before him, Origen makes much of the Joshua/Jesus homonymy of the OT and the NT. Accordingly, Joshua 'does not so much indicate to us the deeds of the son of Nun, as it presents for us the mysteries of Jesus my Lord'.[51] On this premise, the wars of conquest are transposed to the spiritual warfare of Christ and the Christian, a warfare directed not against other human beings but against vices and demons.[52] The Canaanites to be destroyed are 'diabolical races of powerful adversaries against whom we battle'; they are 'within us'.[53]

Origen repeatedly ensures that his audience is clear that 'we do not have to wage physical wars'.[54] In his hermeneutic, the command that 'nothing that draws breath may be left behind' is understood to mean for the Christian that 'not even an impulse of wrath retains a place within you'.[55]

In sum, Origen is committed to the full divine inspiration of every jot and tittle of the OT. Consequently, he rejects a literal interpretation which would produce a meaning that is impossible or unworthy of God. While he rarely questions the historicity of the Joshua accounts, the issue of what actually happened in the past is of almost no importance to him. The only meaning he thinks important for his congregation, i.e. the meaning intended by God, is the spiritual meaning.[56] This meaning can only be discerned with God's help and must be discovered in the light of Jesus Christ.

Origen is by no means alone in the Christian tradition to interpret *ḥērem* texts allegorically. As noted above, Augustine also tends to focus on the 'spiritual meaning' when he addresses his flock. With regards to Deuteronomy specifically, the seven Canaanite nations to be devoted to destruction have traditionally been interpreted as representing the seven deadly sins (e.g. by Isidore of Seville,

---

50. Origen, *On First Principles* (Gloucester: Peter Smith, 1973), IV.ii.1, 271.

51. Origen, *Homilies on Joshua* , I.3.

52. Cf. Eph. 6:12.

53. Origen, *Homilies on Joshua*, I.6.7.

54. Ibid., XV.1.

55. Ibid., XV.3.

56. It should be noted, however, that Origen nowhere denies the historicity of the conquest, and that elsewhere Origen speaks positively of wars and even of acts of *ḥērem*, in a non-spiritualizing context.

the Venerable Bede, the Glossa Ordinaria).[57] The allegorical approach to interpreting the OT also has its contemporary defenders. Richard Swinburne, for instance, suggests that a purely allegorical reading of the command to exterminate the Canaanites would be a perfectly legitimate hermeneutical strategy, though he himself does not feel compelled to adopt it.[58]

The advantage of an allegorical reading is that it allows for an affirmation of all three tenets regarding the justice of God, the truth of the Scriptures and the moral revulsion at genocide. The cost, however, is not insignificant: without proper controls, all of 'biblical history' risks to disappear into allegorical smoke. Further, unless historical referents of the *ḥērem* texts are explicitly denied, the allegories do not address the underlying concern about the nature of God's involvement in human affairs. In addition, they can appear to be fanciful projections of theological data known from elsewhere onto texts addressing entirely different concerns. Using the concept of *theoprepes* (what is worthy of God) as a hermeneutical criterion is perhaps unavoidable, but nonetheless problematic. How can believers guard against simply capitulating to the sensitivities of their own time and imposing the diktats of the zeitgeist onto Holy Writ? How can Scripture ever challenge their preconceived moral intuitions? If believers do not learn what is worthy of God from the Scriptures, whence does their knowledge derive? The historical answer to these questions has, of course, made much of the rule of faith (*regula fidei*), a concept crucial to the hermeneutics of such diverse early church leaders as Irenaeus, Origen and Augustine.

Myth

Not entirely dissimilar from the ancient allegorical approach is a recent proposal to understand *ḥērem* in terms of the anthropological categories of cultural memory and myth.[59] According to Douglas Earl, the significance of OT narratives understood as 'myth' is located in the 'shaping of identity, shaping that may or may not relate straightforwardly to the "literal sense" of the narrative'.[60]

---

57. Cf. D. Earl, 'The Christian Significance of Deuteronomy 7', *Journal of Theological Interpretation* 3.1. (2009), pp. 41–62 (51), and the references there.

58. R. Swinburne, *Revelation: From Metaphor to Analogy* (Oxford/New York: Oxford University Press, 2007), p. 271.

59. Earl, 'The Christian Significance of Deuteronomy 7'; idem, *Reading Joshua as Christian Scripture* (Winona Lake: Eisenbrauns, 2010); idem, *The Joshua Delusion?: Rethinking Genocide in the Bible* (Eugene: Cascade Books, 2010). The latter, more popular treatment contains a critical response by C. J. H. Wright.

60. Earl, *Reading Joshua*, p. 44.

In Deuteronomy, *ḥērem* 'shapes attitudes towards idols – avoid idols and separate yourself from anything that is likely to lead to idolatry'.[61]

Applying neo-structural analysis, Earl suggests that *ḥērem* 'in the "world of the text" of Deuteronomy can be viewed as constructing Israel's identity by denying the possibility of mediation between Israel and the local peoples. Any attempt to "mediate" between categories results in annihilation or death, symbolizing expulsion from the community.'[62] However, if we read Deuteronomy as part of the larger canon of Scripture, we find in Joshua an 'ideological "pushing" of the underlying structures ... to allow for the possibility of mediation and transformation of "non-Israel" and "Israel"', a 'shift in structure that is further developed in the NT'.[63]

In light of this developing canonical perspective, for Earl it is 'possible that the Christian significance of Deut 7 is located primarily in its importance as part of Christian "cultural memory" in that it narrates part of the story through which Christian identity has been constructed'.[64] On such a view, *ḥērem* 'as a metaphor is itself symbolically expressive of the "oldness" of the Old Covenant, being paradigmatic of the denial of transformation and witness'.[65] By contrast, readings that focus on 'allegiance to God and the rejection of idolatry' find 'continuity with the Christian tradition'.[66]

This mythical reading shares many of the strengths of the allegorical approach, in that all three tenets can be maintained at some level. In fact, the concept of 'cultural memory' could be construed within a robust theological framework of progressive revelation, accommodation and the canonical interpretation of Scripture.[67] However, as with allegory, unless a historical referent of these texts is explicitly denied, the moral challenge is not fully addressed. If it is denied, then what stops more and more of biblical history from dissolving into mythical mist?

One might of course argue that in this case there never was a time when these texts were anything other than myth. This option comports well with a

---

61. Ibid., p. 111.

62. Ibid.

63. Earl, 'The Christian Significance of Deuteronomy 7', p. 49.

64. Ibid., p. 52.

65. Ibid., p. 55.

66. Ibid., p. 60.

67. Cf. e.g. C. Seitz, 'The Canonical Approach and Theological Interpretation', in C. G. Bartholomew et al. (eds.), *Canon and Biblical Interpretation* (Grand Rapids: Zondervan, 2006), pp. 58–110.

number of historical-critical hypotheses regarding the dates and circumstances of the formation and redaction of Deuteronomy and the Deuteronomistic History.[68]

Metaphor

Metaphor is a category that is sometimes thought to have the strengths of allegorical and mythical readings, without the concomitant drawbacks. It has recently been suggested as a category by which to make sense of *ḥērem* in Deuteronomy. According to Walter Moberly, 'Deuteronomy 7 contains the fullest exposition within the Old Testament of what is arguably the single most morally and theologically problematic aspect of the Old Testament, God's command to Israel to practice *ḥerem*.'[69] The argument he develops is that '[w]hatever the "literal" implementation of *ḥerem* in certain Old Testament narratives might appear to mean, and whether or not *ḥerem* was ever actually implemented in Israel's warfare, Deuteronomy 7 ... presents *ḥerem* as a metaphor for religious fidelity which has only two primary practical expressions, neither of which involved the taking of life'.[70] According to Moberly, the only practical content given to *ḥērem* in Deuteronomy 7 is the double command to abstain from intermarriage with the Canaanites, which 'presupposes that life is not taken', and to thoroughly destroy their religious objects.[71] Suggesting that '[w]hat we have is a retention of the (in all likelihood) traditional language of *ḥerem* but a shift in the direction of its acquiring significance as a metaphor', Moberly concludes that '[i]f this understanding is on the right lines, then the usage of *ḥerem* terminology elsewhere in Deuteronomy ... is not a problem. For once it is grasped that the term functions as a metaphor for religious faithfulness, then all injunctions are interpreted accordingly.'[72] In fact, Moberly suggests that '[i]t is likely that a grasp of the metaphorical

---

68. Cf. other chapters in this volume; and on *ḥērem* specifically Rachel M. Billings, *'Israel Served the Lord': The Book of Joshua as Paradoxical Portrait of Faithful Israel*, PhD thesis, Harvard University (April 2010), pp. 120–145. This is also the approach suggested by P. Jenkins, *Laying Down the Sword. Why We Can't Ignore the Bible's Violent Verses* (New York: HarperOne, 2011).

69. R. W. L. Moberly, 'Toward an Interpretation of the Shema', in C. R. Seitz et al. (eds.), *Theological Exegesis: Essays in Honor of Brevard S. Childs* (Grand Rapids: Eerdmans, 1999), pp. 124–144 (134).

70. Ibid., p. 135.

71. Ibid.

72. Ibid., p. 136.

nature of *ḥerem* was integral both to the compilation of Deuteronomy in its present form, in which it becomes a primary interpretation of the Shema, and to the preservation and reception of Deuteronomy as Israel's Scripture within the continuing life of Judah'.[73]

Moberly's student Nathan MacDonald further developed this reading of *ḥerem* in Deuteronomy 7 in his doctoral thesis. Noting that a metaphorical reading 'must not be based on preference or emotional reaction to the problems of a "literal" reading',[74] he offers a number of exegetical observations as the basis for his interpretation: if *ḥerem* were not to be taken as metaphorical, its significance would be limited in time (in contrast to the surrounding material in chapters 6 and 8); the names of the seven nations (7:1) 'are not historical descriptions of the ethnic composition of Canaan'; the prohibition of inter-marriage would make little sense if total annihilation were envisaged; and a metaphorical reading 'reduces the tensions between Deuteronomy 7 and the parallel material in Exodus 23 and 34'.[75]

MacDonald goes on to suggest that '[t]he portrayal of *ḥerem* in Deuteronomy 7 and the rest of the book gives substance to the metaphor, and, thus to Deuteronomy's requirement that love be shown towards YHWH'.[76] This substance involves an understanding of 'devotion to YHWH' as an 'act of radical obedience; an obedience that may act against natural impulses',[77] obedience that 'must occur even if this entails material disadvantage' and that 'transcend[s] familial and national ties'.[78]

Like Moberly, MacDonald suggests that the realization of the metaphor was twofold, in the prohibition of intermarriage and the destruction of religious paraphernalia. He concludes that '*ḥerem* is a powerful and evocative metaphor, and as such is a suitable negative expression of the similarly evocative expression of "love"', suggesting an understanding of 'devoted love as radical obedience to YHWH's commands, as the absence of "abomination", as something that must transcend human desires for wealth or family. *Ḥerem* also indicates the need for separation and the importance of education.'[79]

---

73. Ibid., p. 137.

74. N. MacDonald, *Deuteronomy and the Meaning of 'Monotheism'* (Tübingen: Mohr Siebeck, 2003), p. 111.

75. Ibid., p. 111f.

76. Ibid., p. 113.

77. Ibid., p. 115, citing 1 Sam. 15 as the 'most striking example' of this.

78. Ibid., citing Deut. 13 as an example.

79. Ibid., p. 122f.

Moberly and MacDonald thus both argue that the intent of the author(s)/ editor(s)/canonizer(s) was for *ḥērem* to be understood as a metaphor for love of YHWH as enjoined by the *Shema*. The concrete application of the metaphor never had killing in view, it only envisaged abstaining from intermarriage and demolishing cult objects. If this reading can be sustained, it comes with all the benefits of the allegorical reading (i.e. all three tenets can be upheld), while also being closer to the text and less fanciful than the allegories.

There are, however, major obstacles to this view. It is by no means necessary to conclude that the command not to intermarry presupposes survivors; the choice presented by the text could just as easily be between option A (kill everyone) and option B (intermarry and be led into idolatry), with option A being commanded and option B being forbidden. In other words, the command was to kill everyone, lest you might be seduced to marry idolaters and become idolatrous yourself.

Even if the metaphorical reading were found to be sustainable within the confines of Deuteronomy 7, the reader of the canonical book of Deuteronomy would form an opinion on the meaning of *ḥērem* in chapters 2 and 3 already, and neither Moberly nor MacDonald provide a convincing account of why the annihilation of Og and Sihon and their peoples should be read metaphorically. The same can be said for the *ḥērem* passages that follow Deuteronomy 7, which explicitly state that *ḥērem* involves killing human beings (13:15; 20:16). From a wider canonical perspective the use of the war *ḥērem* in Numbers 21:1–3 and throughout Joshua could be added to this critique. It is thus not clear that a strictly metaphorical reading can be justified on internal textual grounds alone.

Hyperbole

A further recent attempt to make sense of *ḥērem* texts from a Christian perspective focuses on the book of Joshua, but is sometimes held to have implications for understanding *ḥērem* in Deuteronomy as well. On this view, Joshua belongs to the genre of ANE conquest accounts, a genre which typically included hyperbolic descriptions of wiping out the enemy.[80] The reports in Joshua 1 – 11 should therefore be read as highly hyperbolic, not as descriptions of a literal extermination campaign. Sometimes appeals are also made to ANE archaeology, contending that Jericho and Ai, for instance, were small military forts that would have had few if any non-combatants in

---

80. K. L. Younger, *Ancient Conquest Accounts: A Study in Near Eastern and Biblical History Writing* (Sheffield: JSOT Press, 1990).

them.[81] Two Christian philosophers have recently argued that this reading of Joshua should also lead to a re-evaluation of the *ḥērem* commands in Deuteronomy. The argument runs like this: 'Scripture clearly indicates that Joshua fulfilled Moses' charge to him. So *if* Joshua did just as Moses commanded, and *if* Joshua's described destruction was really the hyperbole common in ANE warfare language and familiar to Moses, *then* clearly Moses himself didn't intend a literal, comprehensive Canaanite destruction. He, like Joshua, was merely following the literary convention of the day.'[82]

Since this view depends largely on the interpretation of Joshua, rather than of Deuteronomy, this is not the place to engage with a detailed critique. However, two things should be noted. Even if this view should be found persuasive for Joshua, the retrojective interpretation of *ḥērem* in Deuteronomy will not convince everyone; and even if this were accepted, it would only mitigate rather than obviate the problem. God would still have commanded mass killings, even if not the extinction of each individual life.

Conclusion

This brief historical overview of Christian responses to the moral challenge of *ḥērem* texts has had to be selective. Among hermeneutical strategies not covered in any detail are various cultural relativist, 'canon within the canon', paradigmatic and reader-response approaches. Many of these more recent reading strategies, however, have similar strengths and weaknesses to the historic ones.

As the analysis above has shown, some historic approaches such as Augustine's solve the tension by exhorting Christian readers to give up their moral intuitions regarding genocide. A paramount danger of this approach is that, if wrong, it may lead one to 'believe such things about [God] as would not be believed of the most savage and unjust of men', to use Origen's phrase. By contrast, other approaches risk, in Augustine's phrase, to 'remove all authority from the heart of the scriptures and to make each person his own authority for what he approves or disapproves of in any scripture'. Tracing a path between this Scylla and Charybdis is fraught with the real risk of shipwreck. Whether one should

---

81. R. S. Hess, 'The Jericho and Ai of the Book of Joshua', in R. S. Hess et al. (eds.), *Critical Issues in Early Israelite History* (Winona Lake: Eisenbrauns, 2008), pp. 33–46.

82. P. Copan, *Is God a Moral Monster?: Making Sense of the Old Testament God* (Grand Rapids: Baker Books, 2011), p. 182; similarly N. Wolterstorff, 'Reading Joshua', in M. Bergman et al. (eds.), *Divine Evil?*, p. 252.

search for guidance in navigating these treacherous passages primarily in the church's rule of faith, or with one or other ancient interpreter, or in traditional, modern or postmodern reworkings of the concepts of revelation and accommodation, or in various literary and historical-critical approaches, depends on considerations too far reaching to be fully explored here.

One final point, however, should be noted in closing: Christians did not have to wait for the often ill-informed tirades of the so-called New Atheists, or, for that matter, for Enlightenment critics, to know that certain biblical texts pose enormous moral challenges. History shows that it was the very life and teaching of Jesus Christ that made these texts problematic in the first place. That some who claimed to be Christ's followers, like the crusaders who massacred the population of Jerusalem in July 1099, appealed to the Scriptures to justify their atrocities is a fact that Christians cannot and must not deny or forget. To suggest, however, that their 'interpretation' was in any meaningful sense an expression of being a disciple of Jesus Christ is blasphemous.[83]

© Christian Hofreiter, 2012

---

83. I am grateful for feedback from participants at the Tyndale Fellowship OT Study Group in July 2011 and from my supervisor Professor John Barton on earlier drafts of this chapter. Special thanks are also due to the Arts & Humanities Research Council (http://www.ahrc.ac.uk), which generously supported my research with a doctoral studentship held at Oxford University (2009–2012).

INDEX OF AUTHORS

INDEX OF SCRIPTURE REFERENCES

INDEX OF OTHER ANCIENT SOURCES

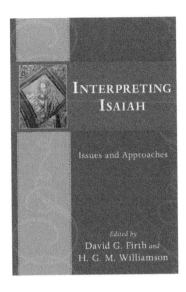

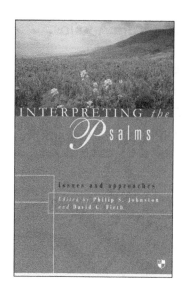

Interpreting the Psalms

Issues and approaches

Philip S. Johnston and
David G. Firth (editors)

ISBN: 978-1-84474-077-2
336 pages, paperback

The book of Psalms has been precious to countless Jewish and Christian believers in many different languages and countries over many centuries. It has expressed their hopes and fears, inspired their faith, and renewed their trust in God. In this way, the spiritual insight and religious heritage of a small number of ancient Israelites has had a profound and lasting impact on humanity.

The book of Psalms is also of great importance in biblical scholarship. In the twentieth century, Psalms study was dominated by two approaches, but now it is in the midst of a sea change, and the older perspectives jostle for attention alongside newer interests.

This volume aims to bridge the gap between basic introductions and specialized literature.

The authors are Craig Broyles, Dale Brueggemann, Jerome Creach, Timothy Edwards, David Firth, Jamie Grant, David Howard, James Hely Hutchinson, Philip Johnston, Michael LeFebvre, Tremper Longman, Dwight Swanson, Andy Warren-Rothlin, Gordon Wenham and Gerald Wilson. They have already published many books and articles, and made significant contributions to Old Testament scholarship.

related titles from Apollos

APOLLOS OLD TESTAMENT COMMENTARIES

Deuteronomy

J. G. McConville

ISBN: 978-0-85111-779-9
544 pages, hardback

In this outstanding commentary, Gordon McConville offers a theological interpretation of the Old Testament book of Deuteronomy in the context of the biblical canon. He gives due attention to historical issues where these bear on what can be known about the settings in which the text emerged. His dominant method is one that approaches Deuteronomy as a finished work.

Dr McConville argues that, in the context of the ancient world, Deuteronomy should be understood as the radical blueprint for the life of a people, at the same time both spiritual and political, and profoundly different from every other social, political and religious programme. The book incorporates the tension between an open-ended vision of a perfectly ordered society under God, and practical provisions for dealing with the frailty and imperfections of real people. Hence, it is capable of informing our thinking about the organization of societies, while maintaining a vision of the kingdom of God.

Available from your local Christian bookshop or **www.thinkivp.com**

related titles from IVP

TYNDALE OLD TESTAMENT COMMENTARIES

Deuteronomy
Edward J. Woods

ISBN: 978-1-84474-533-3
336 pages, paperback

Deuteronomy has been aptly described as a book 'on the boundary': it addresses the possibilities of new life 'beyond the Jordan' as dependent upon Israel's keeping of the law and acknowledgment of Yahweh's supremacy. Moses leaves the people with his last will and testament that would ensure their success and well-being in the new land. Ted Woods expounds this book's breathtaking and all-encompassing vision, and shows how the Israelites, from king to ordinary citizen, were exhorted to make its words the interpreter of their life's story within the land.

Tyndale Commentaries are designed to help the reader of the Bible understand what the text says and what it means. The Introduction to each book gives a concise but thorough treatment of its authorship, date , original setting and purpose. Following a structural Analysis, the Commentary takes the book section by section, drawing out its main themes, and also comments on individual verses and problems of interpretation. Additional Notes provide fuller discussion of particular difficulties. In the new Old Testament volumes, the commentary on each section of the text is structured under three headings: Context, Comment and Meaning. The goal is to explain the true meaning of the Bible and make its message plain.

Available from your local Christian bookshop or **www.thinkivp.com**

Printed and bound by CPI Group (UK) Ltd, Croydon, CR0 4YY

13/04/2025

14656474-0004